ROSS RICHIE Chief Executive Officer • **MATT GAGNON** Editor-in-Chief • **FILIP SABLIK** VP-Publishing & Marketing • **LANCE KREITER** VP-Licensing & Merchandising • **PHIL BARBARO** Director of Finance
BRYCE CARLSON Managing Editor • **DAFNA PLEBAN** Editor • **SHANNON WATTERS** Editor • **ERIC HARBURN** Assistant Editor • **ADAM STAFFARONI** Assistant Editor • **CHRIS ROSA** Assistant Editor
STEPHANIE GONZAGA Graphic Designer • **CAROL THOMPSON** Production Designer • **JASMINE AMIRI** Operations Coordinator • **DEVIN FUNCHES** Marketing & Sales Assistant

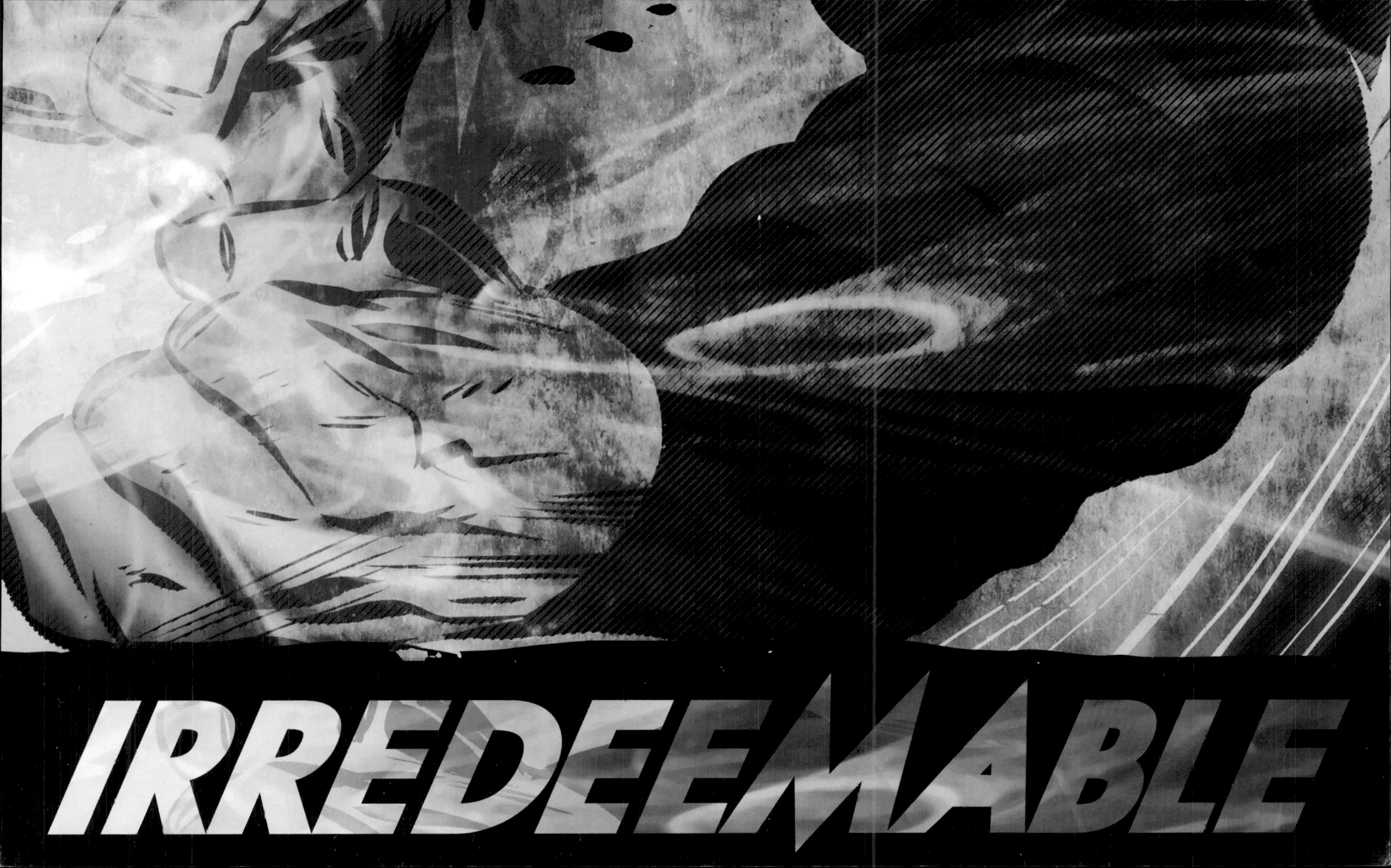
IRREDEEMABLE

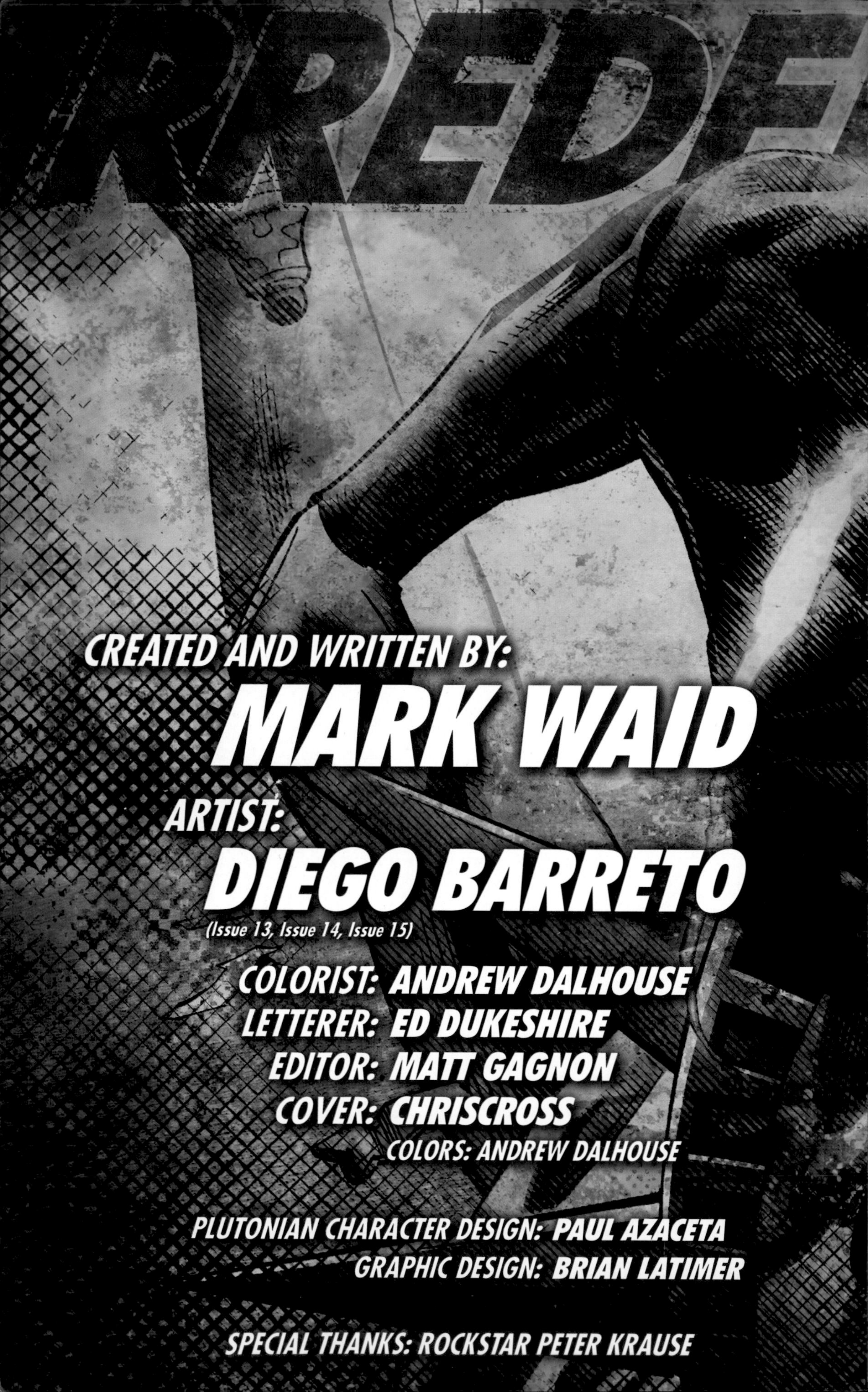

CREATED AND WRITTEN BY:
MARK WAID

ARTIST:
DIEGO BARRETO
(Issue 13, Issue 14, Issue 15)

COLORIST: **ANDREW DALHOUSE**
LETTERER: **ED DUKESHIRE**
EDITOR: **MATT GAGNON**
COVER: **CHRISCROSS**
COLORS: ANDREW DALHOUSE

PLUTONIAN CHARACTER DESIGN: **PAUL AZACETA**
GRAPHIC DESIGN: **BRIAN LATIMER**

SPECIAL THANKS: ROCKSTAR PETER KRAUSE

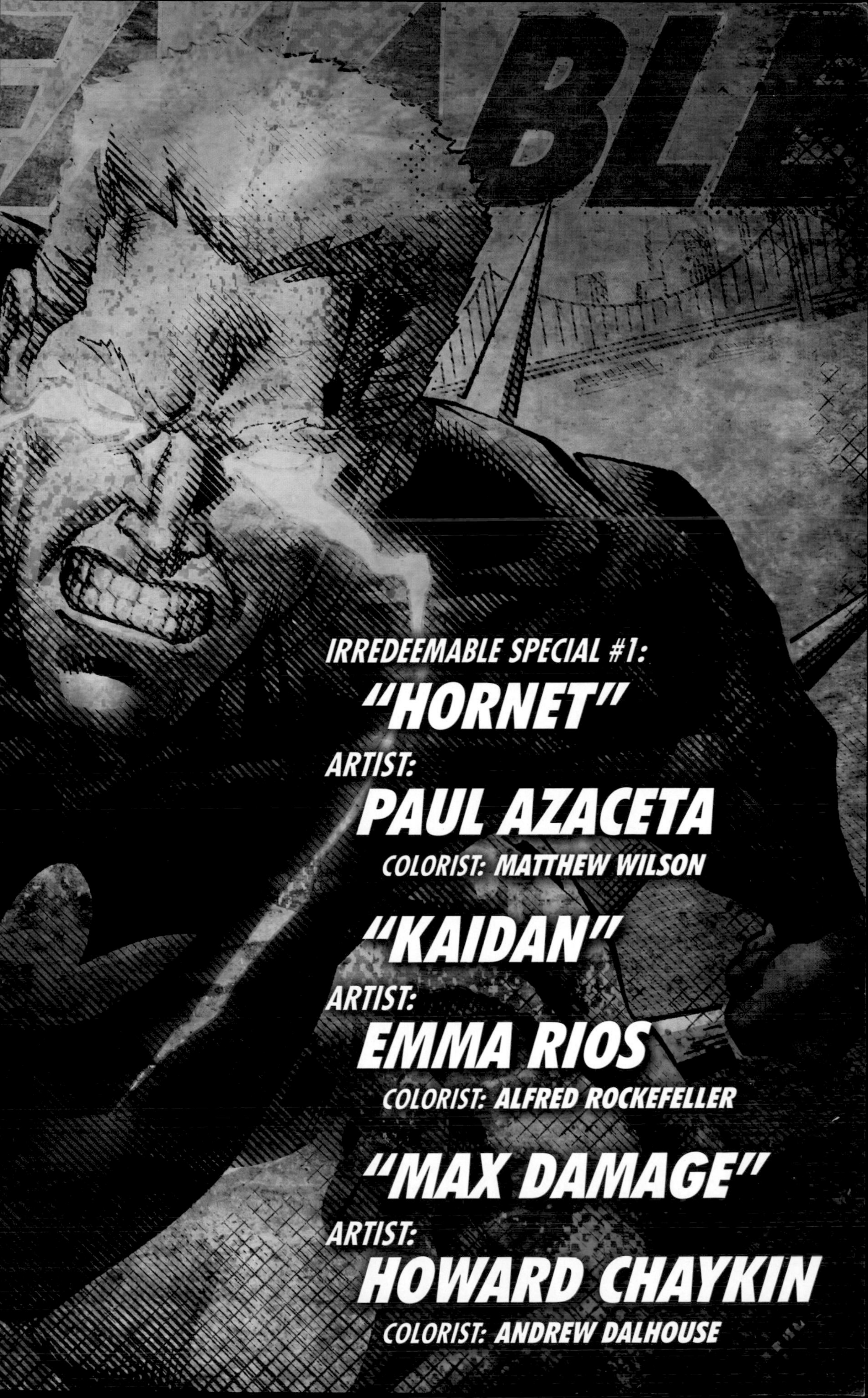

IRREDEEMABLE SPECIAL #1:

"HORNET"

ARTIST:

PAUL AZACETA

COLORIST: MATTHEW WILSON

"KAIDAN"

ARTIST:

EMMA RIOS

COLORIST: ALFRED ROCKEFELLER

"MAX DAMAGE"

ARTIST:

HOWARD CHAYKIN

COLORIST: ANDREW DALHOUSE

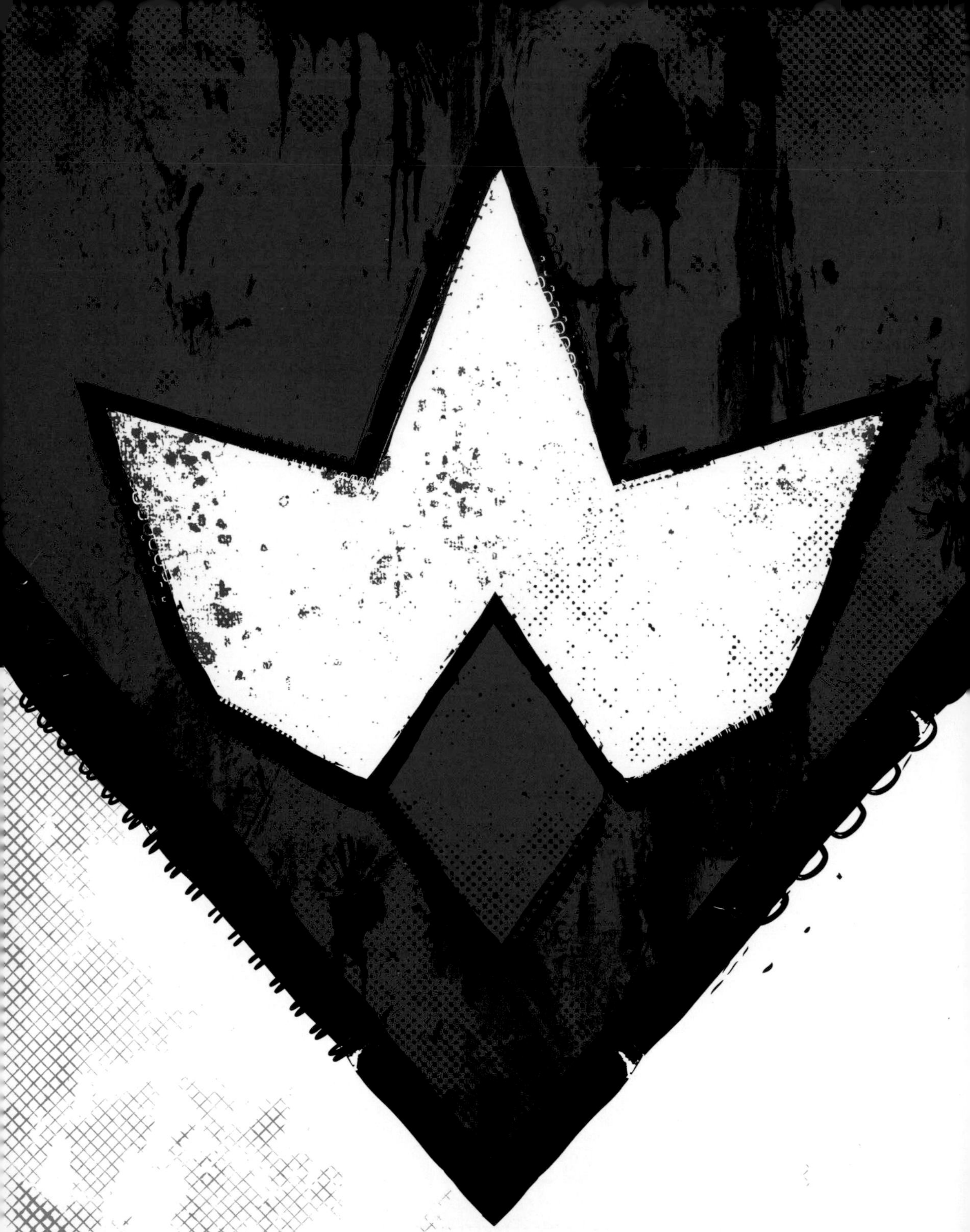

IRREDEEMABLE SPECIAL

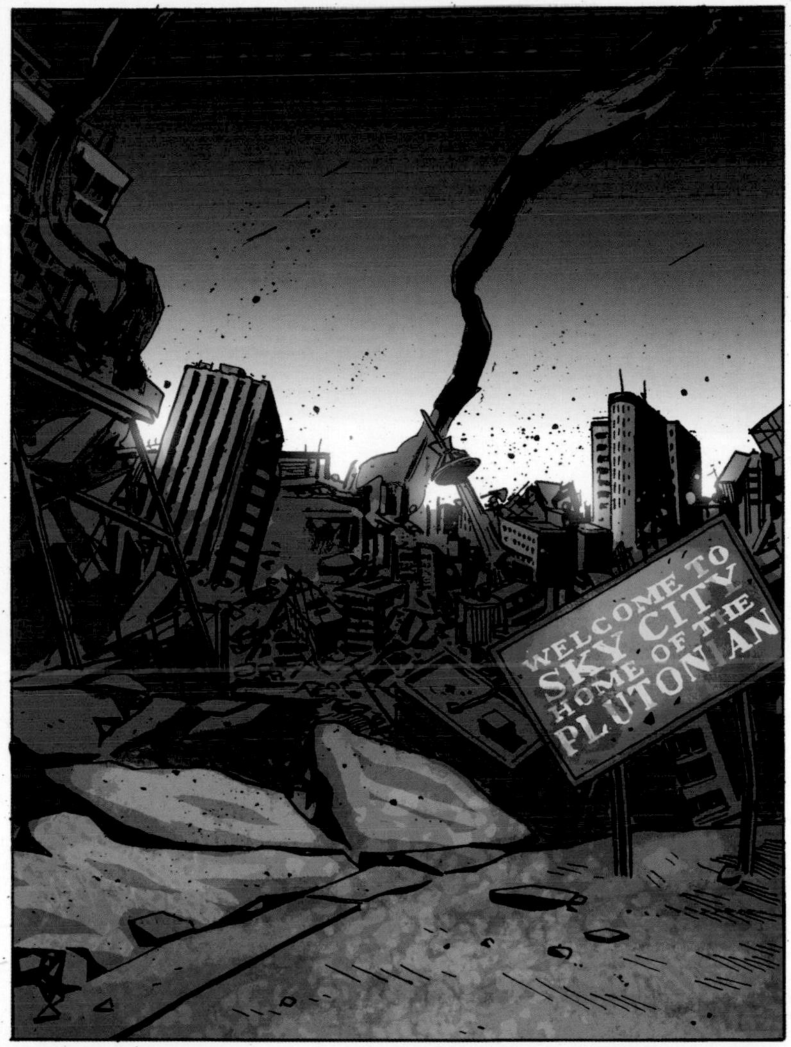
WELCOME TO
SKY CITY
HOME OF THE
PLUTONIAN

THE WORLD

IS IN TATTERS. FOR YEARS, EARTH'S FOREMOST HERO WAS ***THE PLUTONIAN,*** A NEAR-OMNIPOTENT BEING WHO WATCHED OVER US AS A KIND AND BENEVOLENT PROTECTOR. EVERYONE TRUSTED HIM.

AND THEN HE SNAPPED.

ABSOLUTE POWER

BRINGS WITH IT ABSOLUTE RESPONSIBILITY. AND THE PRESSURE PLUTONIAN FELT TO NEVER MAKE THE SLIGHTEST MISTAKE FOR FEAR HE'D HURT PEOPLE AND LOSE THEIR LOVE WAS INCALCULABLE. IT FINALLY BROKE HIM...AND WHEN IT DID, IT UNLEASHED IN HIM A LIFETIME OF PENT-UP RAGE AND FRUSTRATION.

KILLING MILLIONS,

PLUTONIAN LEVELED CITIES AND ENTIRE COUNTRIES. HE QUICKLY BECAME THE GREATEST MASS-MURDERER IN HISTORY, AND THE WORLD NOW LIVES UNDER THE CONSTANT THREAT OF AN INVULNERABLE GOD WHO LOOMS IN THE SKIES AND CAN INCINERATE ENTIRE VILLAGES WITH A GLANCE.

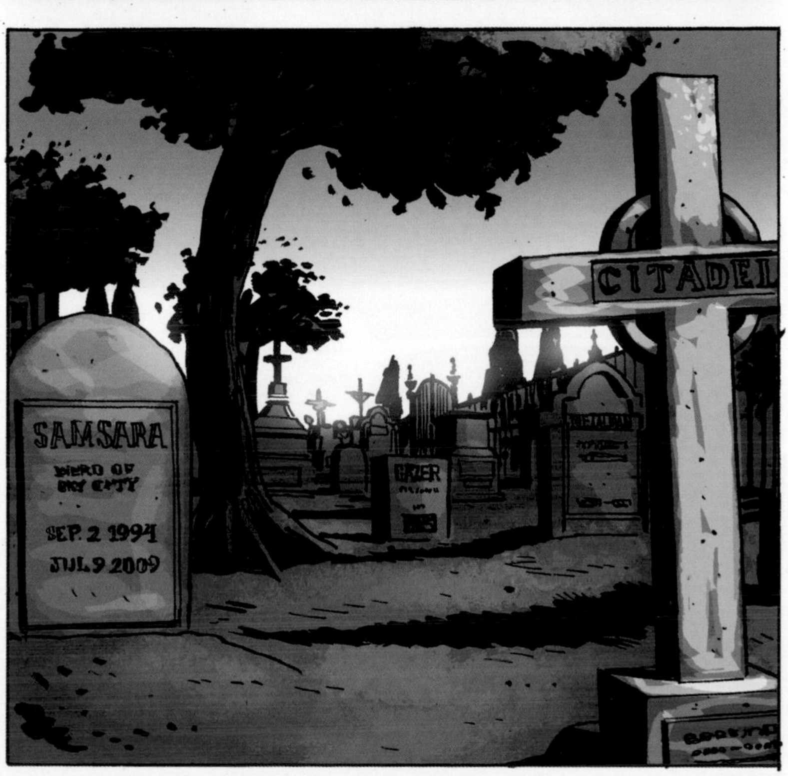
CITADEL
SAMSARA
SEP. 2 1994
JUL 9 2009

EARTH'S ONLY HOPE

LIES WITH A HANDFUL OF SUPERHUMANS, THREE OF WHOM IN THE COMING MONTHS WILL PLAY ESPECIALLY CRITICAL ROLES IN SAVING THE EARTH FROM DESTRUCTION. ONE IS A REFORMED ENEMY OF THE PLUTONIAN'S. ONE IS A YOUNG WOMAN WHOSE HERITAGE WILL TURN THE TIDE AT A CRUCIAL MOMENT.

THE THIRD

IS ALREADY DEAD.

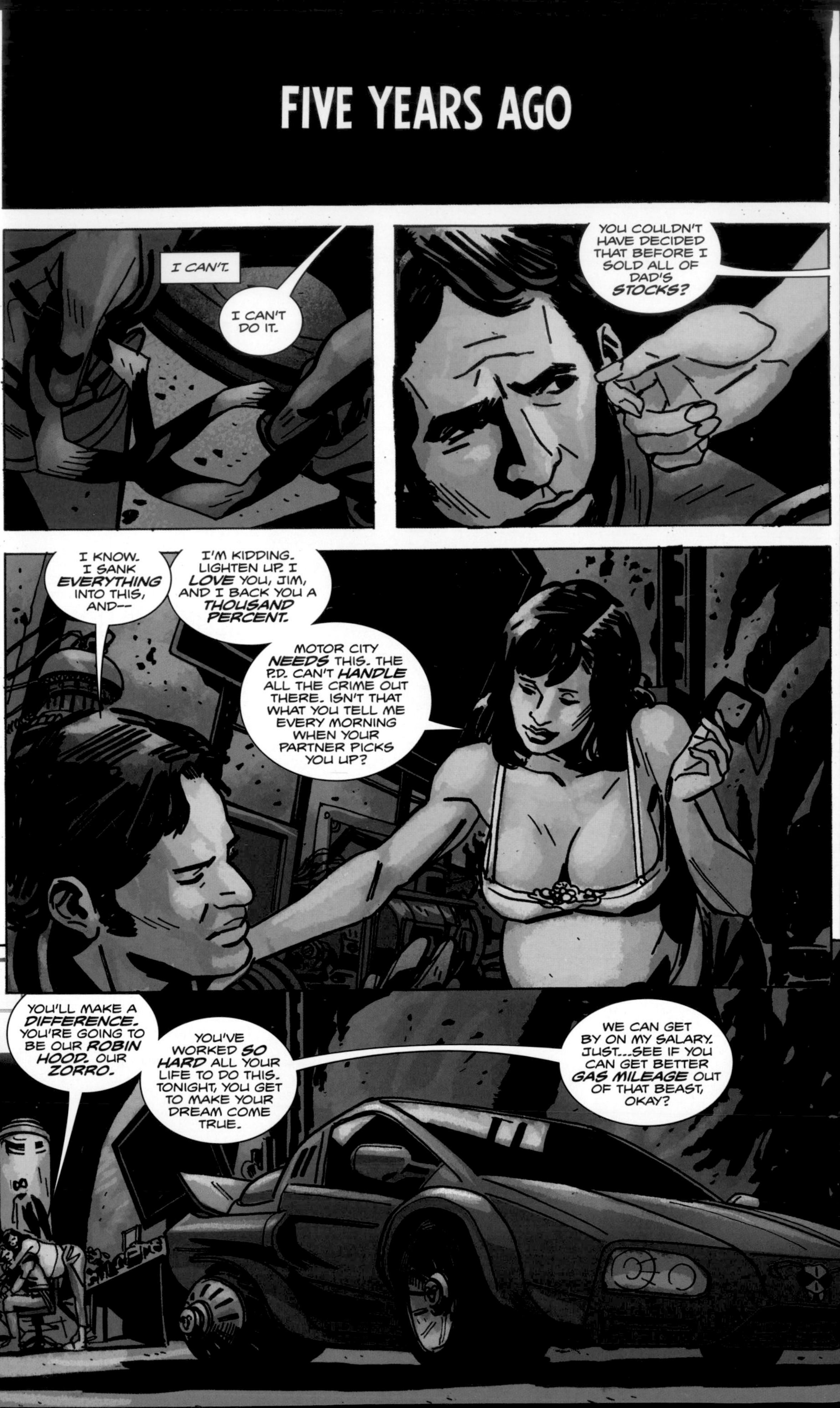

FIVE YEARS AGO
I CAN'T.
I CAN'T DO IT.
YOU COULDN'T HAVE DECIDED THAT BEFORE I SOLD ALL OF DAD'S STOCKS?
I KNOW. I SANK EVERYTHING INTO THIS, AND--
I'M KIDDING. LIGHTEN UP. I LOVE YOU, JIM, AND I BACK YOU A THOUSAND PERCENT.
MOTOR CITY NEEDS THIS. THE P.D. CAN'T HANDLE ALL THE CRIME OUT THERE. ISN'T THAT WHAT YOU TELL ME EVERY MORNING WHEN YOUR PARTNER PICKS YOU UP?
YOU'LL MAKE A DIFFERENCE. YOU'RE GOING TO BE OUR ROBIN HOOD. OUR ZORRO.
YOU'VE WORKED SO HARD ALL YOUR LIFE TO DO THIS. TONIGHT, YOU GET TO MAKE YOUR DREAM COME TRUE.
WE CAN GET BY ON MY SALARY. JUST...SEE IF YOU CAN GET BETTER GAS MILEAGE OUT OF THAT BEAST, OKAY?

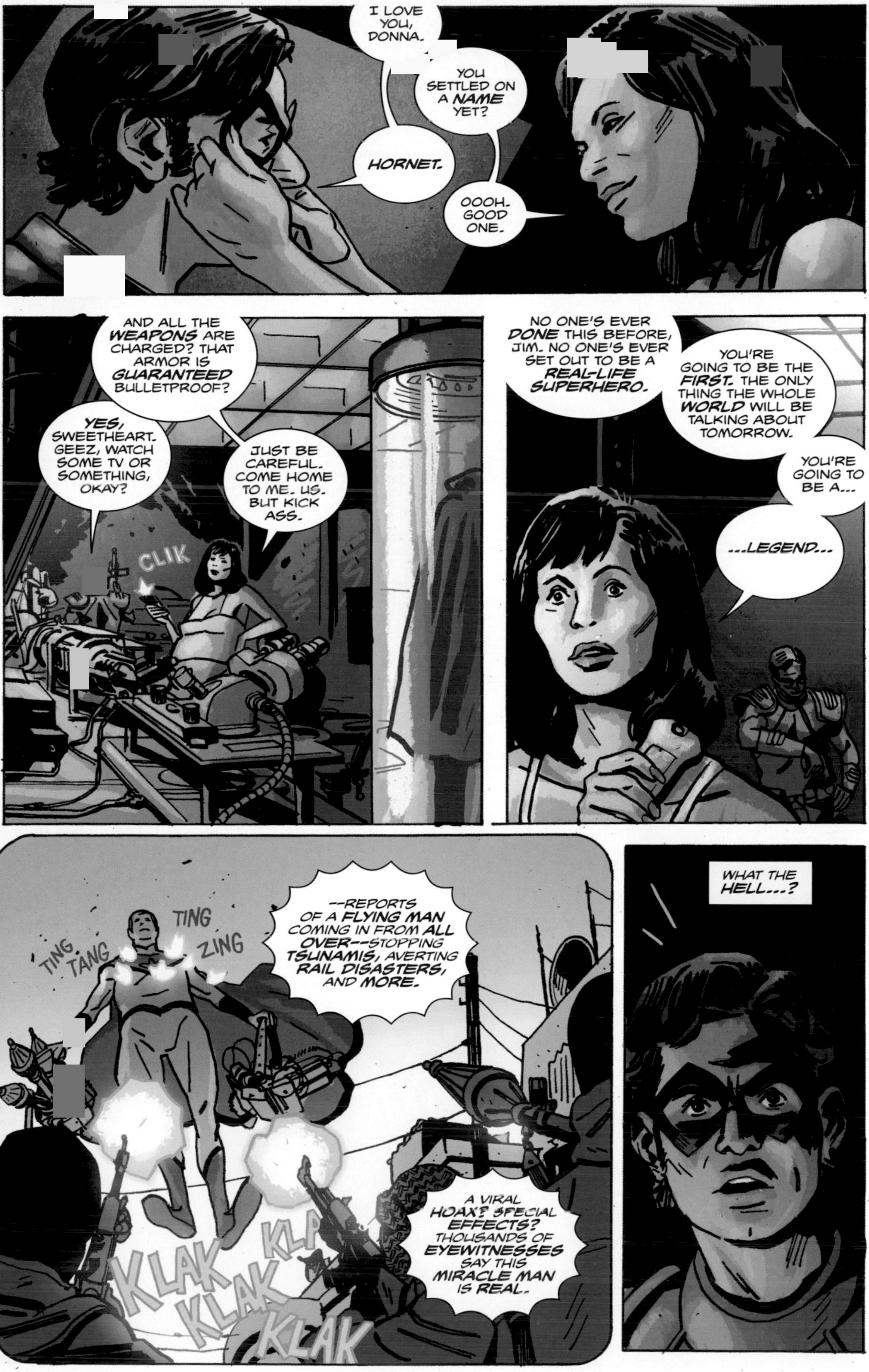
I LOVE YOU, DONNA.
YOU SETTLED ON A NAME YET?
HORNET.
OOOH. GOOD ONE.
AND ALL THE WEAPONS ARE CHARGED? THAT ARMOR IS GUARANTEED BULLETPROOF?
YES, SWEETHEART. GEEZ, WATCH SOME TV OR SOMETHING, OKAY?
JUST BE CAREFUL. COME HOME TO ME. US. BUT KICK ASS.
CLIK
NO ONE'S EVER DONE THIS BEFORE, JIM. NO ONE'S EVER SET OUT TO BE A REAL-LIFE SUPERHERO.
YOU'RE GOING TO BE THE FIRST. THE ONLY THING THE WHOLE WORLD WILL BE TALKING ABOUT TOMORROW.
YOU'RE GOING TO BE A...
...LEGEND...
--REPORTS OF A FLYING MAN COMING IN FROM ALL OVER--STOPPING TSUNAMIS, AVERTING RAIL DISASTERS, AND MORE.
TING
TING
TANG
ZING
A VIRAL HOAX? SPECIAL EFFECTS? THOUSANDS OF EYEWITNESSES SAY THIS MIRACLE MAN IS REAL.
KLAK
KLAK
KLAK
WHAT THE HELL...?

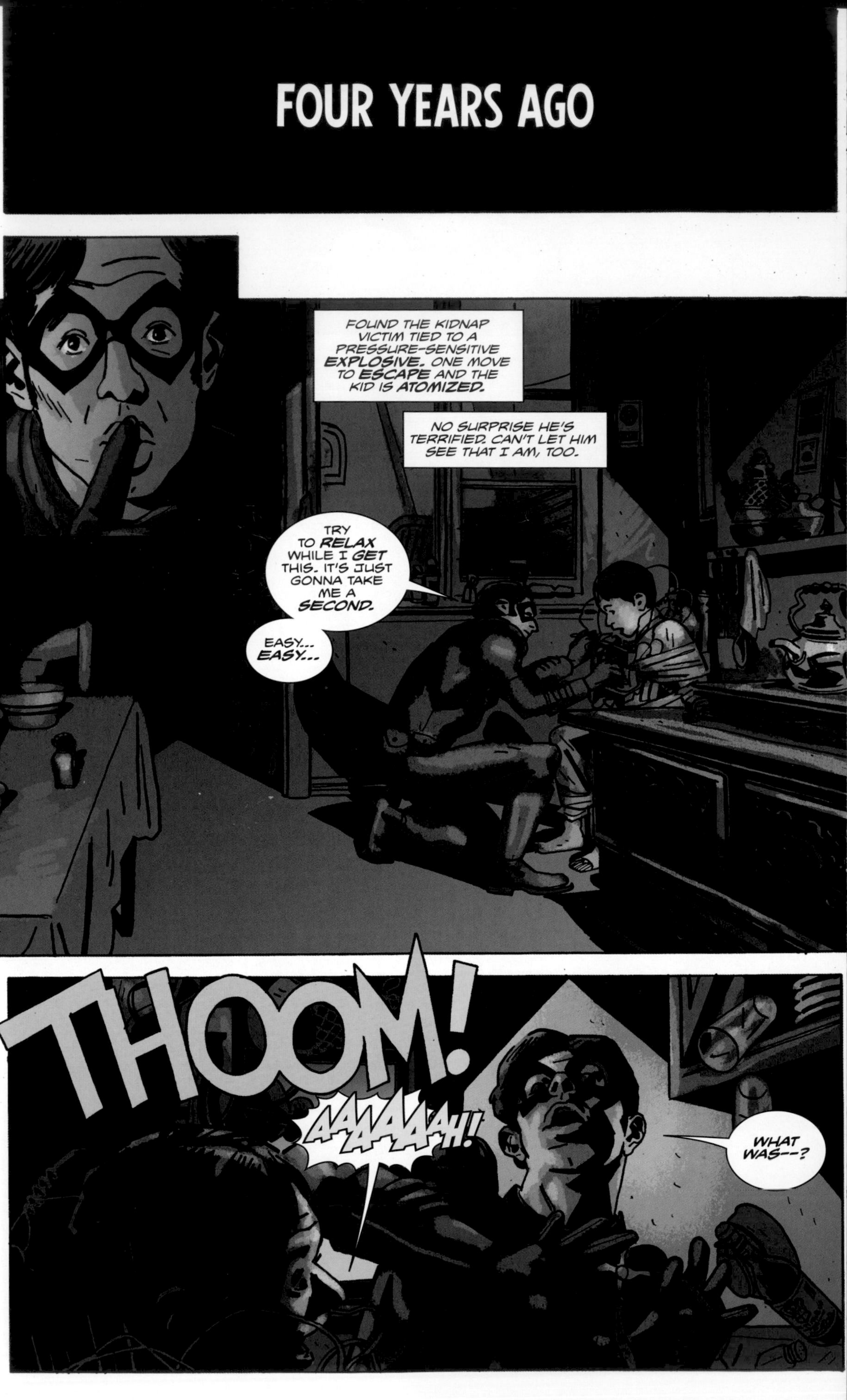
FOUR YEARS AGO
FOUND THE KIDNAP VICTIM TIED TO A PRESSURE-SENSITIVE EXPLOSIVE. ONE MOVE TO ESCAPE AND THE KID IS ATOMIZED.
NO SURPRISE HE'S TERRIFIED. CAN'T LET HIM SEE THAT I AM, TOO.
TRY TO RELAX WHILE I GET THIS. IT'S JUST GONNA TAKE ME A SECOND.
EASY... EASY...
THOOM!
AAAAAAH!
WHAT WAS--?

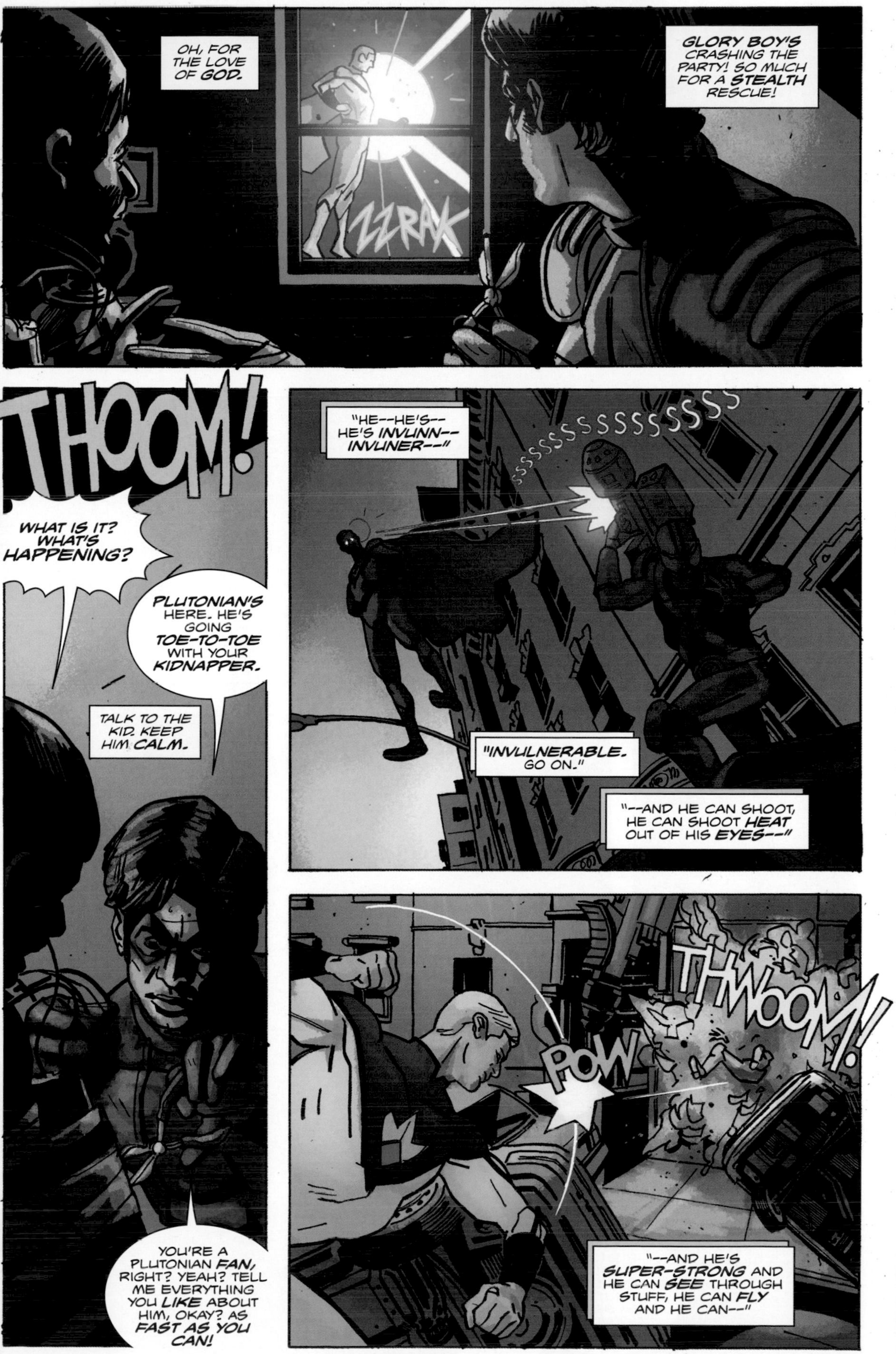
OH, FOR THE LOVE OF GOD.
ZZRAK
GLORY BOY'S CRASHING THE PARTY! SO MUCH FOR A STEALTH RESCUE!
THOOM!
WHAT IS IT? WHAT'S HAPPENING?
PLUTONIAN'S HERE. HE'S GOING TOE-TO-TOE WITH YOUR KIDNAPPER.
TALK TO THE KID. KEEP HIM CALM.
"HE--HE'S--HE'S INVUNN--INVUNER--"
SSSSSSSSSSSSSSSSSS
"INVULNERABLE. GO ON."
"--AND HE CAN SHOOT, HE CAN SHOOT HEAT OUT OF HIS EYES--"
THWOOM!
POW
YOU'RE A PLUTONIAN FAN, RIGHT? YEAH? TELL ME EVERYTHING YOU LIKE ABOUT HIM, OKAY? AS FAST AS YOU CAN!
"--AND HE'S SUPER-STRONG AND HE CAN SEE THROUGH STUFF, HE CAN FLY AND HE CAN--"

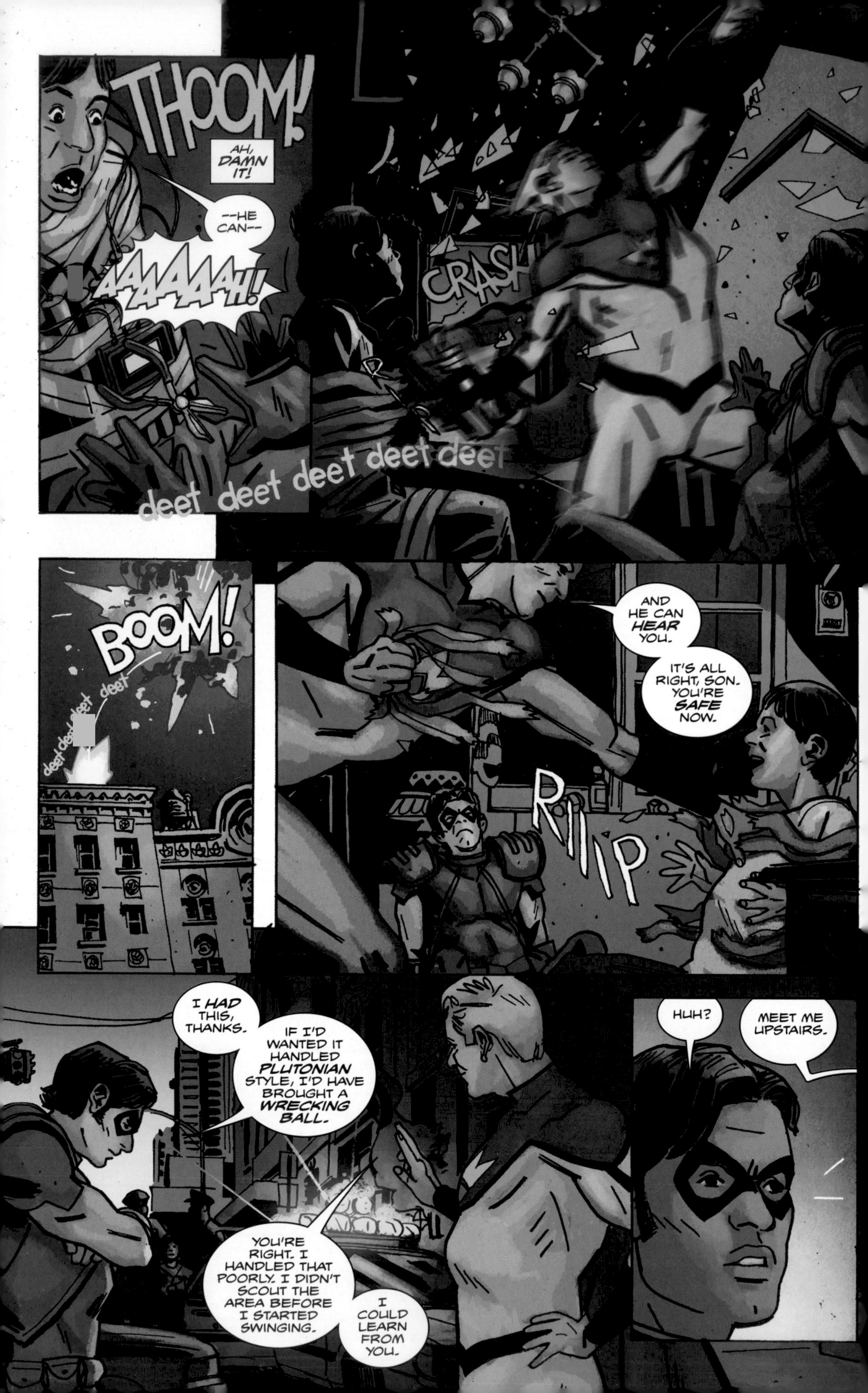
THOOM!
AH, DAMN IT!
--HE CAN--
AAAAAAH!
CRASH
RIP
deet deet deet deet deet
BOOM!
deet deet deet deet
AND HE CAN HEAR YOU.
IT'S ALL RIGHT, SON. YOU'RE SAFE NOW.
RIIIP
I HAD THIS, THANKS.
IF I'D WANTED IT HANDLED PLUTONIAN STYLE, I'D HAVE BROUGHT A WRECKING BALL.
YOU'RE RIGHT. I HANDLED THAT POORLY. I DIDN'T SCOUT THE AREA BEFORE I STARTED SWINGING.
I COULD LEARN FROM YOU.
HUH?
MEET ME UPSTAIRS.

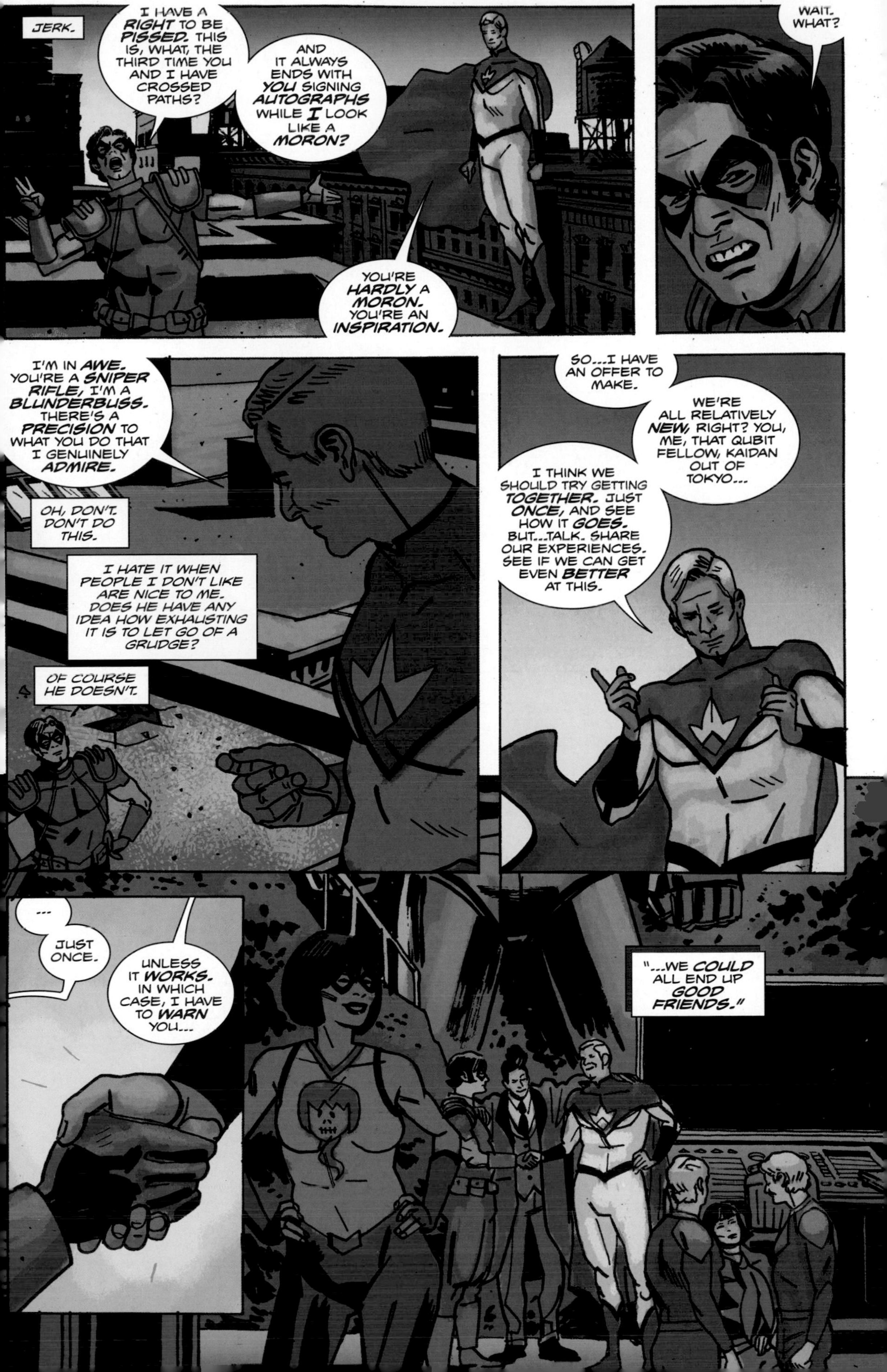
JERK.
I HAVE A RIGHT TO BE PISSED. THIS IS, WHAT, THE THIRD TIME YOU AND I HAVE CROSSED PATHS?
AND IT ALWAYS ENDS WITH YOU SIGNING AUTOGRAPHS WHILE I LOOK LIKE A MORON?
YOU'RE HARDLY A MORON. YOU'RE AN INSPIRATION.
WAIT. WHAT?
I'M IN AWE. YOU'RE A SNIPER RIFLE, I'M A BLUNDERBUSS. THERE'S A PRECISION TO WHAT YOU DO THAT I GENUINELY ADMIRE.
OH, DON'T. DON'T DO THIS.
I HATE IT WHEN PEOPLE I DON'T LIKE ARE NICE TO ME. DOES HE HAVE ANY IDEA HOW EXHAUSTING IT IS TO LET GO OF A GRUDGE?
OF COURSE HE DOESN'T.
SO...I HAVE AN OFFER TO MAKE.
WE'RE ALL RELATIVELY NEW, RIGHT? YOU, ME, THAT QUBIT FELLOW, KAIDAN OUT OF TOKYO...
I THINK WE SHOULD TRY GETTING TOGETHER. JUST ONCE, AND SEE HOW IT GOES. BUT...TALK. SHARE OUR EXPERIENCES. SEE IF WE CAN GET EVEN BETTER AT THIS.
...
JUST ONCE.
UNLESS IT WORKS. IN WHICH CASE, I HAVE TO WARN YOU...
"...WE COULD ALL END UP GOOD FRIENDS."

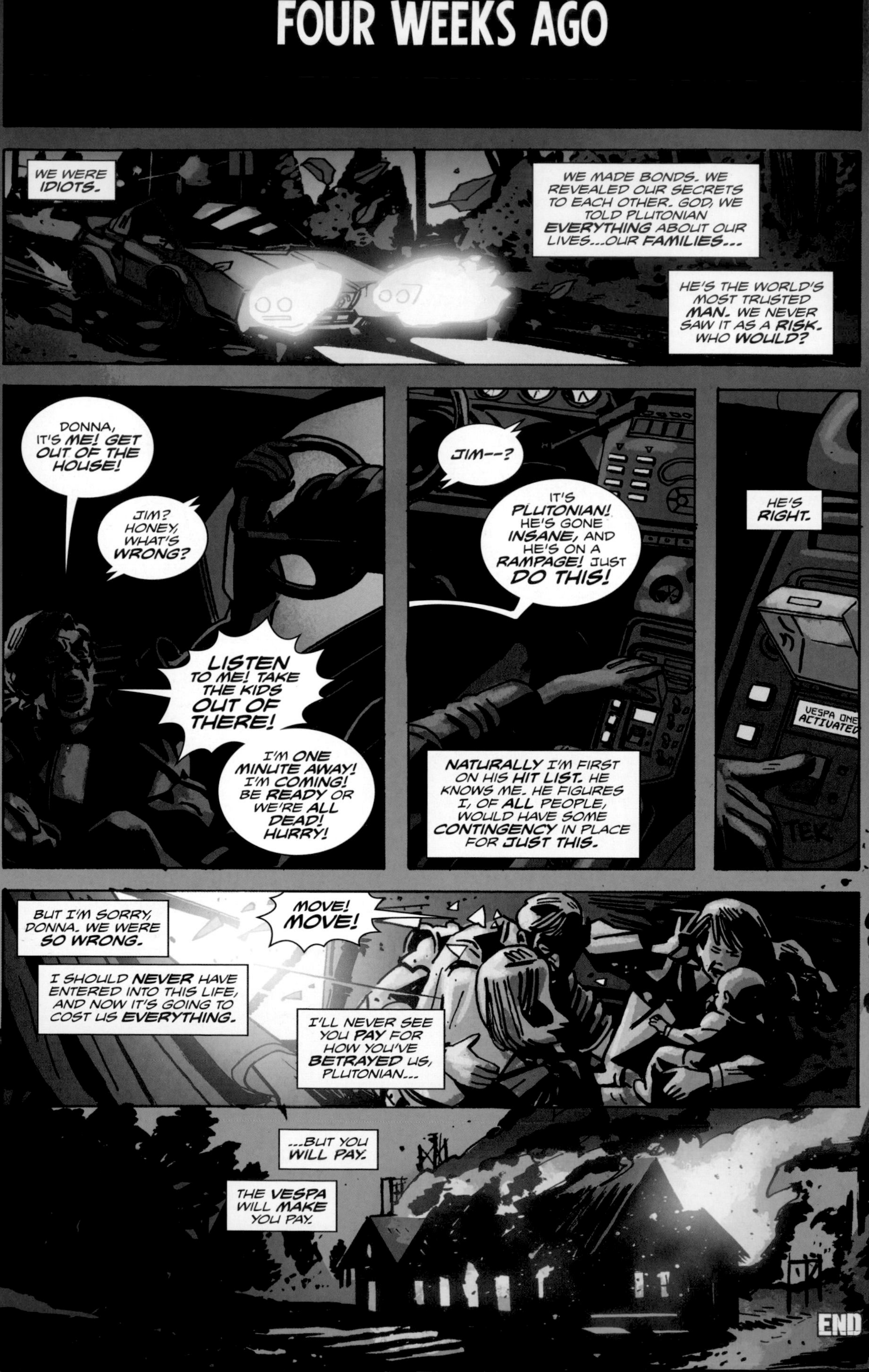
FOUR WEEKS AGO
WE WERE IDIOTS.
WE MADE BONDS. WE REVEALED OUR SECRETS TO EACH OTHER. GOD, WE TOLD PLUTONIAN EVERYTHING ABOUT OUR LIVES...OUR FAMILIES...
HE'S THE WORLD'S MOST TRUSTED MAN. WE NEVER SAW IT AS A RISK. WHO WOULD?
DONNA, IT'S ME! GET OUT OF THE HOUSE!
JIM? HONEY, WHAT'S WRONG?
LISTEN TO ME! TAKE THE KIDS OUT OF THERE!
I'M ONE MINUTE AWAY! I'M COMING! BE READY OR WE'RE ALL DEAD! HURRY!
JIM--?
IT'S PLUTONIAN! HE'S GONE INSANE, AND HE'S ON A RAMPAGE! JUST DO THIS!
NATURALLY I'M FIRST ON HIS HIT LIST. HE KNOWS ME. HE FIGURES I, OF ALL PEOPLE, WOULD HAVE SOME CONTINGENCY IN PLACE FOR JUST THIS.
HE'S RIGHT.
VESPA ONE ACTIVATED
BUT I'M SORRY, DONNA. WE WERE SO WRONG.
MOVE! MOVE!
I SHOULD NEVER HAVE ENTERED INTO THIS LIFE, AND NOW IT'S GOING TO COST US EVERYTHING.
I'LL NEVER SEE YOU PAY FOR HOW YOU'VE BETRAYED US, PLUTONIAN...
...BUT YOU WILL PAY.
THE VESPA WILL MAKE YOU PAY.
END

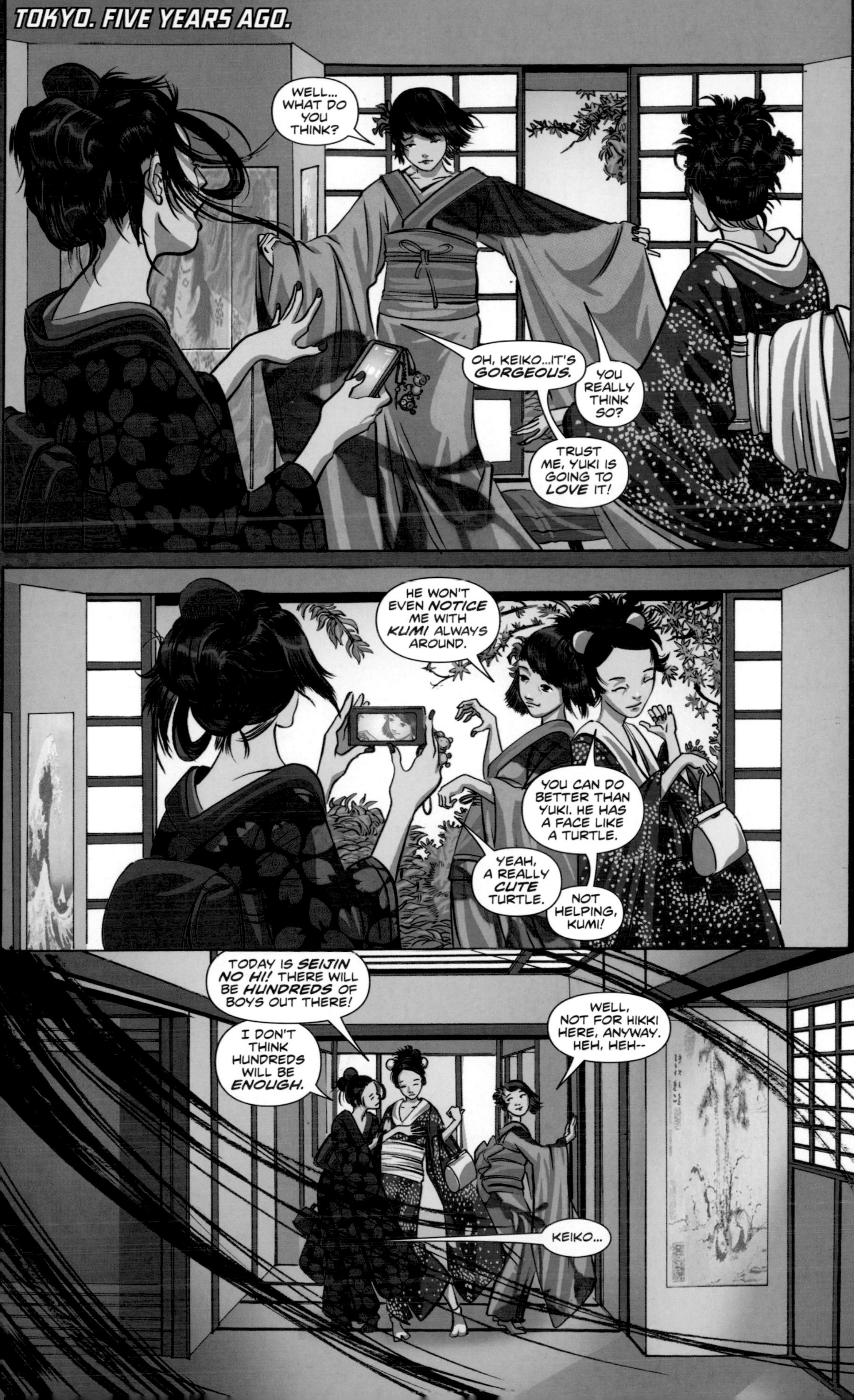
TOKYO. FIVE YEARS AGO.
WELL... WHAT DO YOU THINK?
OH, KEIKO...IT'S GORGEOUS.
YOU REALLY THINK SO?
TRUST ME, YUKI IS GOING TO LOVE IT!
HE WON'T EVEN NOTICE ME WITH KUMI ALWAYS AROUND.
YOU CAN DO BETTER THAN YUKI. HE HAS A FACE LIKE A TURTLE.
YEAH, A REALLY CUTE TURTLE.
NOT HELPING, KUMI!
TODAY IS SEIJIN NO HI! THERE WILL BE HUNDREDS OF BOYS OUT THERE!
I DON'T THINK HUNDREDS WILL BE ENOUGH.
WELL, NOT FOR HIKKI HERE, ANYWAY. HEH, HEH--
KEIKO...

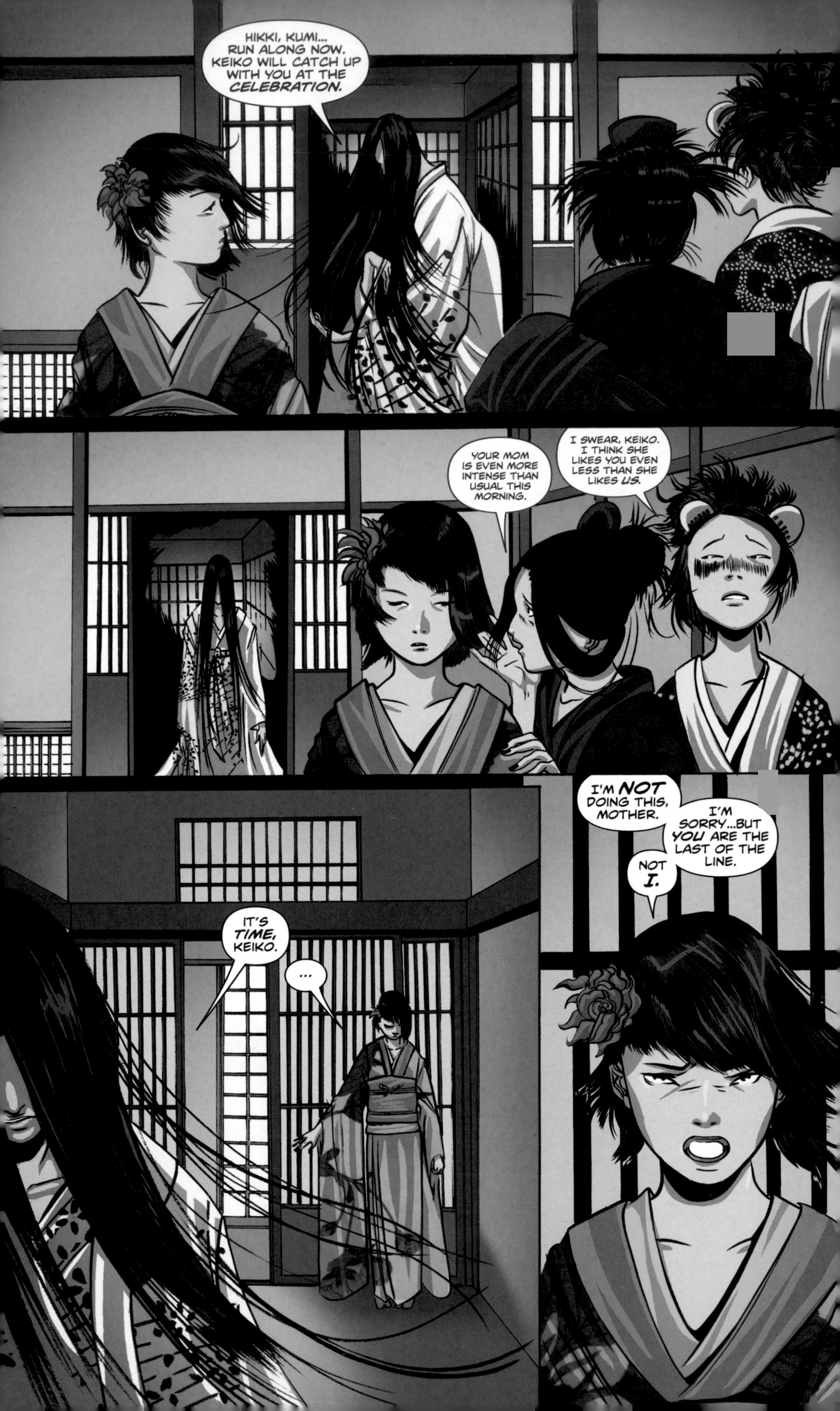
HIKKI, KUMI... RUN ALONG NOW. KEIKO WILL CATCH UP WITH YOU AT THE CELEBRATION.
YOUR MOM IS EVEN MORE INTENSE THAN USUAL THIS MORNING.
I SWEAR, KEIKO. I THINK SHE LIKES YOU EVEN LESS THAN SHE LIKES US.
IT'S TIME, KEIKO.
...
I'M NOT DOING THIS, MOTHER.
I'M SORRY...BUT YOU ARE THE LAST OF THE LINE.
NOT I.

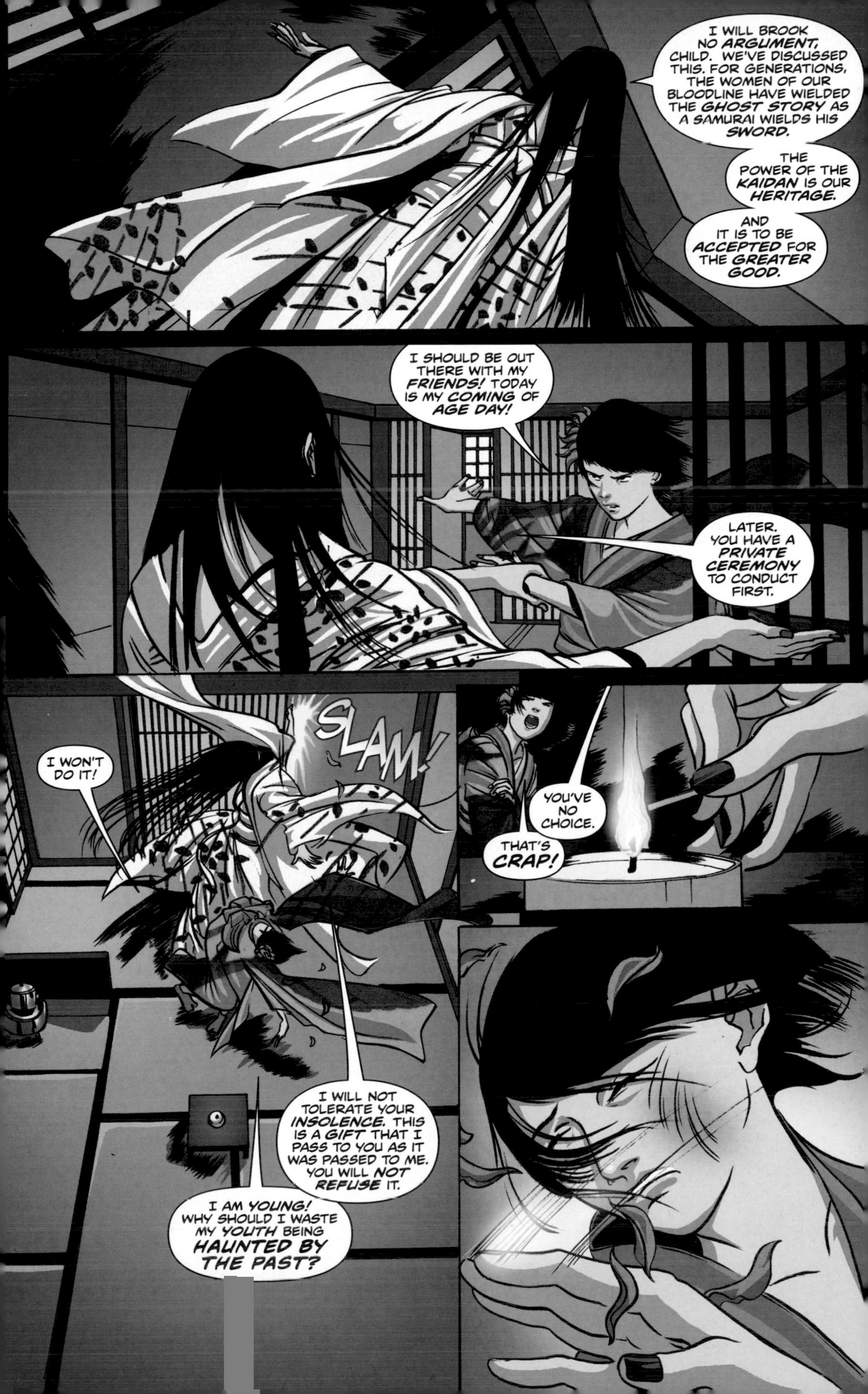

I WILL BROOK NO ARGUMENT, CHILD. WE'VE DISCUSSED THIS. FOR GENERATIONS, THE WOMEN OF OUR BLOODLINE HAVE WIELDED THE GHOST STORY AS A SAMURAI WIELDS HIS SWORD.
THE POWER OF THE KAIDAN IS OUR HERITAGE.
AND IT IS TO BE ACCEPTED FOR THE GREATER GOOD.
I SHOULD BE OUT THERE WITH MY FRIENDS! TODAY IS MY COMING OF AGE DAY!
LATER. YOU HAVE A PRIVATE CEREMONY TO CONDUCT FIRST.
SLAM!
I WON'T DO IT!
I WILL NOT TOLERATE YOUR INSOLENCE. THIS IS A GIFT THAT I PASS TO YOU AS IT WAS PASSED TO ME. YOU WILL NOT REFUSE IT.
I AM YOUNG! WHY SHOULD I WASTE MY YOUTH BEING HAUNTED BY THE PAST?
YOU'VE NO CHOICE.
THAT'S CRAP!

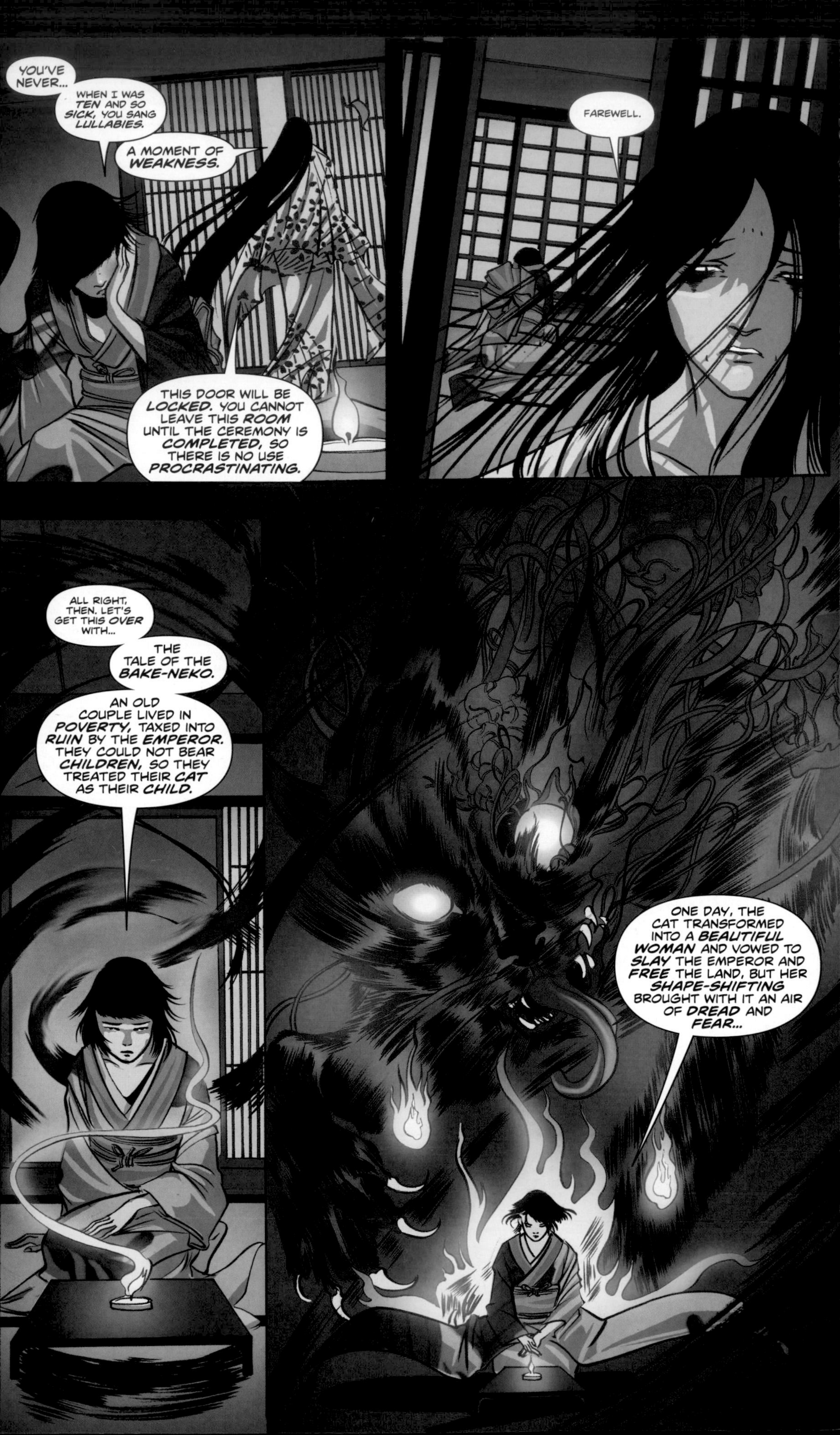
YOU'VE NEVER...
WHEN I WAS TEN AND SO SICK, YOU SANG LULLABIES.
A MOMENT OF WEAKNESS.
THIS DOOR WILL BE LOCKED. YOU CANNOT LEAVE THIS ROOM UNTIL THE CEREMONY IS COMPLETED, SO THERE IS NO USE PROCRASTINATING.
FAREWELL.
ALL RIGHT, THEN. LET'S GET THIS OVER WITH...
THE TALE OF THE BAKE-NEKO.
AN OLD COUPLE LIVED IN POVERTY, TAXED INTO RUIN BY THE EMPEROR. THEY COULD NOT BEAR CHILDREN, SO THEY TREATED THEIR CAT AS THEIR CHILD.
ONE DAY, THE CAT TRANSFORMED INTO A BEAUTIFUL WOMAN AND VOWED TO SLAY THE EMPEROR AND FREE THE LAND, BUT HER SHAPE-SHIFTING BROUGHT WITH IT AN AIR OF DREAD AND FEAR...

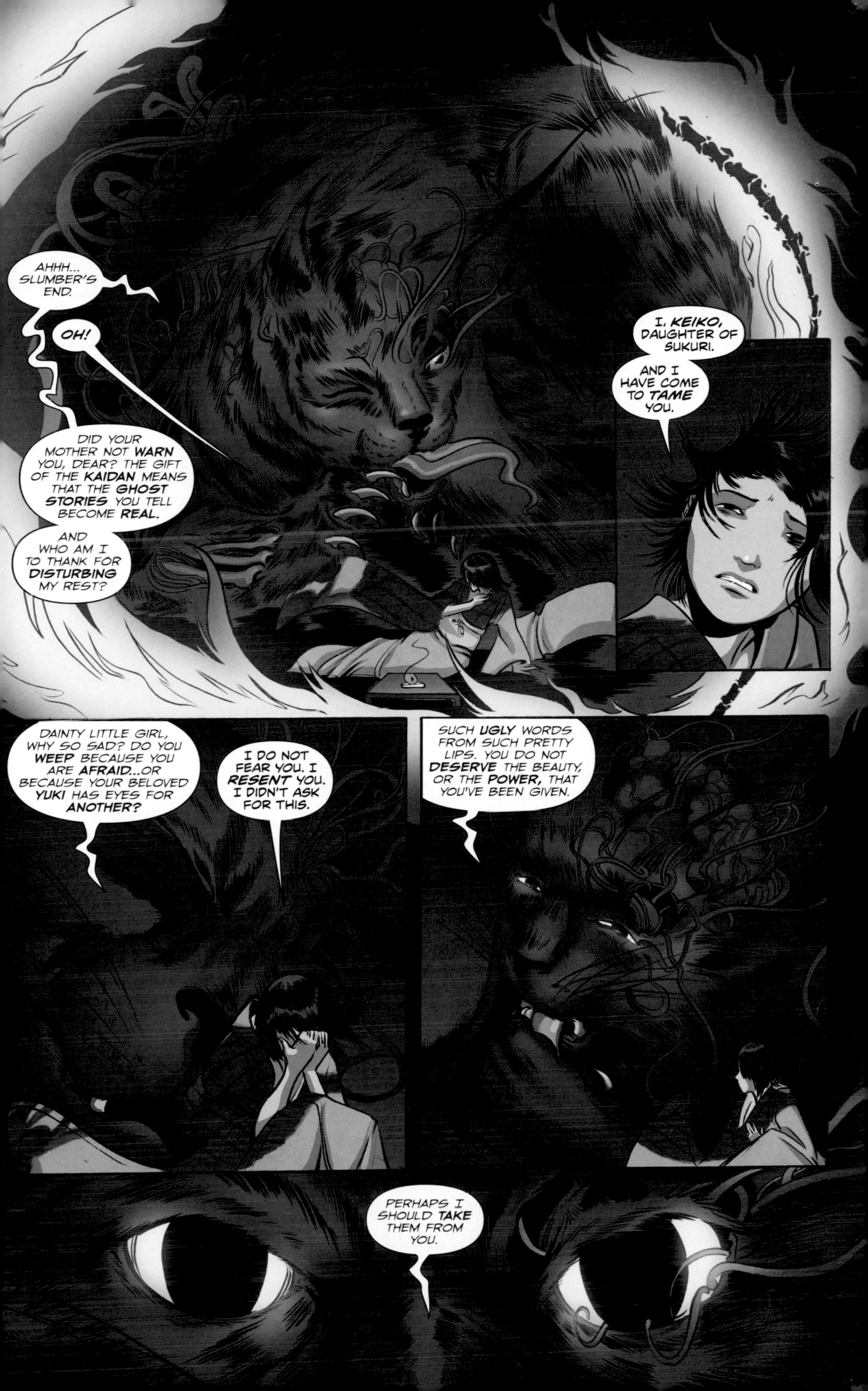
AHHH... SLUMBER'S END.
OH!
DID YOUR MOTHER NOT WARN YOU, DEAR? THE GIFT OF THE KAIDAN MEANS THAT THE GHOST STORIES YOU TELL BECOME REAL.
AND WHO AM I TO THANK FOR DISTURBING MY REST?
I, KEIKO, DAUGHTER OF SUKURI.
AND I HAVE COME TO TAME YOU.
DAINTY LITTLE GIRL, WHY SO SAD? DO YOU WEEP BECAUSE YOU ARE AFRAID...OR BECAUSE YOUR BELOVED YUKI HAS EYES FOR ANOTHER?
I DO NOT FEAR YOU. I RESENT YOU. I DIDN'T ASK FOR THIS.
SUCH UGLY WORDS FROM SUCH PRETTY LIPS. YOU DO NOT DESERVE THE BEAUTY, OR THE POWER, THAT YOU'VE BEEN GIVEN.
PERHAPS I SHOULD TAKE THEM FROM YOU.

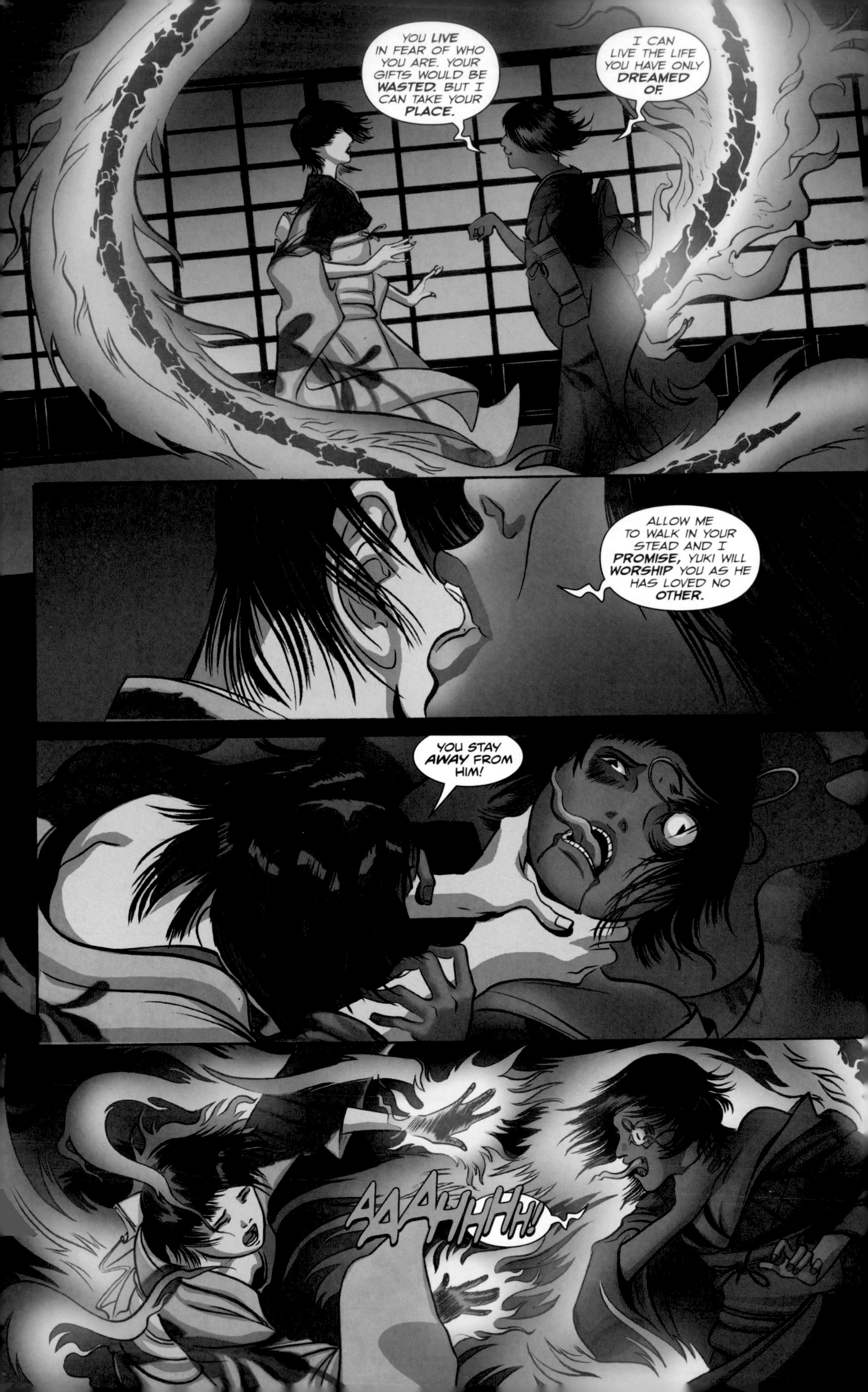
YOU LIVE IN FEAR OF WHO YOU ARE. YOUR GIFTS WOULD BE WASTED. BUT I CAN TAKE YOUR PLACE.
I CAN LIVE THE LIFE YOU HAVE ONLY DREAMED OF.
ALLOW ME TO WALK IN YOUR STEAD AND I PROMISE, YUKI WILL WORSHIP YOU AS HE HAS LOVED NO OTHER.
YOU STAY AWAY FROM HIM!
AAAHHHH!

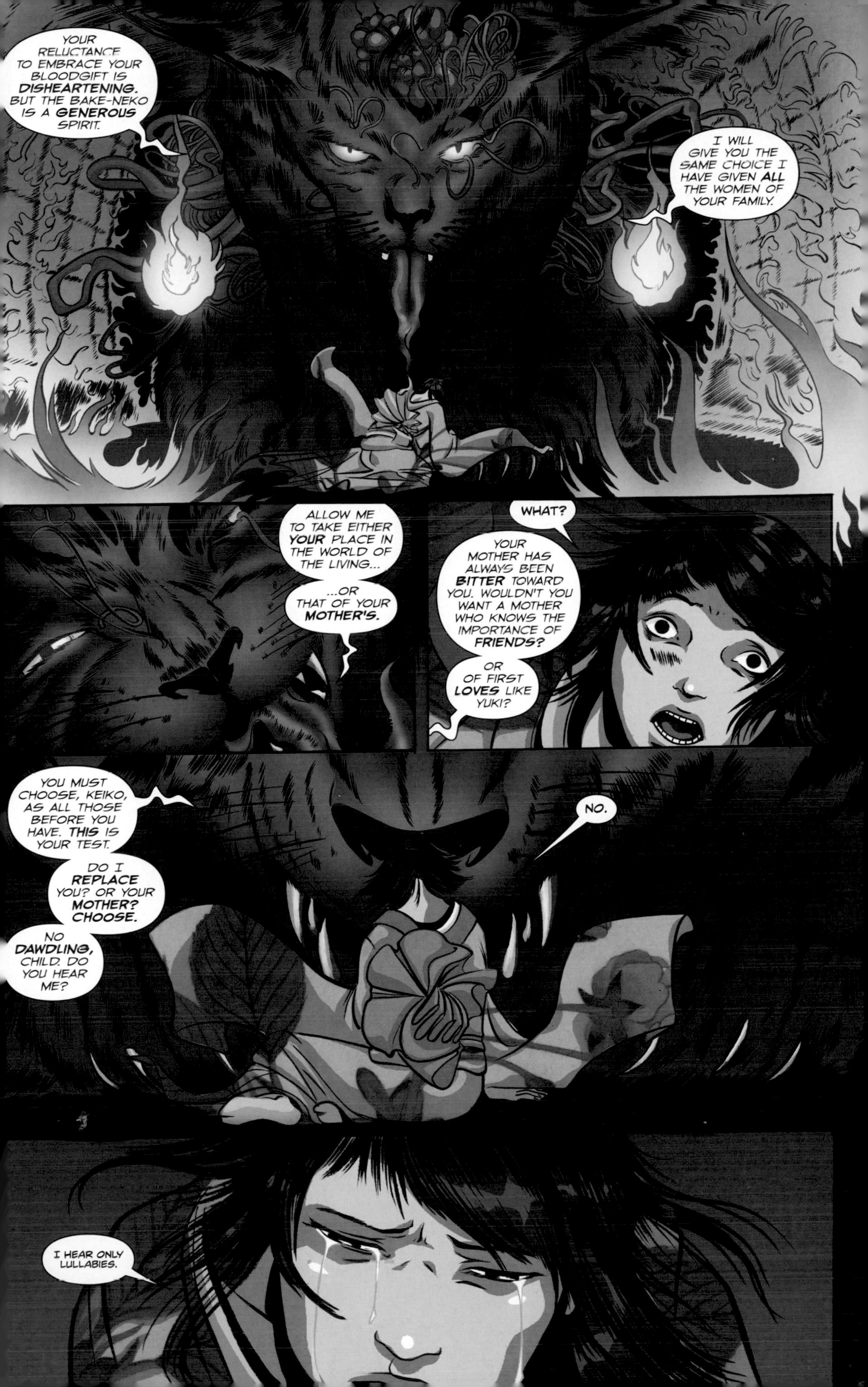
YOUR RELUCTANCE TO EMBRACE YOUR BLOODGIFT IS DISHEARTENING. BUT THE BAKE-NEKO IS A GENEROUS SPIRIT.
I WILL GIVE YOU THE SAME CHOICE I HAVE GIVEN ALL THE WOMEN OF YOUR FAMILY.
ALLOW ME TO TAKE EITHER YOUR PLACE IN THE WORLD OF THE LIVING...
...OR THAT OF YOUR MOTHER'S.
WHAT?
YOUR MOTHER HAS ALWAYS BEEN BITTER TOWARD YOU. WOULDN'T YOU WANT A MOTHER WHO KNOWS THE IMPORTANCE OF FRIENDS?
OR OF FIRST LOVES LIKE YUKI?
YOU MUST CHOOSE, KEIKO, AS ALL THOSE BEFORE YOU HAVE. THIS IS YOUR TEST.
DO I REPLACE YOU? OR YOUR MOTHER? CHOOSE.
NO DAWDLING, CHILD. DO YOU HEAR ME?
NO.
I HEAR ONLY LULLABIES.

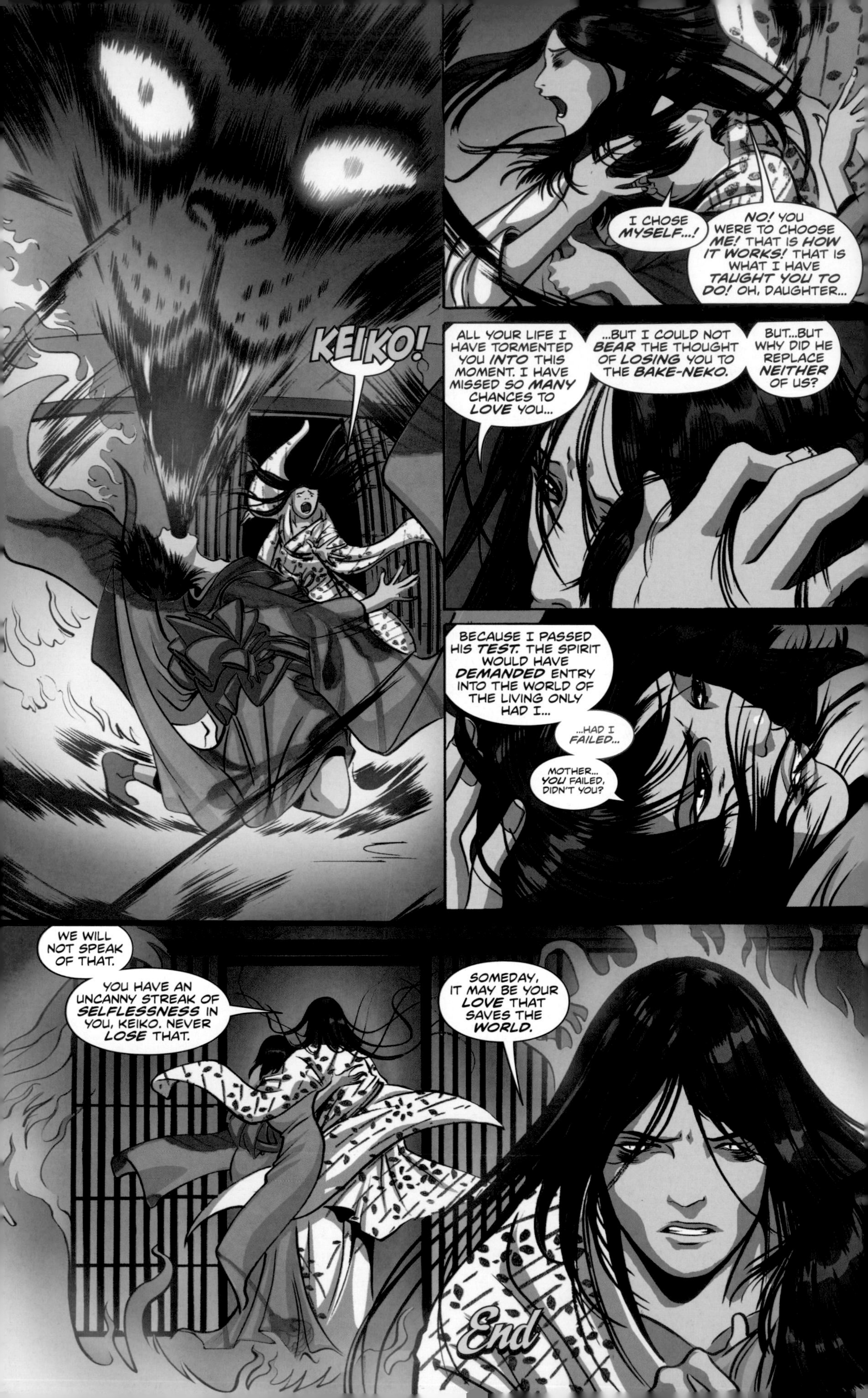
KEIKO!
I CHOSE MYSELF...!
NO! YOU WERE TO CHOOSE ME! THAT IS HOW IT WORKS! THAT IS WHAT I HAVE TAUGHT YOU TO DO! OH, DAUGHTER...
ALL YOUR LIFE I HAVE TORMENTED YOU INTO THIS MOMENT. I HAVE MISSED SO MANY CHANCES TO LOVE YOU...
...BUT I COULD NOT BEAR THE THOUGHT OF LOSING YOU TO THE BAKE-NEKO.
BUT...BUT WHY DID HE REPLACE NEITHER OF US?
BECAUSE I PASSED HIS TEST. THE SPIRIT WOULD HAVE DEMANDED ENTRY INTO THE WORLD OF THE LIVING ONLY HAD I...
...HAD I FAILED...
MOTHER... YOU FAILED, DIDN'T YOU?
WE WILL NOT SPEAK OF THAT.
YOU HAVE AN UNCANNY STREAK OF SELFLESSNESS IN YOU, KEIKO. NEVER LOSE THAT.
SOMEDAY, IT MAY BE YOUR LOVE THAT SAVES THE WORLD.
End

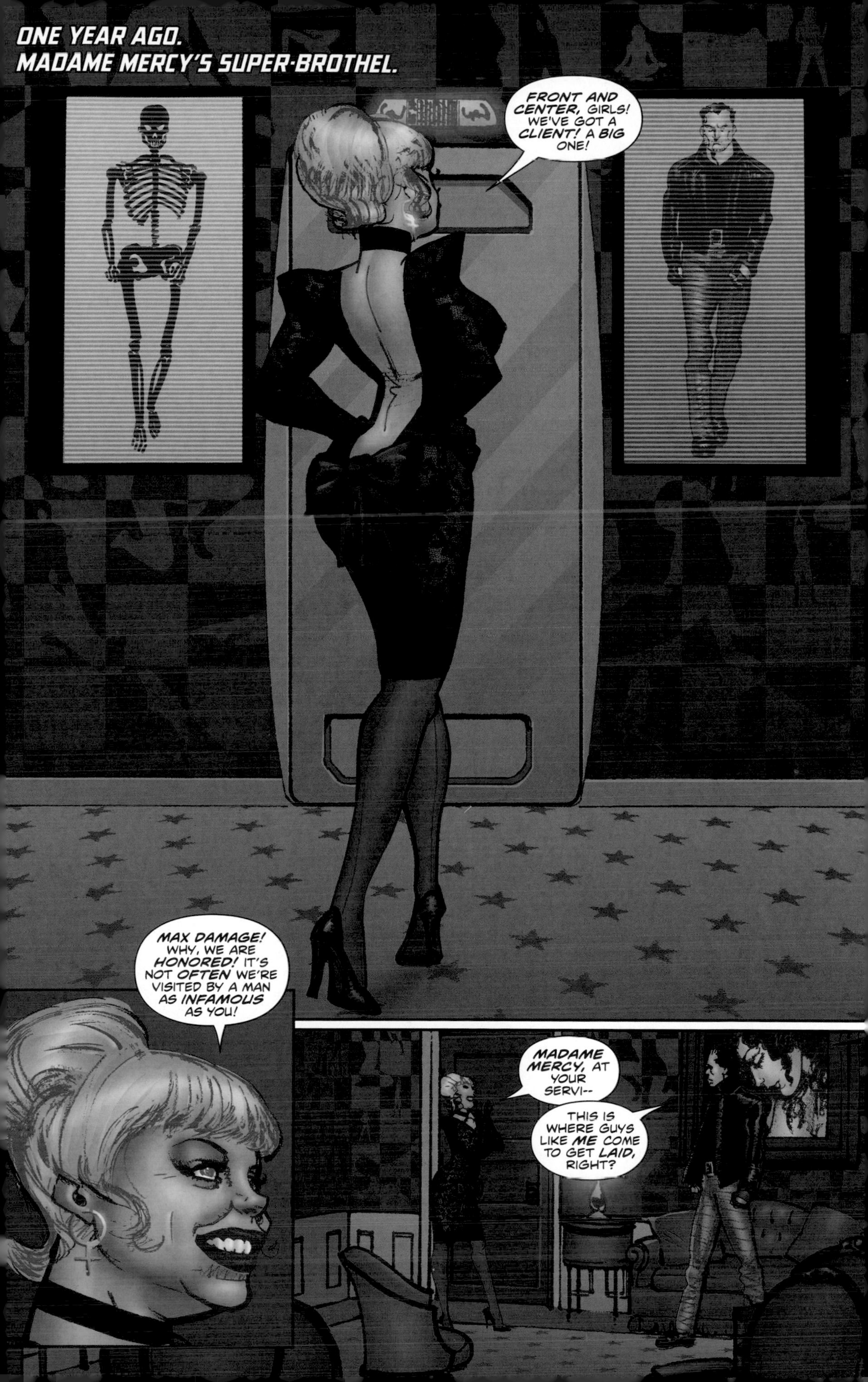

ONE YEAR AGO.
MADAME MERCY'S SUPER-BROTHEL.
FRONT AND CENTER, GIRLS! WE'VE GOT A CLIENT! A BIG ONE!
MAX DAMAGE! WHY, WE ARE HONORED! IT'S NOT OFTEN WE'RE VISITED BY A MAN AS INFAMOUS AS YOU!
MADAME MERCY, AT YOUR SERVI--
THIS IS WHERE GUYS LIKE ME COME TO GET LAID, RIGHT?

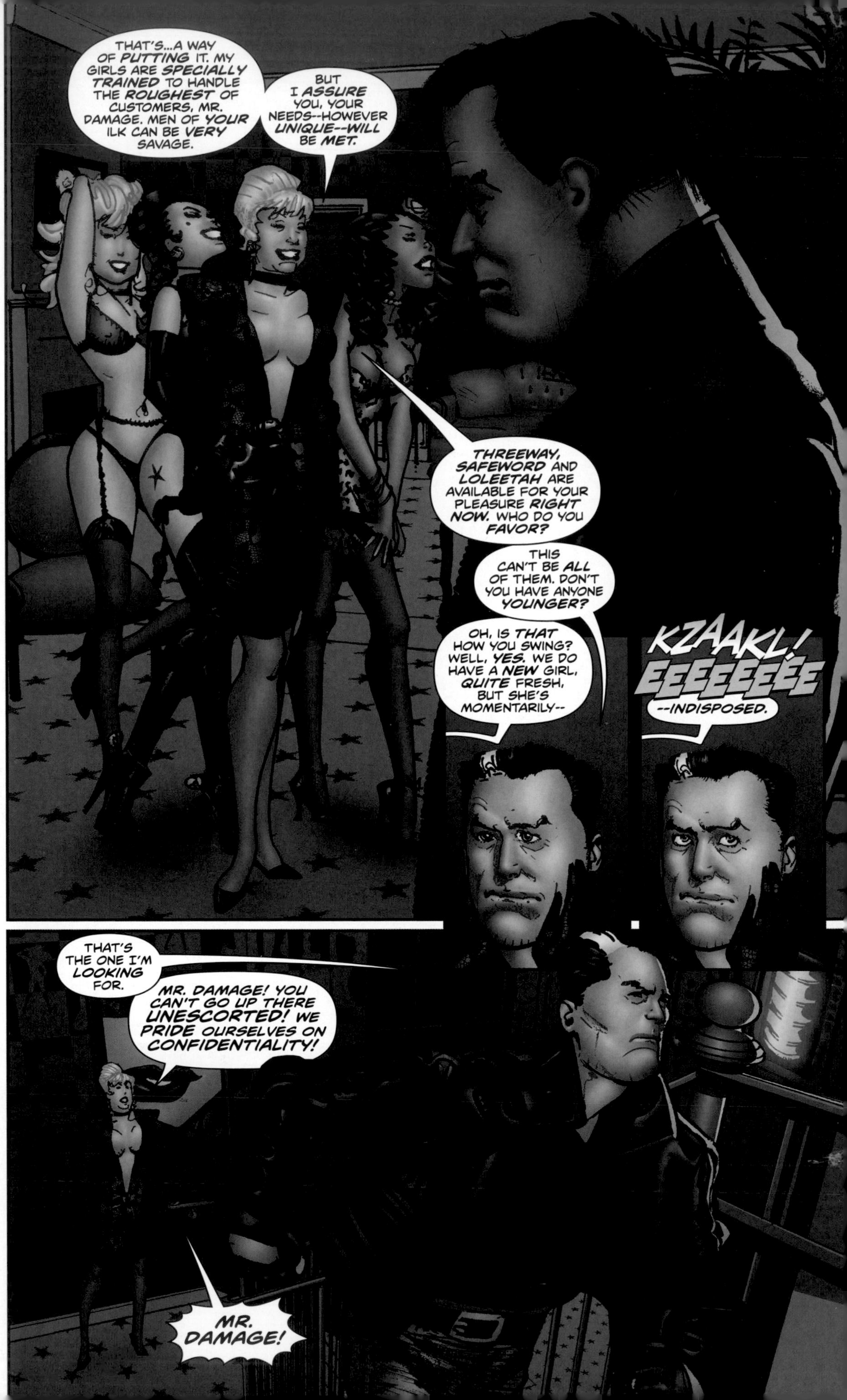
THAT'S...A WAY OF PUTTING IT. MY GIRLS ARE SPECIALLY TRAINED TO HANDLE THE ROUGHEST OF CUSTOMERS, MR. DAMAGE. MEN OF YOUR ILK CAN BE VERY SAVAGE.
BUT I ASSURE YOU, YOUR NEEDS--HOWEVER UNIQUE--WILL BE MET.
THREEWAY, SAFEWORD AND LOLEETAH ARE AVAILABLE FOR YOUR PLEASURE RIGHT NOW. WHO DO YOU FAVOR?
THIS CAN'T BE ALL OF THEM. DON'T YOU HAVE ANYONE YOUNGER?
OH, IS THAT HOW YOU SWING? WELL, YES. WE DO HAVE A NEW GIRL, QUITE FRESH, BUT SHE'S MOMENTARILY--
KZAAKL! EEEEEEEE
--INDISPOSED.
THAT'S THE ONE I'M LOOKING FOR.
MR. DAMAGE! YOU CAN'T GO UP THERE UNESCORTED! WE PRIDE OURSELVES ON CONFIDENTIALITY!
MR. DAMAGE!

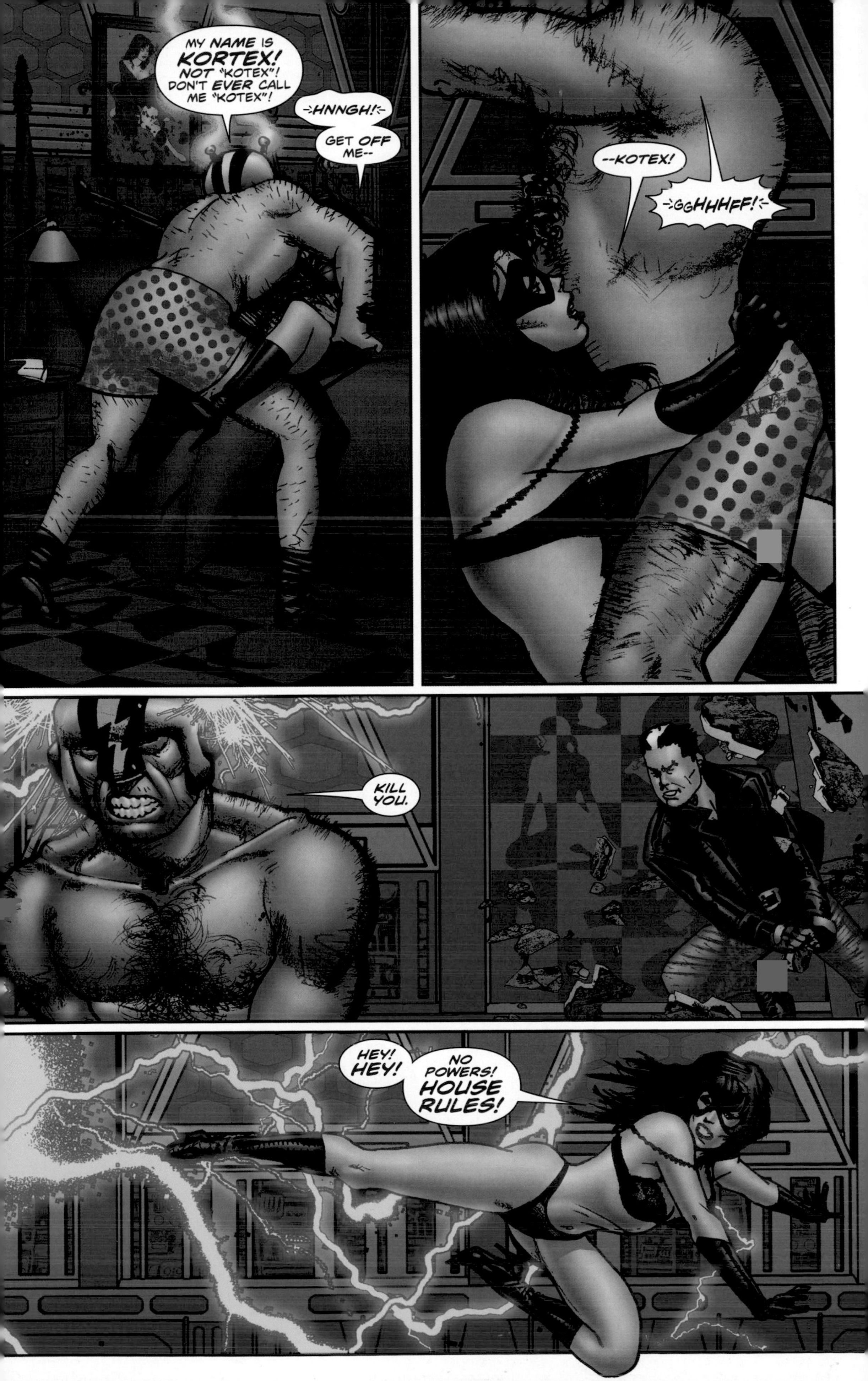

MY NAME IS KORTEX! NOT "KOTEX"! DON'T EVER CALL ME "KOTEX"!
-HNNGH!-
GET OFF ME--
--KOTEX!
-GGHHHFF!-
KILL YOU.
HEY! HEY!
NO POWERS! HOUSE RULES!

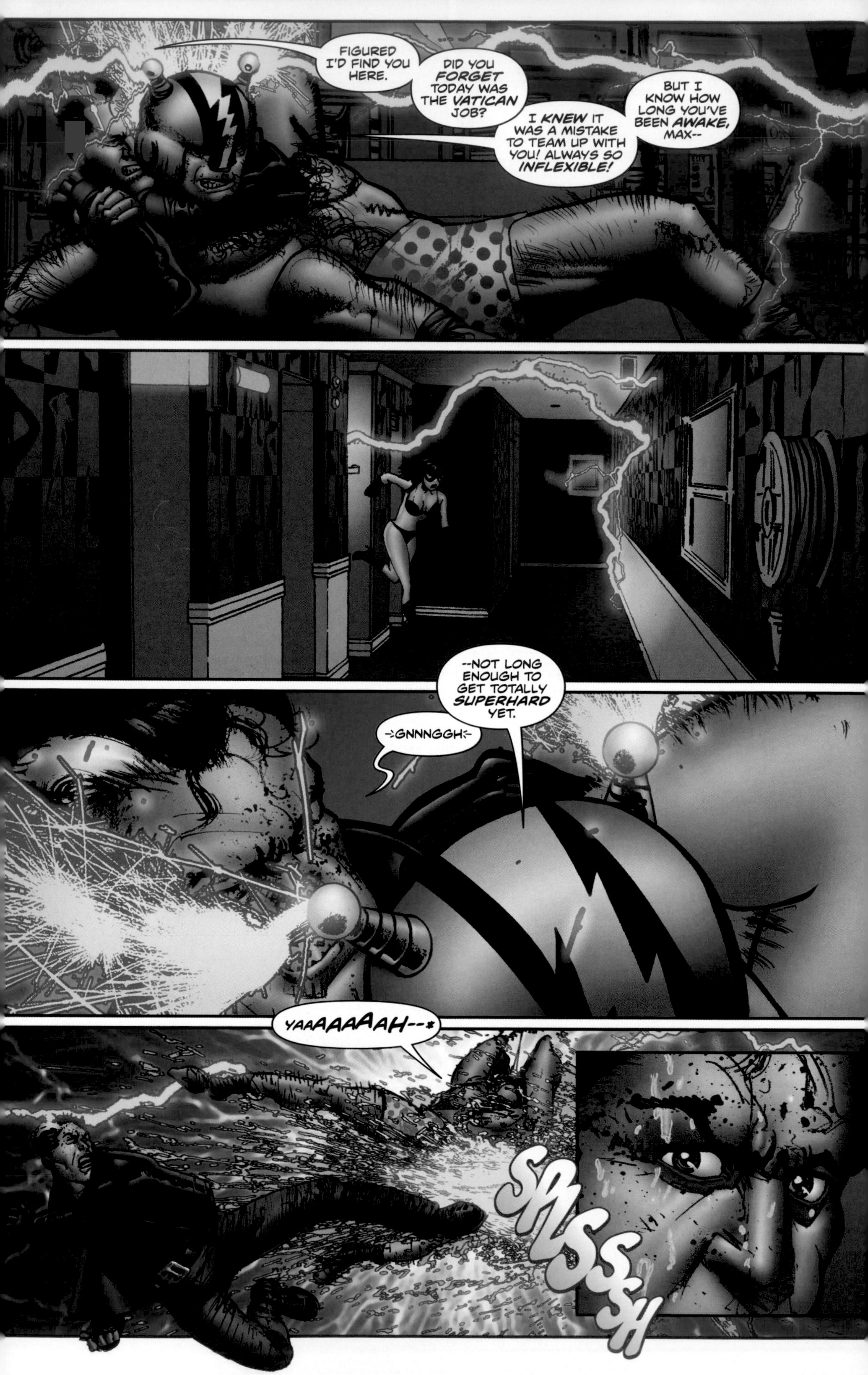
FIGURED I'D FIND YOU HERE.
DID YOU FORGET TODAY WAS THE VATICAN JOB?
I KNEW IT WAS A MISTAKE TO TEAM UP WITH YOU! ALWAYS SO INFLEXIBLE!
BUT I KNOW HOW LONG YOU'VE BEEN AWAKE, MAX--
--NOT LONG ENOUGH TO GET TOTALLY SUPERHARD YET.
-GNNNGGH-
YAAAAAAAH--*
SNSSSH

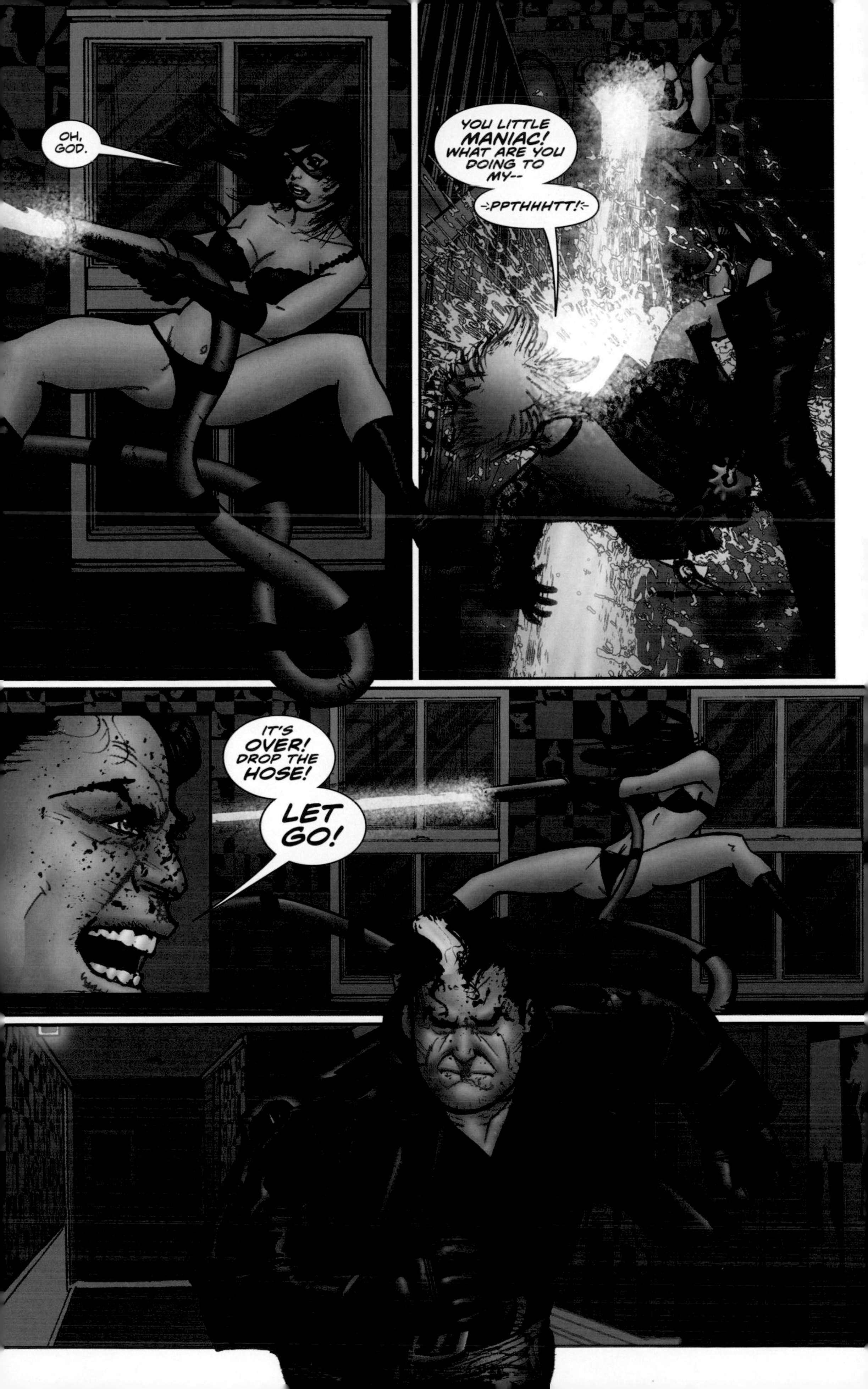
OH, GOD.
YOU LITTLE MANIAC! WHAT ARE YOU DOING TO MY--
-PPTHHHTT!-
IT'S OVER! DROP THE HOSE!
LET GO!

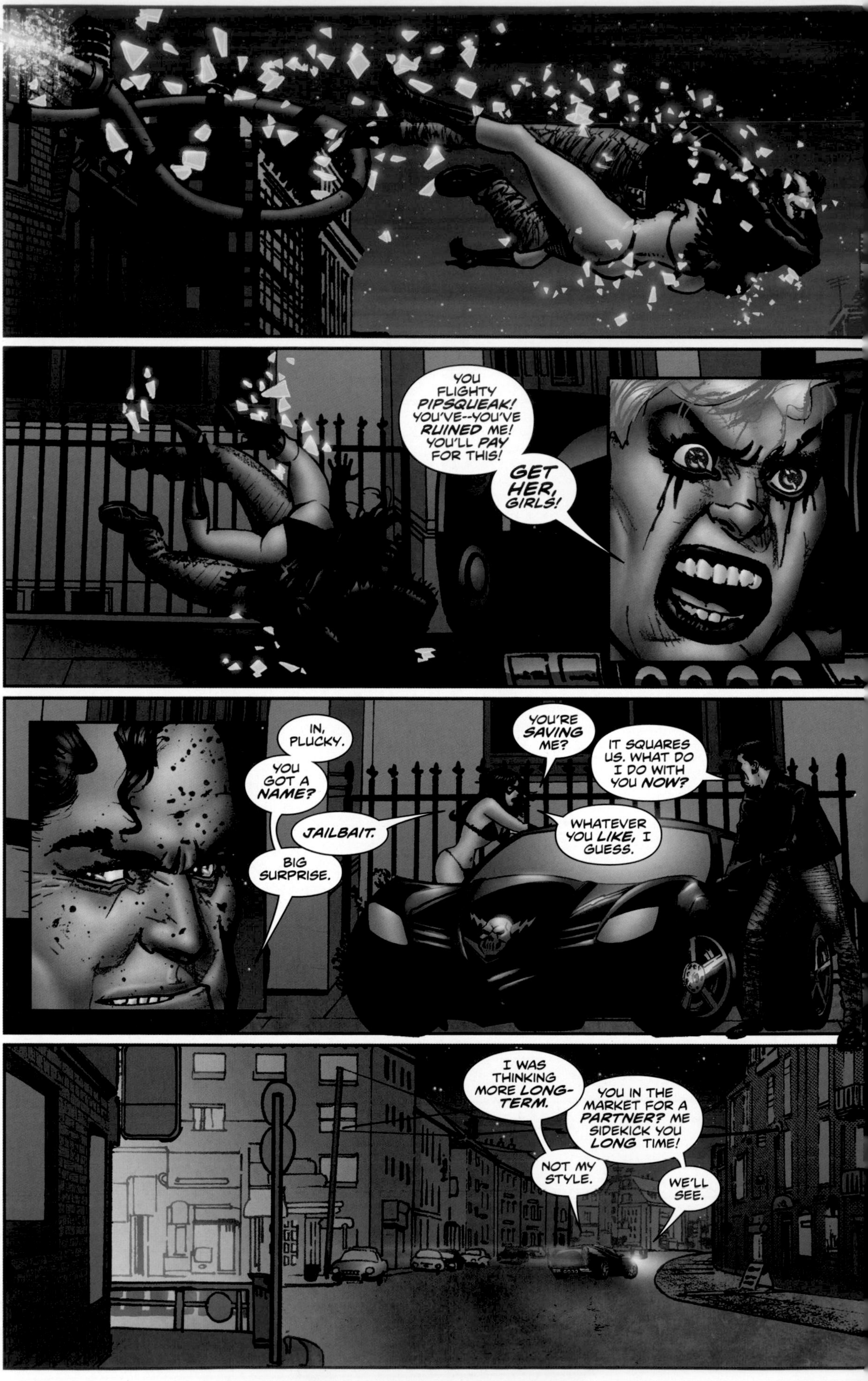

YOU FLIGHTY PIPSQUEAK! YOU'VE--YOU'VE RUINED ME! YOU'LL PAY FOR THIS!
GET HER, GIRLS!
IN, PLUCKY.
YOU GOT A NAME?
JAILBAIT.
BIG SURPRISE.
YOU'RE SAVING ME?
IT SQUARES US. WHAT DO I DO WITH YOU NOW?
WHATEVER YOU LIKE, I GUESS.
I WAS THINKING MORE LONG-TERM.
YOU IN THE MARKET FOR A PARTNER? ME SIDEKICK YOU LONG TIME!
NOT MY STYLE.
WE'LL SEE.

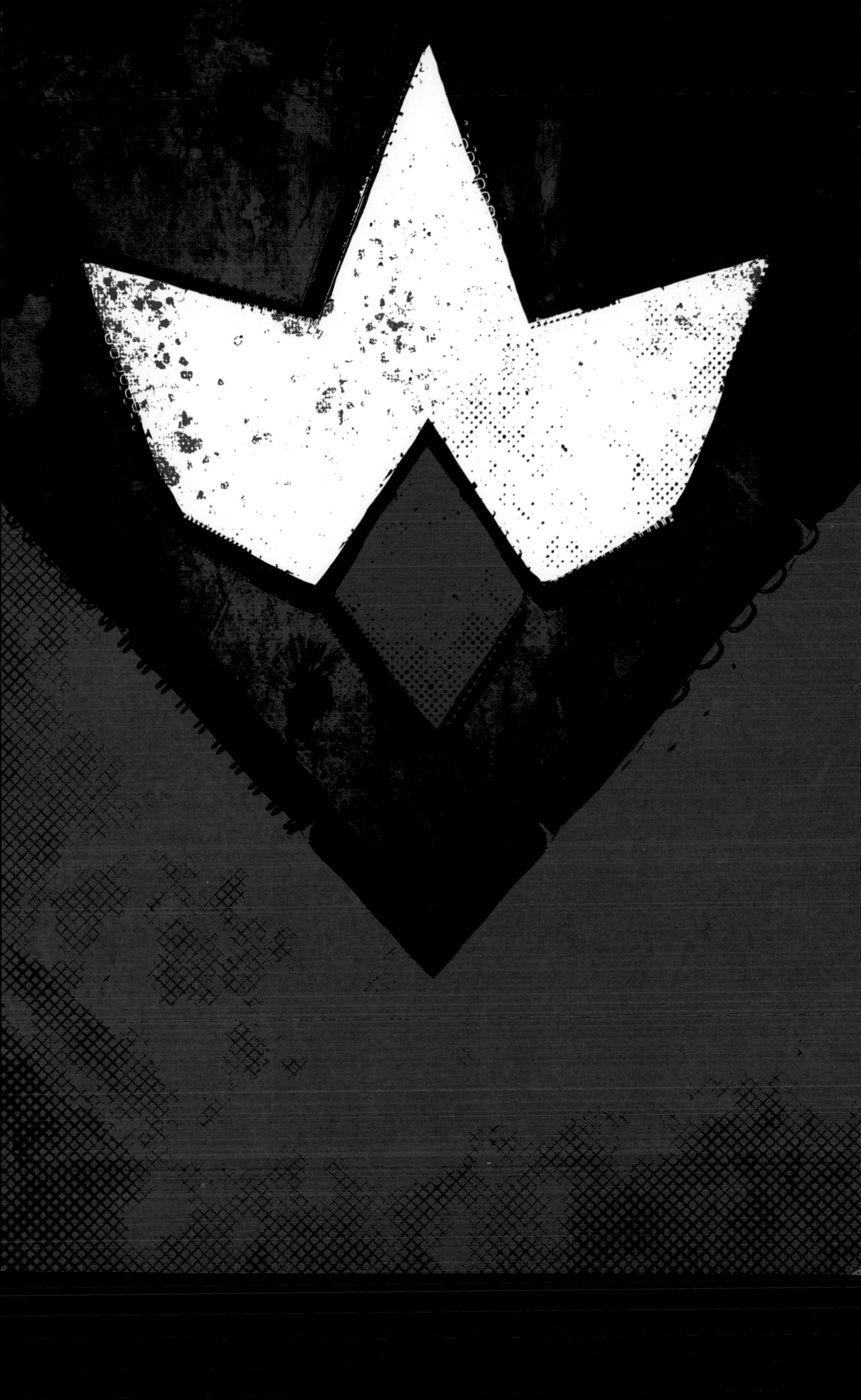

CHAPTER 13

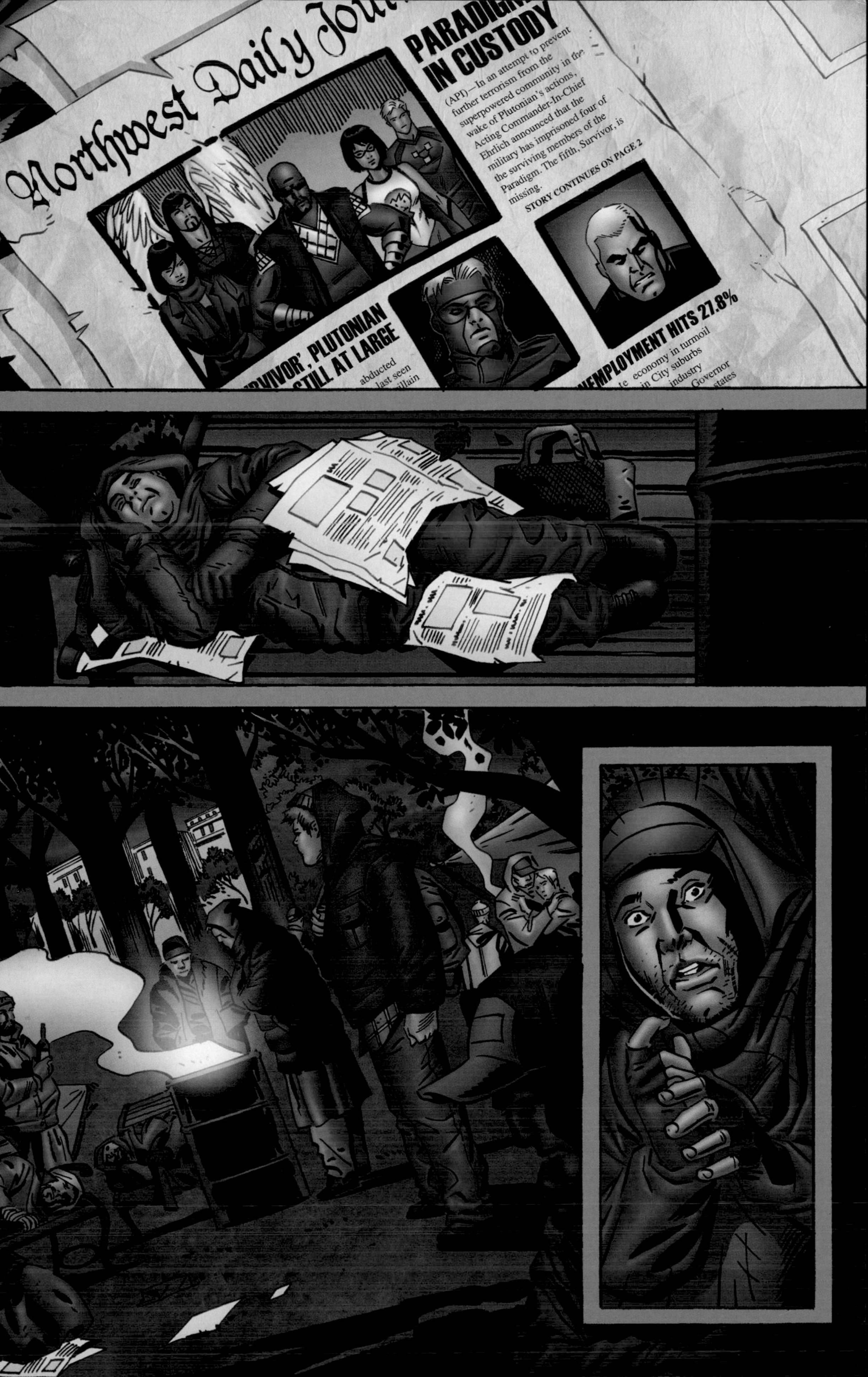
Northwest Daily Jou
PARADIGM
IN CUSTODY
(API)—In an attempt to prevent further terrorism from the superpowered community in the wake of Plutonian's actions, Acting Commander-In-Chief Ehrlich announced that the military has imprisoned four of the surviving members of the Paradigm. The fifth, Survivor, is missing.
STORY CONTINUES ON PAGE 2
URVIVOR', PLUTONIAN
STILL AT LARGE
abducted
last seen
NEMPLOYMENT HITS 27.8%
economy in turmoil
in City suburbs
industry
Governor
states

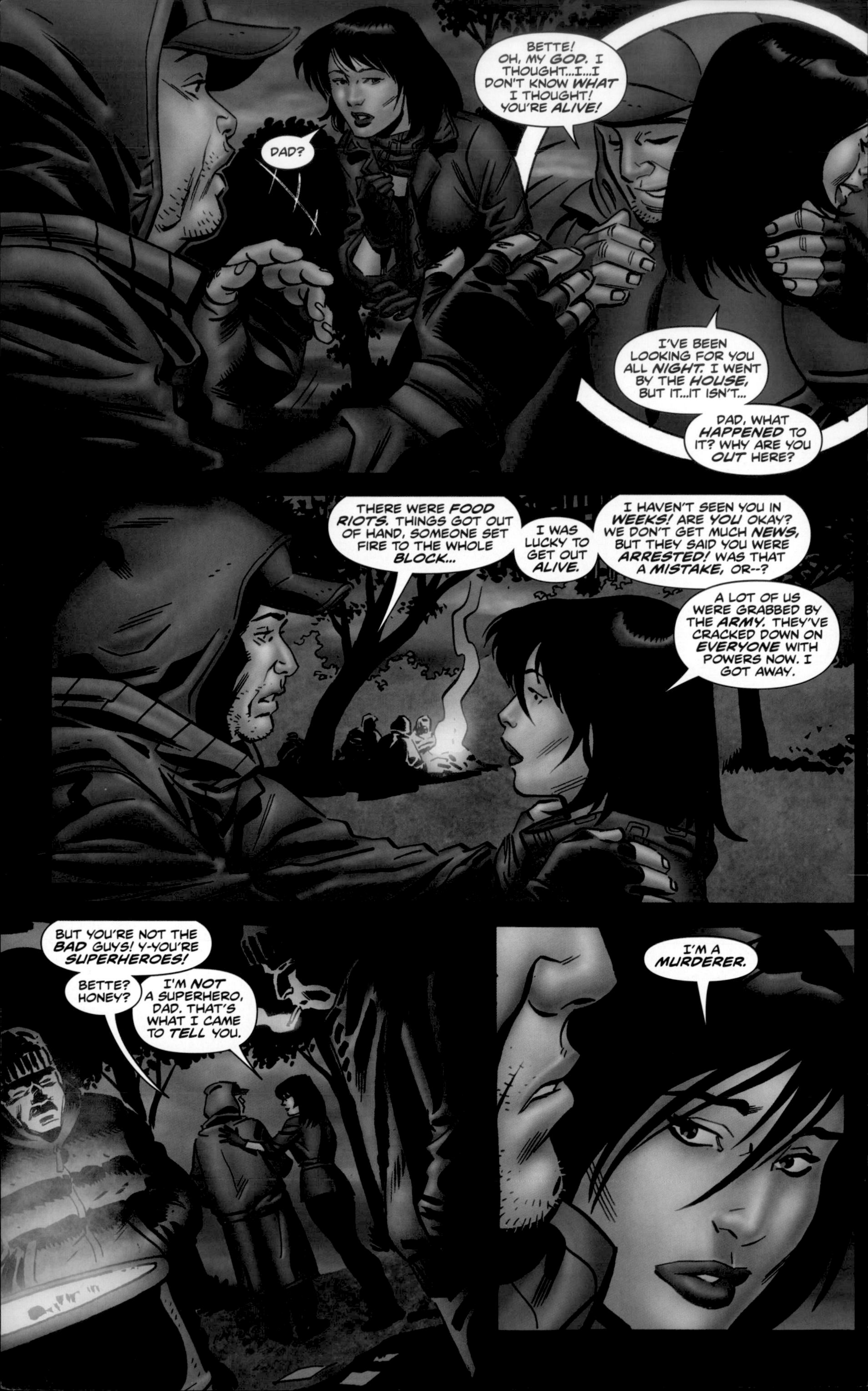
DAD?
BETTE! OH, MY GOD. I THOUGHT...I...I DON'T KNOW WHAT I THOUGHT! YOU'RE ALIVE!
I'VE BEEN LOOKING FOR YOU ALL NIGHT. I WENT BY THE HOUSE, BUT IT...IT ISN'T...
DAD, WHAT HAPPENED TO IT? WHY ARE YOU OUT HERE?
THERE WERE FOOD RIOTS. THINGS GOT OUT OF HAND, SOMEONE SET FIRE TO THE WHOLE BLOCK...
I WAS LUCKY TO GET OUT ALIVE.
I HAVEN'T SEEN YOU IN WEEKS! ARE YOU OKAY? WE DON'T GET MUCH NEWS, BUT THEY SAID YOU WERE ARRESTED! WAS THAT A MISTAKE, OR--?
A LOT OF US WERE GRABBED BY THE ARMY. THEY'VE CRACKED DOWN ON EVERYONE WITH POWERS NOW. I GOT AWAY.
BUT YOU'RE NOT THE BAD GUYS! Y-YOU'RE SUPERHEROES!
BETTE? HONEY?
I'M NOT A SUPERHERO, DAD. THAT'S WHAT I CAME TO TELL YOU.
I'M A MURDERER.

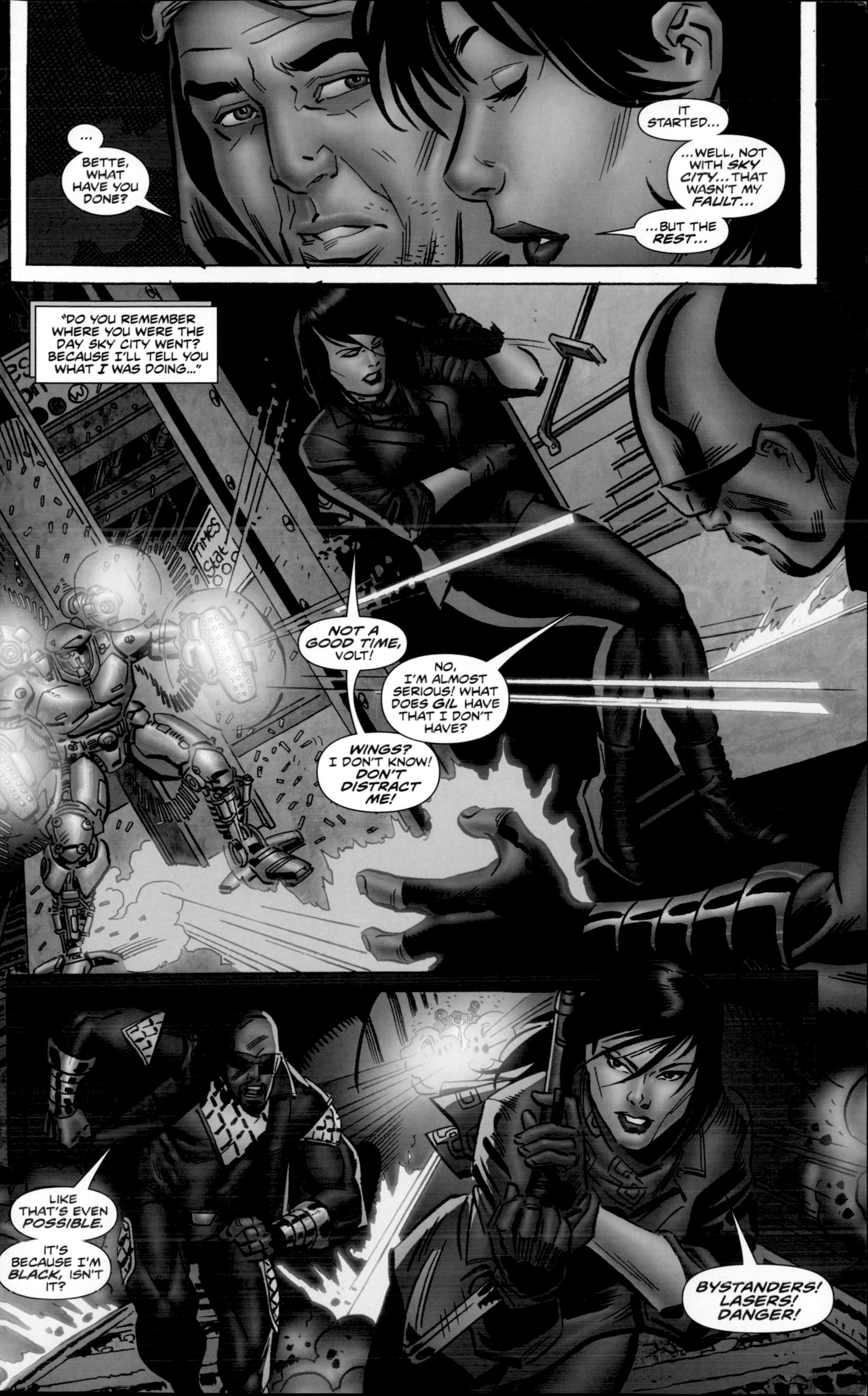
...
BETTE, WHAT HAVE YOU DONE?
IT STARTED...
...WELL, NOT WITH SKY CITY... THAT WASN'T MY FAULT...
...BUT THE REST...
"DO YOU REMEMBER WHERE YOU WERE THE DAY SKY CITY WENT? BECAUSE I'LL TELL YOU WHAT I WAS DOING..."
TIMES Stat
NOT A GOOD TIME, VOLT!
NO, I'M ALMOST SERIOUS! WHAT DOES GIL HAVE THAT I DON'T HAVE?
WINGS? I DON'T KNOW! DON'T DISTRACT ME!
LIKE THAT'S EVEN POSSIBLE.
IT'S BECAUSE I'M BLACK, ISN'T IT?
BYSTANDERS! LASERS! DANGER!

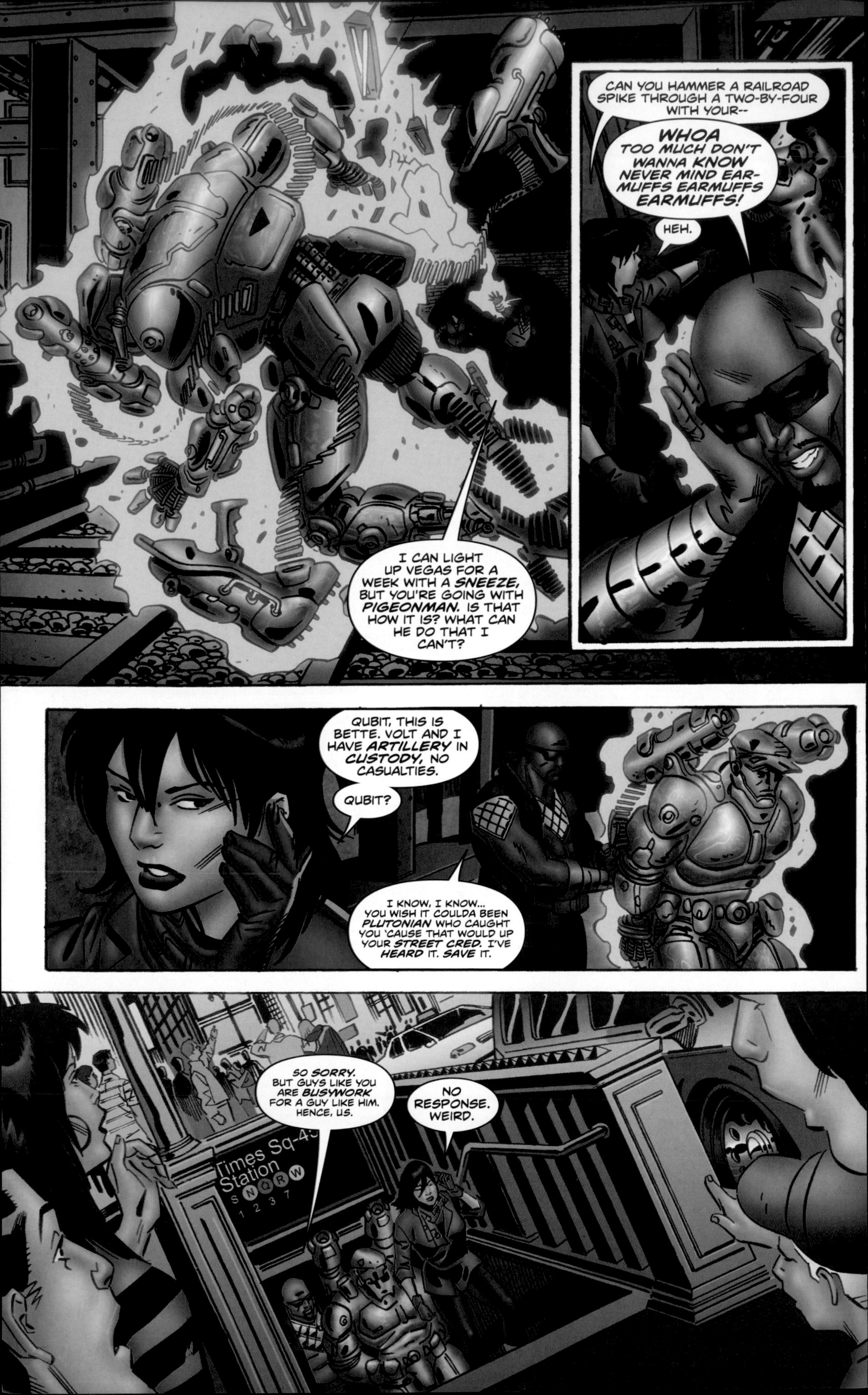
CAN YOU HAMMER A RAILROAD SPIKE THROUGH A TWO-BY-FOUR WITH YOUR--
WHOA TOO MUCH DON'T WANNA KNOW NEVER MIND EAR-MUFFS EARMUFFS EARMUFFS!
HEH.
I CAN LIGHT UP VEGAS FOR A WEEK WITH A SNEEZE, BUT YOU'RE GOING WITH PIGEONMAN. IS THAT HOW IT IS? WHAT CAN HE DO THAT I CAN'T?
QUBIT, THIS IS BETTE. VOLT AND I HAVE ARTILLERY IN CUSTODY, NO CASUALTIES.
QUBIT?
I KNOW, I KNOW... YOU WISH IT COULDA BEEN PLUTONIAN WHO CAUGHT YOU 'CAUSE THAT WOULD UP YOUR STREET CRED. I'VE HEARD IT. SAVE IT.
SO SORRY. BUT GUYS LIKE YOU ARE BUSYWORK FOR A GUY LIKE HIM. HENCE, US.
NO RESPONSE. WEIRD.
Times Sq-42 Station
S N Q R W
1 2 3 7

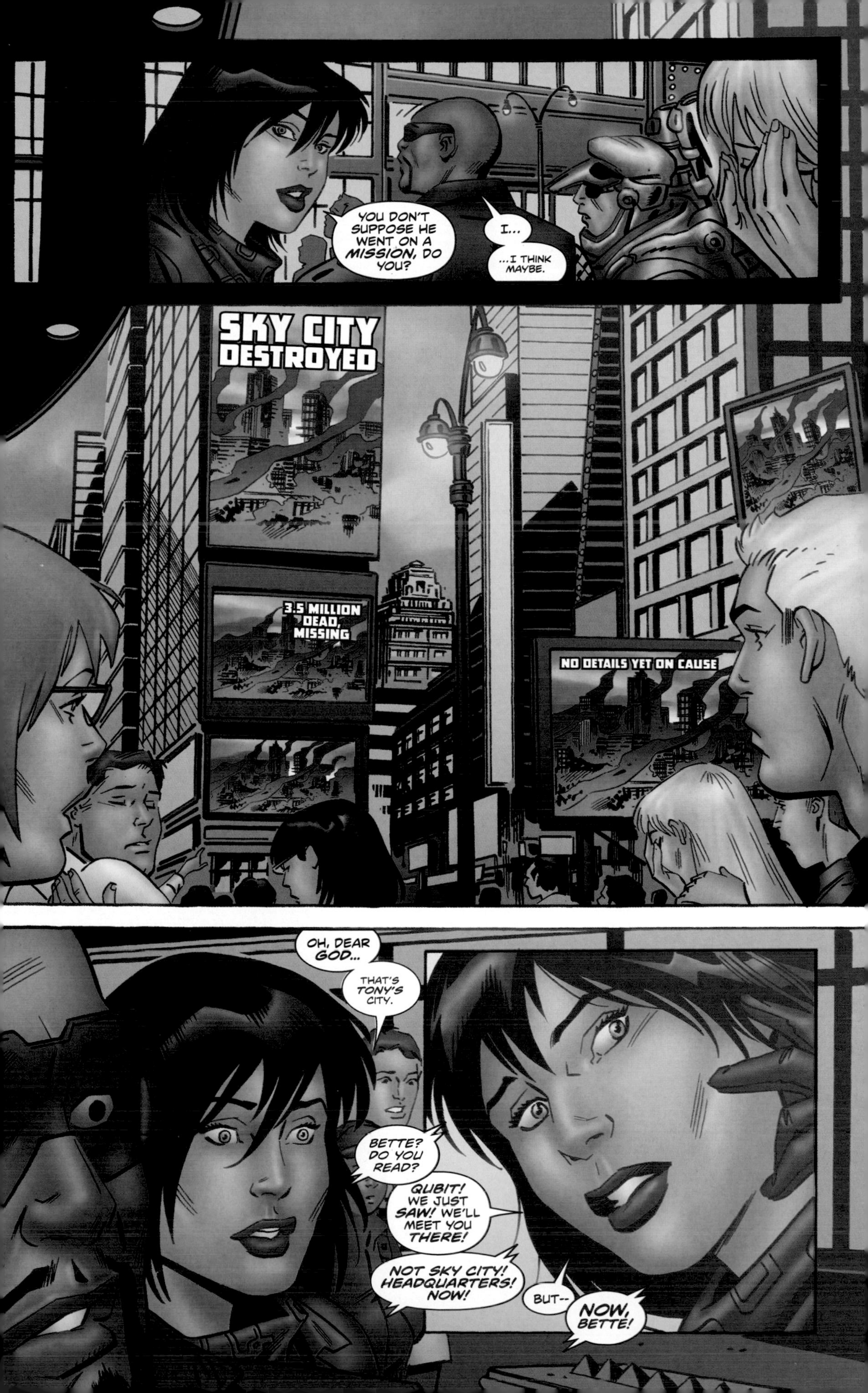
YOU DON'T SUPPOSE HE WENT ON A MISSION, DO YOU?
I...
...I THINK MAYBE.
SKY CITY DESTROYED
3.5 MILLION DEAD, MISSING
NO DETAILS YET ON CAUSE
OH, DEAR GOD...
THAT'S TONY'S CITY.
BETTE? DO YOU READ?
QUBIT! WE JUST SAW! WE'LL MEET YOU THERE!
NOT SKY CITY! HEADQUARTERS! NOW!
BUT--
NOW, BETTE!

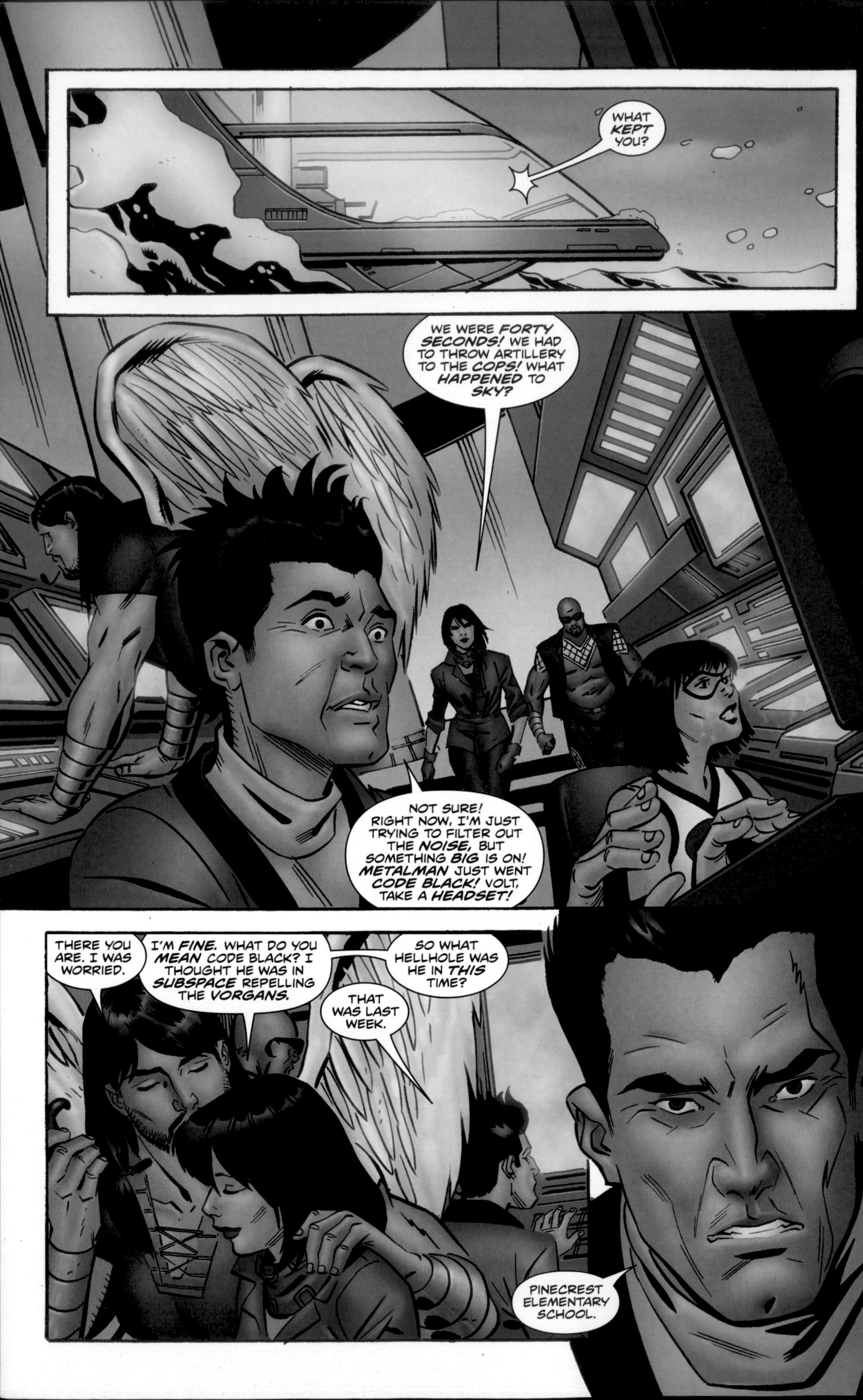
WHAT KEPT YOU?
WE WERE FORTY SECONDS! WE HAD TO THROW ARTILLERY TO THE COPS! WHAT HAPPENED TO SKY?
NOT SURE! RIGHT NOW, I'M JUST TRYING TO FILTER OUT THE NOISE, BUT SOMETHING BIG IS ON! METALMAN JUST WENT CODE BLACK! VOLT, TAKE A HEADSET!
THERE YOU ARE. I WAS WORRIED.
I'M FINE. WHAT DO YOU MEAN CODE BLACK? I THOUGHT HE WAS IN SUBSPACE REPELLING THE VORGANS.
SO WHAT HELLHOLE WAS HE IN THIS TIME?
THAT WAS LAST WEEK.
PINECREST ELEMENTARY SCHOOL.

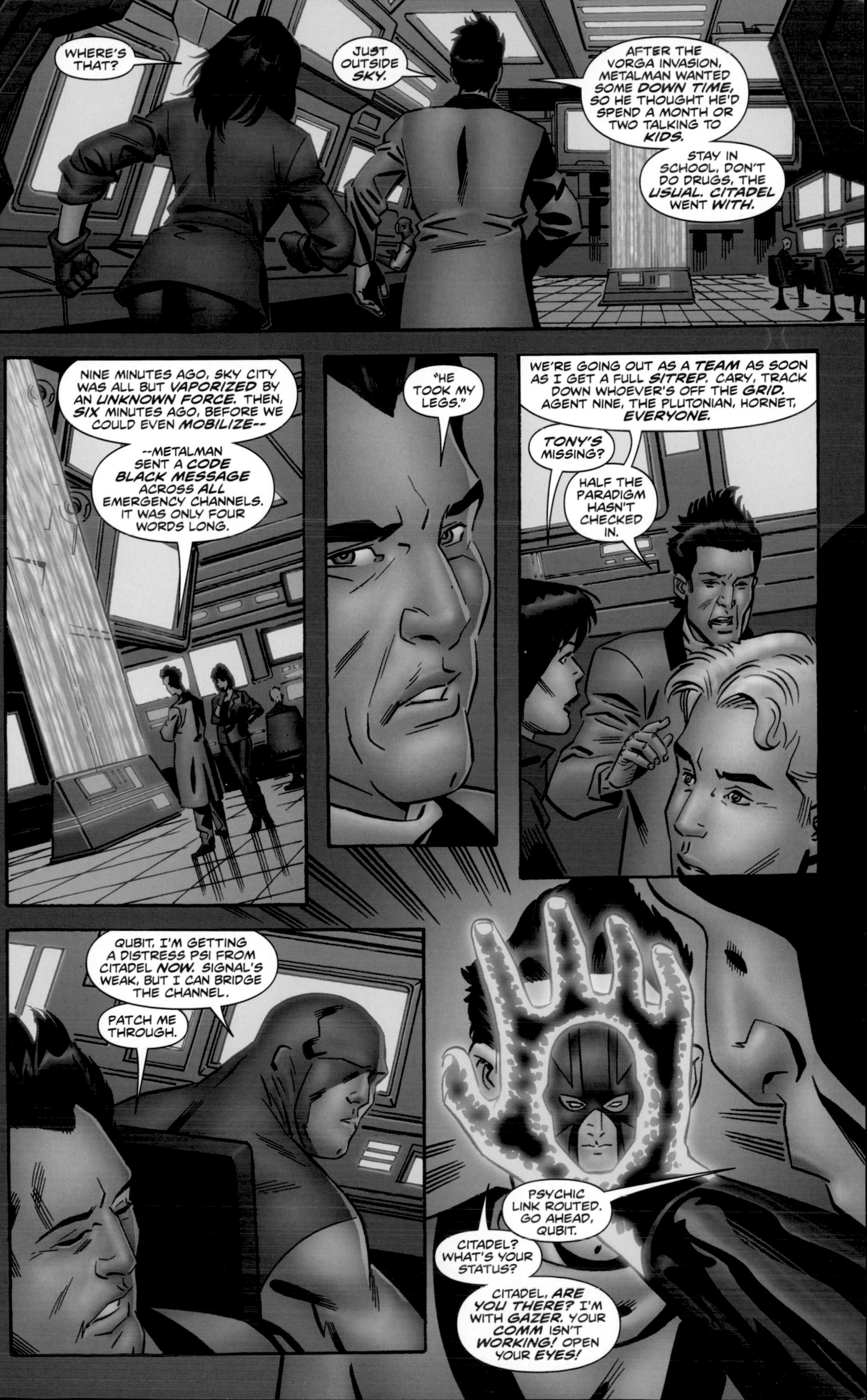
WHERE'S THAT?
JUST OUTSIDE SKY.
AFTER THE VORGA INVASION, METALMAN WANTED SOME DOWN TIME, SO HE THOUGHT HE'D SPEND A MONTH OR TWO TALKING TO KIDS.
STAY IN SCHOOL, DON'T DO DRUGS, THE USUAL. CITADEL WENT WITH.
NINE MINUTES AGO, SKY CITY WAS ALL BUT VAPORIZED BY AN UNKNOWN FORCE. THEN, SIX MINUTES AGO, BEFORE WE COULD EVEN MOBILIZE--
--METALMAN SENT A CODE BLACK MESSAGE ACROSS ALL EMERGENCY CHANNELS. IT WAS ONLY FOUR WORDS LONG.
"HE TOOK MY LEGS."
WE'RE GOING OUT AS A TEAM AS SOON AS I GET A FULL SITREP. CARY, TRACK DOWN WHOEVER'S OFF THE GRID. AGENT NINE, THE PLUTONIAN, HORNET, EVERYONE.
TONY'S MISSING?
HALF THE PARADIGM HASN'T CHECKED IN.
QUBIT, I'M GETTING A DISTRESS PSI FROM CITADEL NOW. SIGNAL'S WEAK, BUT I CAN BRIDGE THE CHANNEL.
PATCH ME THROUGH.
PSYCHIC LINK ROUTED. GO AHEAD, QUBIT.
CITADEL? WHAT'S YOUR STATUS?
CITADEL, ARE YOU THERE? I'M WITH GAZER. YOUR COMM ISN'T WORKING! OPEN YOUR EYES!

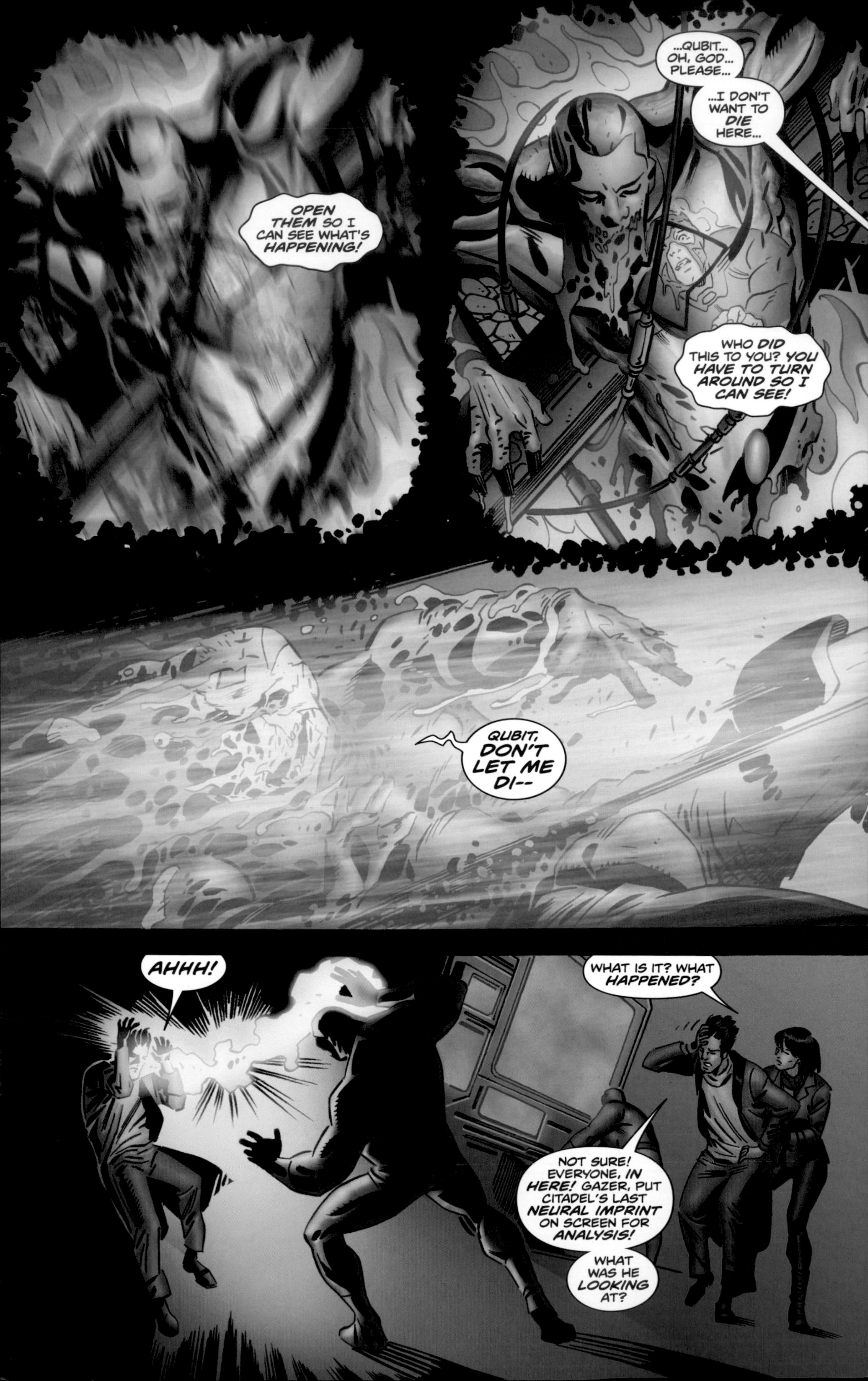
OPEN THEM SO I CAN SEE WHAT'S HAPPENING!
...QUBIT... OH, GOD... PLEASE...
...I DON'T WANT TO DIE HERE...
WHO DID THIS TO YOU? YOU HAVE TO TURN AROUND SO I CAN SEE!
QUBIT, DON'T LET ME DI--
AHHH!
WHAT IS IT? WHAT HAPPENED?
NOT SURE! EVERYONE, IN HERE! GAZER, PUT CITADEL'S LAST NEURAL IMPRINT ON SCREEN FOR ANALYSIS!
WHAT WAS HE LOOKING AT?

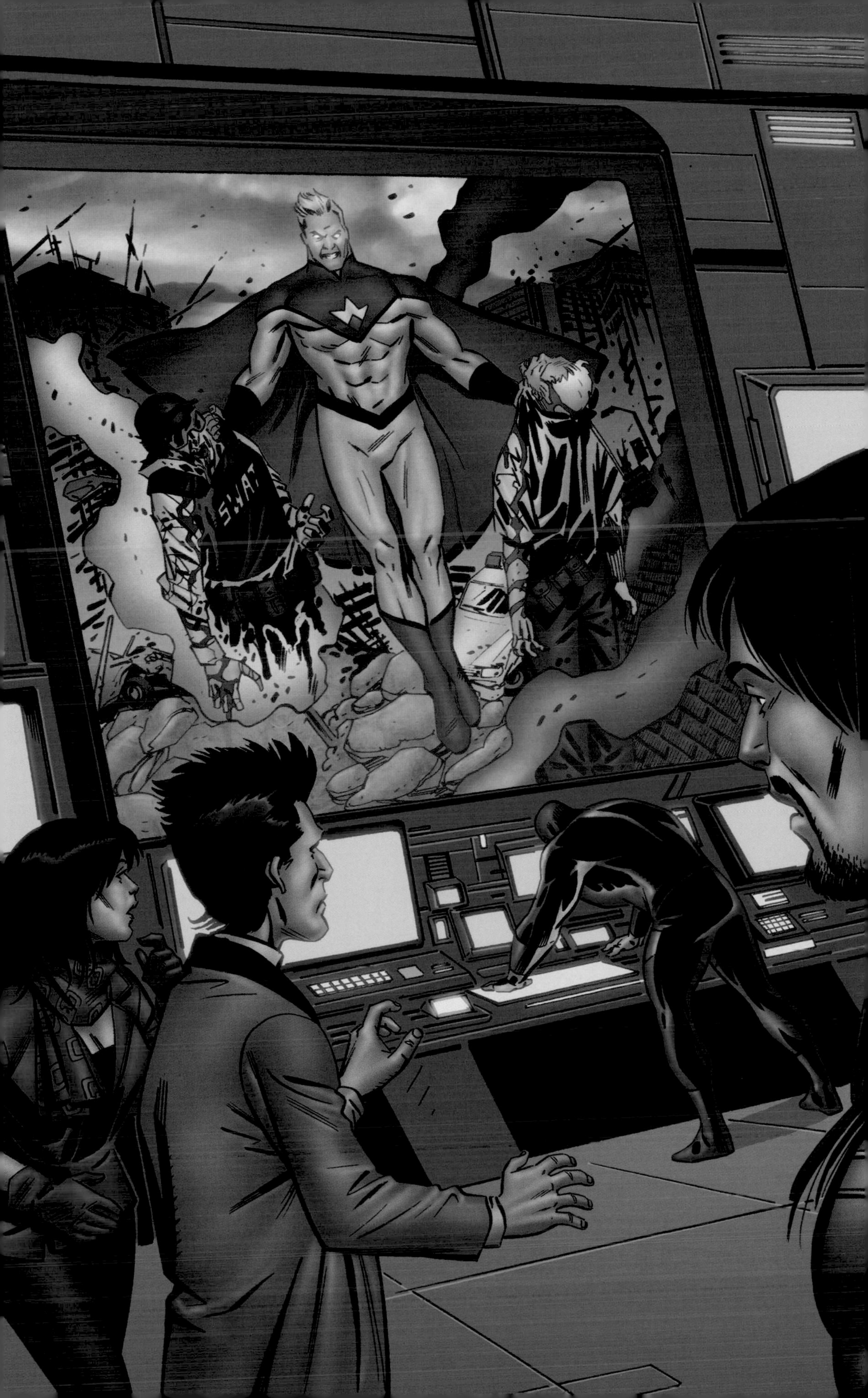

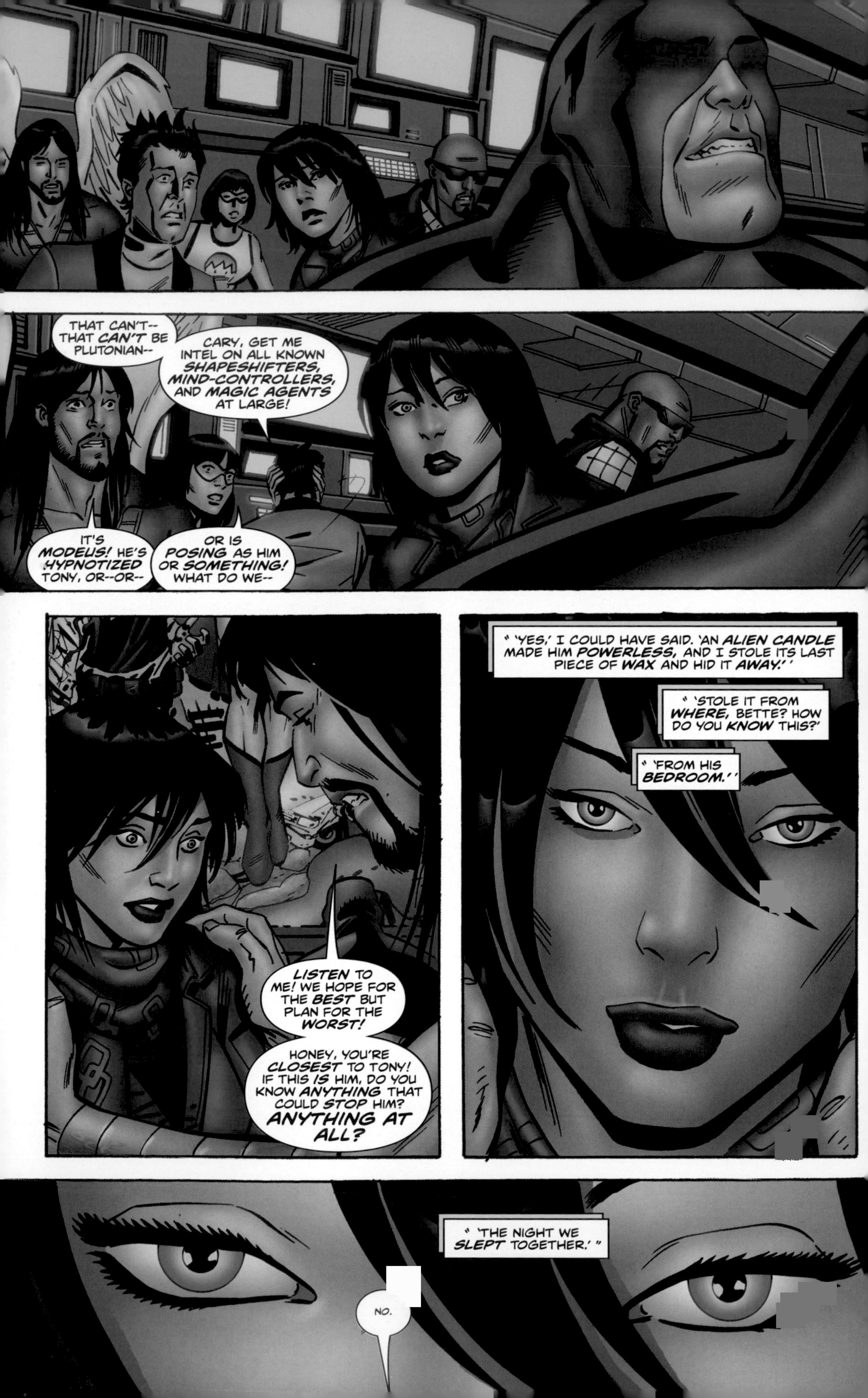
THAT CAN'T-- THAT CAN'T BE PLUTONIAN--
CARY, GET ME INTEL ON ALL KNOWN SHAPESHIFTERS, MIND-CONTROLLERS, AND MAGIC AGENTS AT LARGE!
IT'S MODEUS! HE'S HYPNOTIZED TONY, OR--OR--
OR IS POSING AS HIM OR SOMETHING! WHAT DO WE--
LISTEN TO ME! WE HOPE FOR THE BEST BUT PLAN FOR THE WORST!
HONEY, YOU'RE CLOSEST TO TONY! IF THIS IS HIM, DO YOU KNOW ANYTHING THAT COULD STOP HIM? ANYTHING AT ALL?
" 'YES,' I COULD HAVE SAID. 'AN ALIEN CANDLE MADE HIM POWERLESS, AND I STOLE ITS LAST PIECE OF WAX AND HID IT AWAY.' '
" 'STOLE IT FROM WHERE, BETTE? HOW DO YOU KNOW THIS?'
" 'FROM HIS BEDROOM.' '
" 'THE NIGHT WE SLEPT TOGETHER.' "
NO.

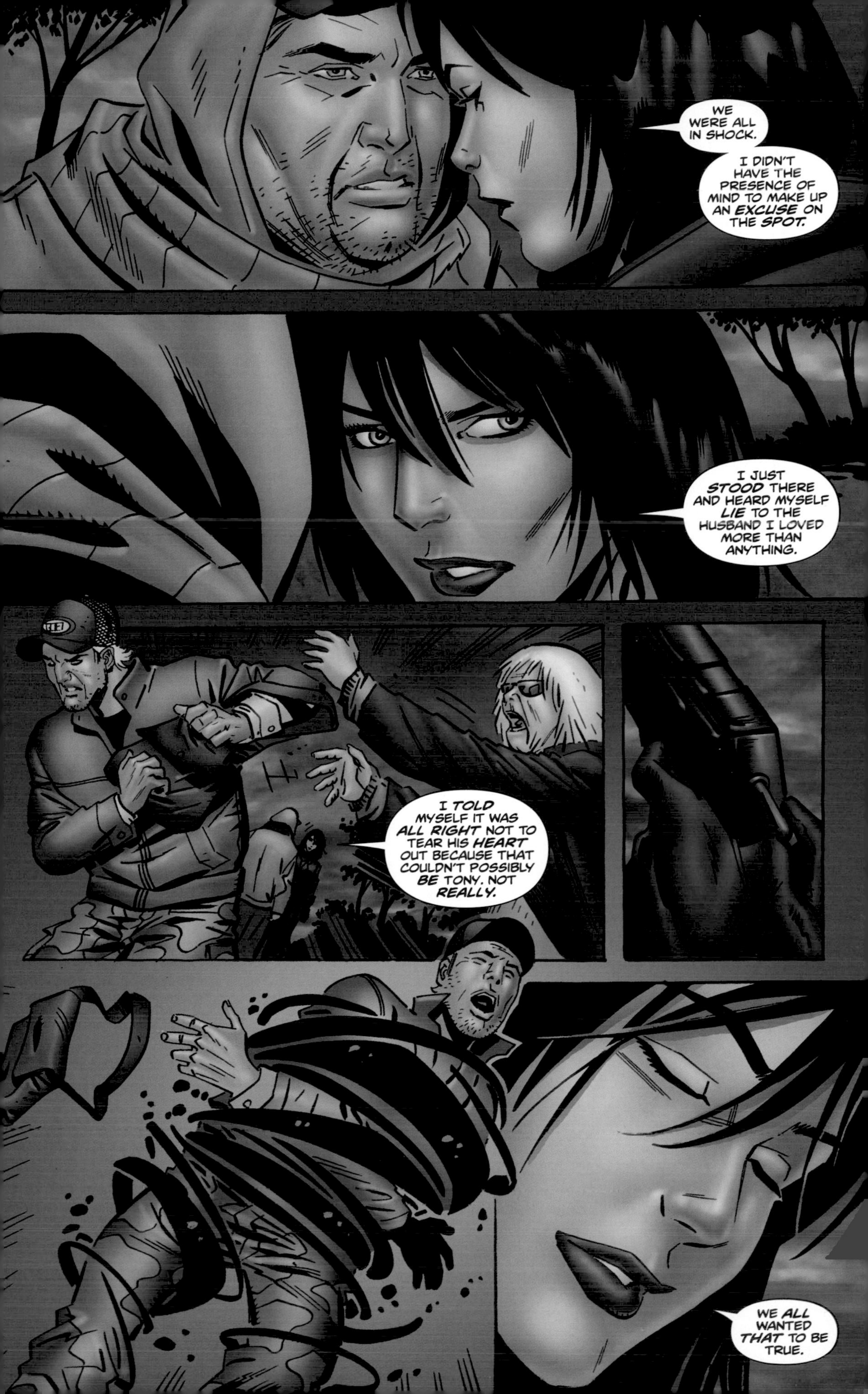
WE WERE ALL IN SHOCK.
I DIDN'T HAVE THE PRESENCE OF MIND TO MAKE UP AN EXCUSE ON THE SPOT.
I JUST STOOD THERE AND HEARD MYSELF LIE TO THE HUSBAND I LOVED MORE THAN ANYTHING.
I TOLD MYSELF IT WAS ALL RIGHT NOT TO TEAR HIS HEART OUT BECAUSE THAT COULDN'T POSSIBLY BE TONY. NOT REALLY.
WE ALL WANTED THAT TO BE TRUE.

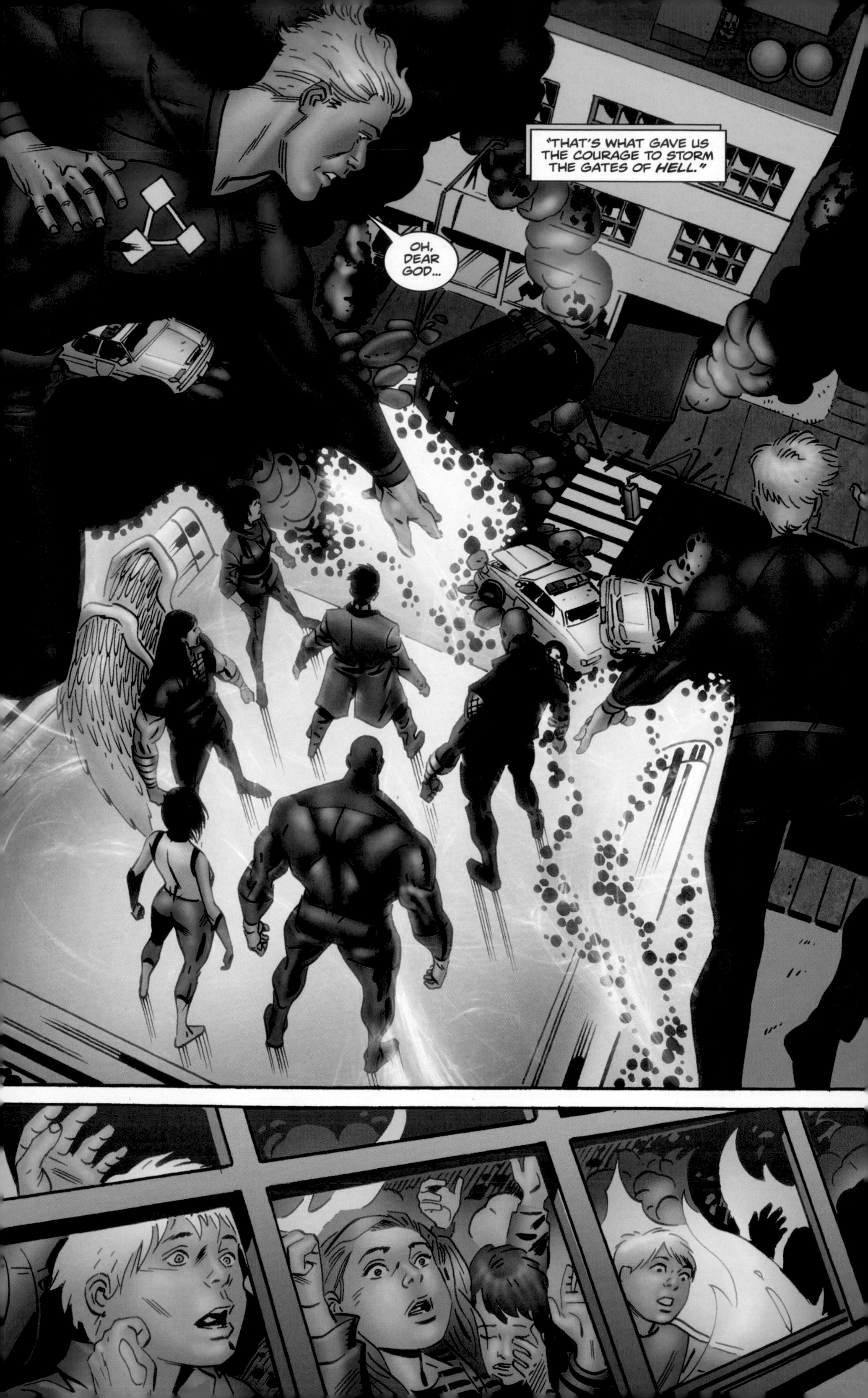
"THAT'S WHAT GAVE US THE COURAGE TO STORM THE GATES OF HELL."
OH, DEAR GOD...

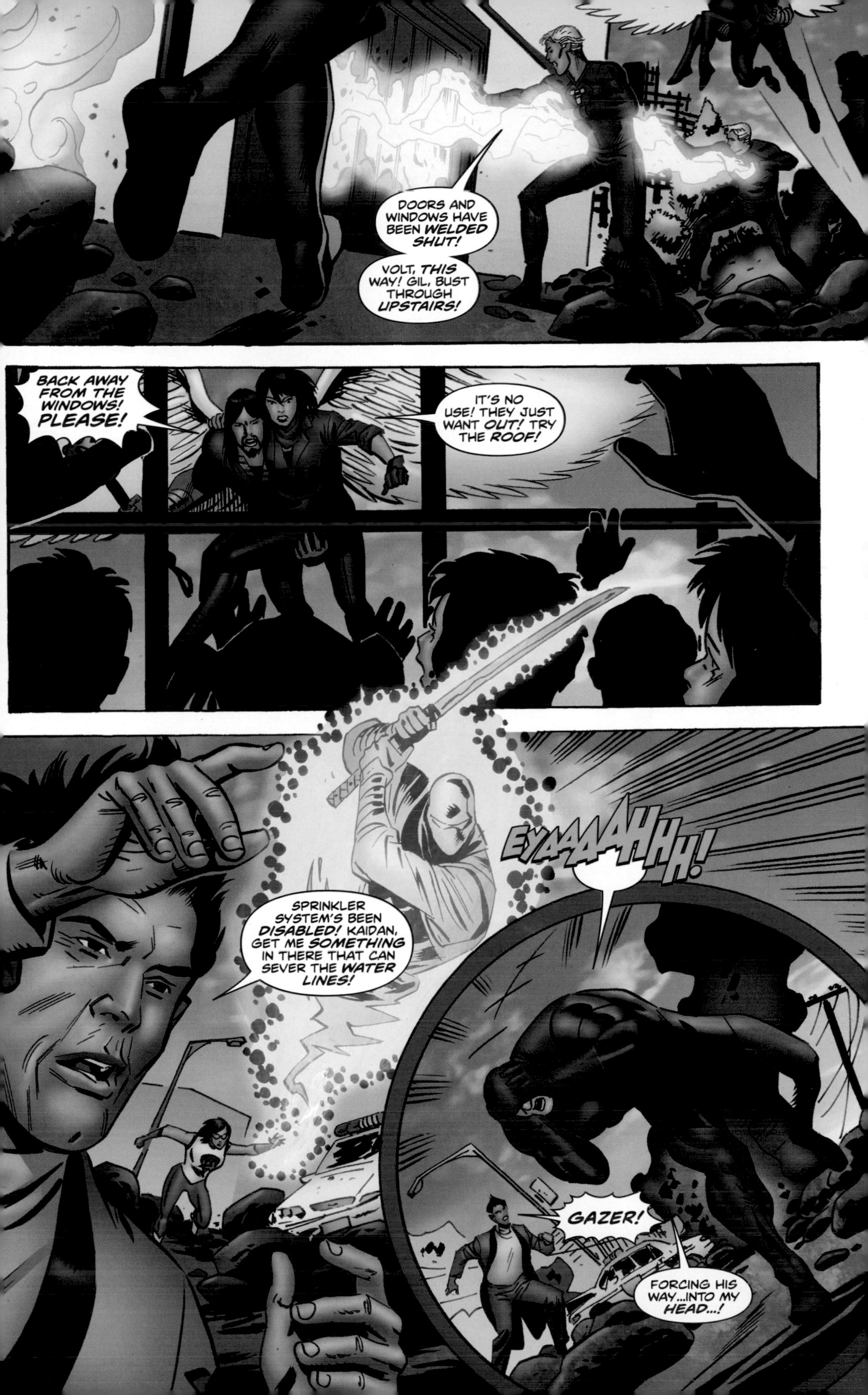
DOORS AND WINDOWS HAVE BEEN WELDED SHUT!
VOLT, THIS WAY! GIL, BUST THROUGH UPSTAIRS!
BACK AWAY FROM THE WINDOWS! PLEASE!
IT'S NO USE! THEY JUST WANT OUT! TRY THE ROOF!
SPRINKLER SYSTEM'S BEEN DISABLED! KAIDAN, GET ME SOMETHING IN THERE THAT CAN SEVER THE WATER LINES!
EYAAAAHHH!
GAZER!
FORCING HIS WAY...INTO MY HEAD...!

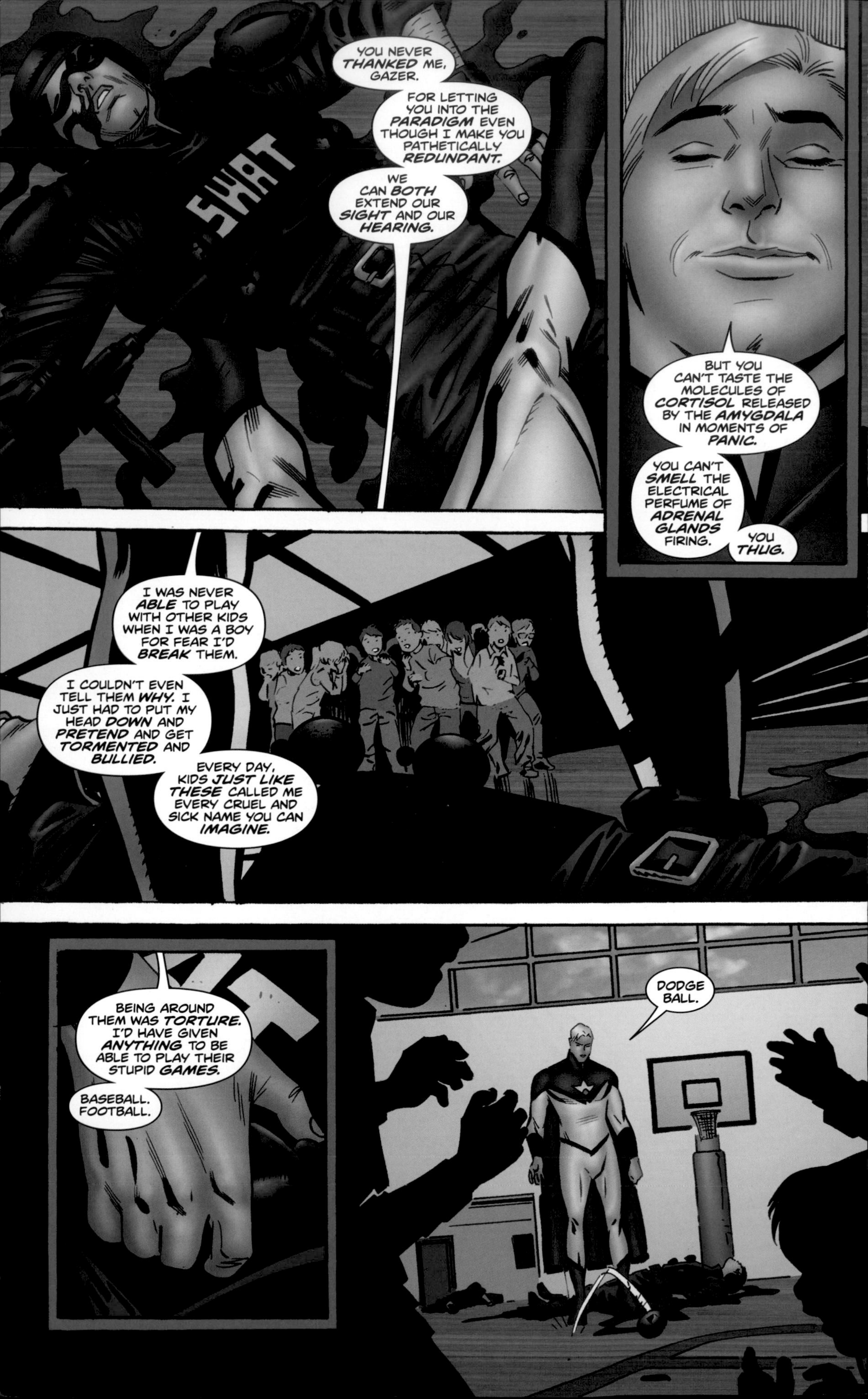
YOU NEVER THANKED ME, GAZER.
FOR LETTING YOU INTO THE PARADIGM EVEN THOUGH I MAKE YOU PATHETICALLY REDUNDANT.
WE CAN BOTH EXTEND OUR SIGHT AND OUR HEARING.
SWAT
BUT YOU CAN'T TASTE THE MOLECULES OF CORTISOL RELEASED BY THE AMYGDALA IN MOMENTS OF PANIC.
YOU CAN'T SMELL THE ELECTRICAL PERFUME OF ADRENAL GLANDS FIRING.
YOU THUG.
I WAS NEVER ABLE TO PLAY WITH OTHER KIDS WHEN I WAS A BOY FOR FEAR I'D BREAK THEM.
I COULDN'T EVEN TELL THEM WHY. I JUST HAD TO PUT MY HEAD DOWN AND PRETEND AND GET TORMENTED AND BULLIED.
EVERY DAY, KIDS JUST LIKE THESE CALLED ME EVERY CRUEL AND SICK NAME YOU CAN IMAGINE.
BEING AROUND THEM WAS TORTURE. I'D HAVE GIVEN ANYTHING TO BE ABLE TO PLAY THEIR STUPID GAMES.
BASEBALL. FOOTBALL.
DODGE BALL.

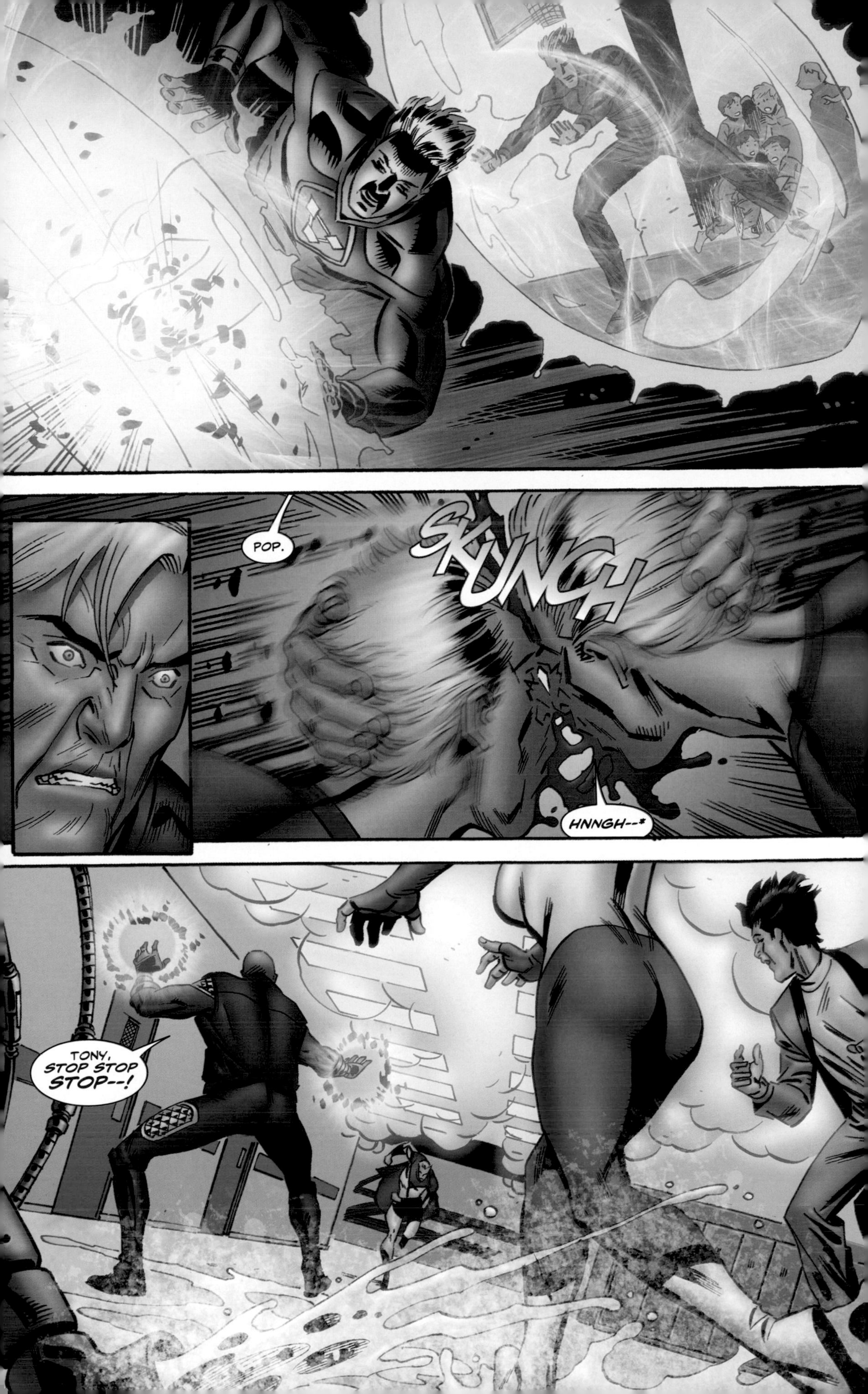
POP.
SKUNCH
HNNGH--*
TONY, STOP STOP STOP--!

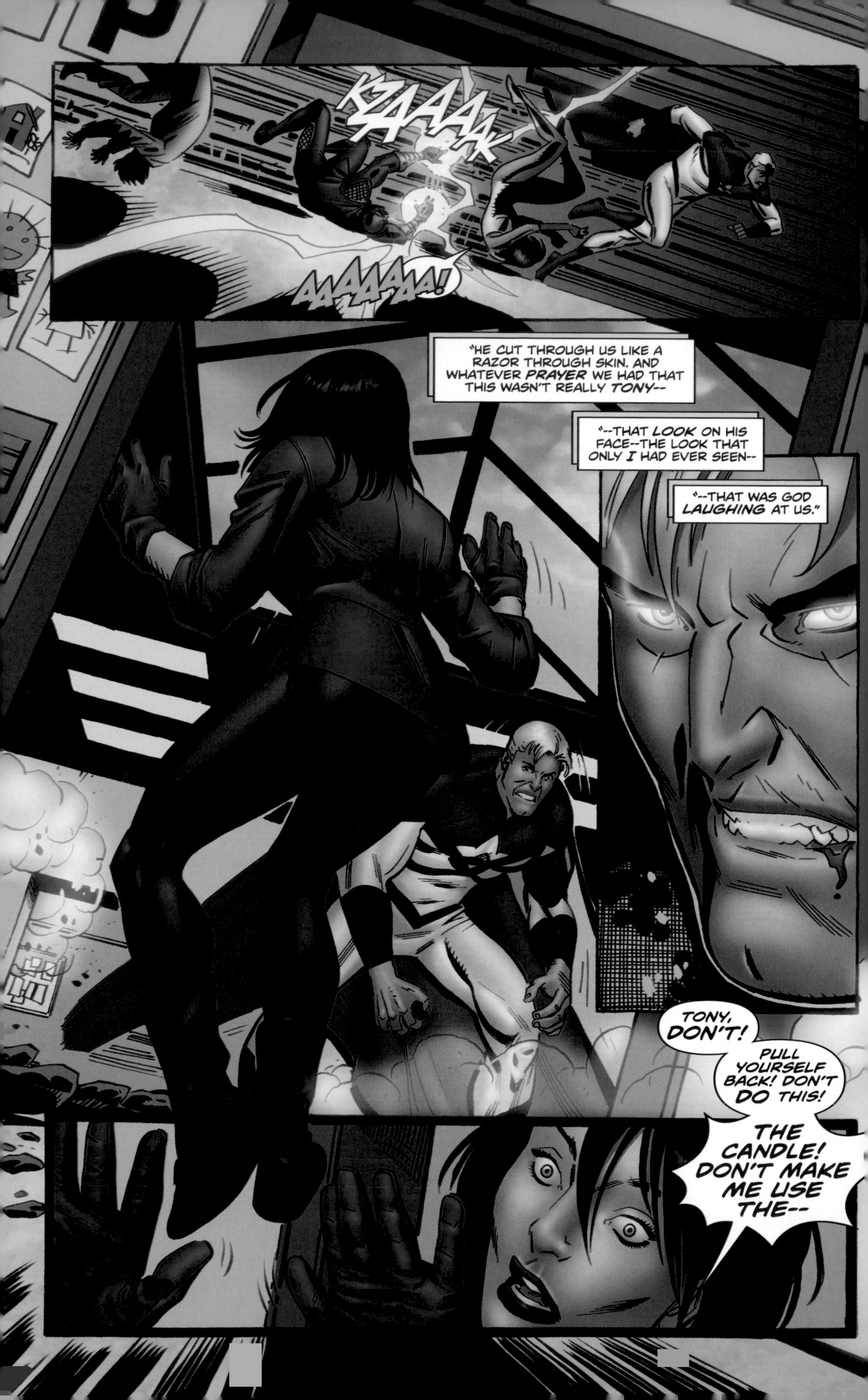
KZAAAAAK
AAAAAAA!
"HE CUT THROUGH US LIKE A RAZOR THROUGH SKIN. AND WHATEVER PRAYER WE HAD THAT THIS WASN'T REALLY TONY--
"--THAT LOOK ON HIS FACE--THE LOOK THAT ONLY I HAD EVER SEEN--
"--THAT WAS GOD LAUGHING AT US."
TONY, DON'T!
PULL YOURSELF BACK! DON'T DO THIS!
THE CANDLE! DON'T MAKE ME USE THE--

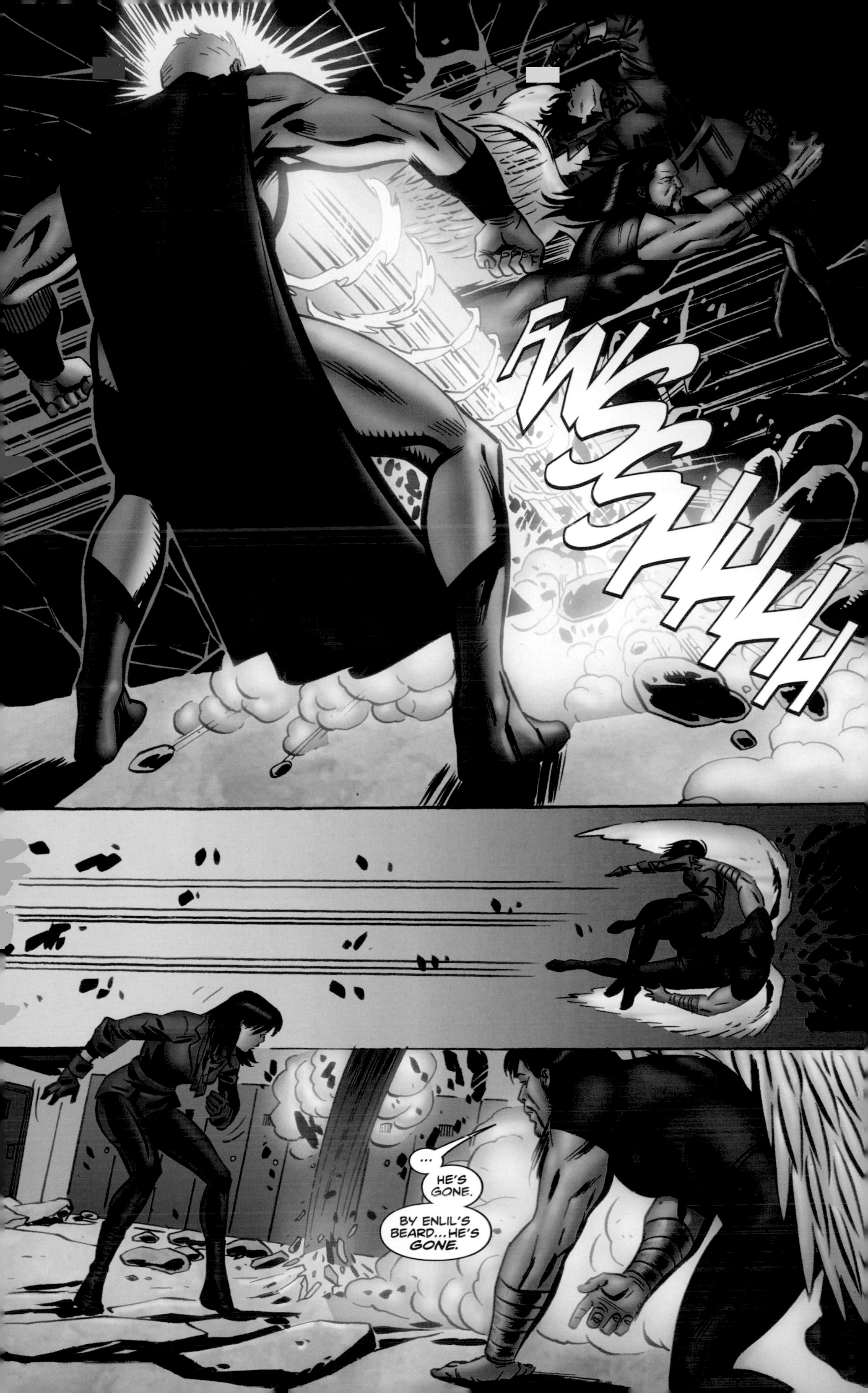
FWSSHHHH
...
HE'S GONE.
BY ENLIL'S BEARD... HE'S GONE.

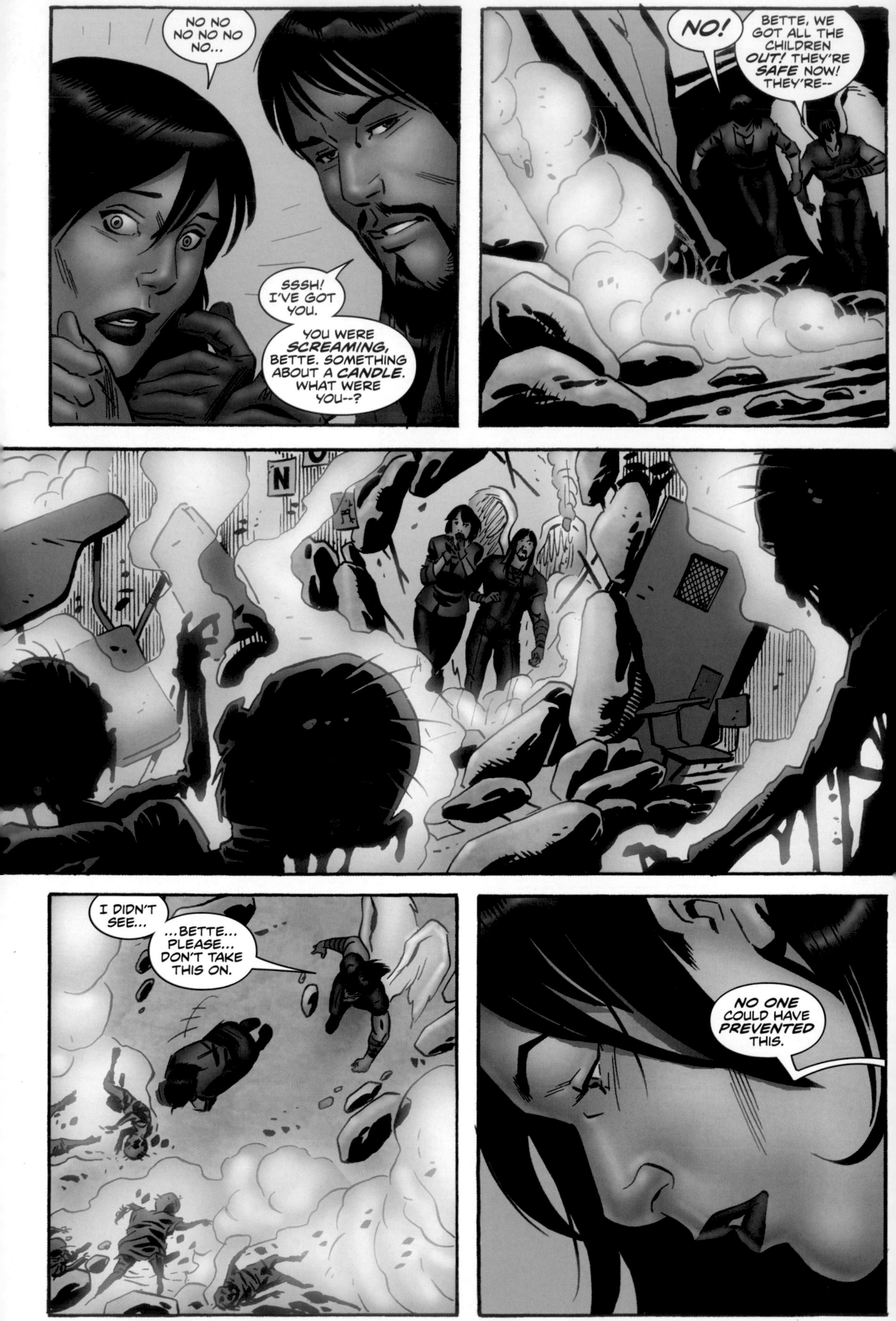
NO NO
NO NO NO
NO...
SSSH! I'VE GOT YOU.
YOU WERE SCREAMING, BETTE. SOMETHING ABOUT A CANDLE. WHAT WERE YOU--?
NO!
BETTE, WE GOT ALL THE CHILDREN OUT! THEY'RE SAFE NOW! THEY'RE--
N
I DIDN'T SEE...
...BETTE... PLEASE... DON'T TAKE THIS ON.
NO ONE COULD HAVE PREVENTED THIS.

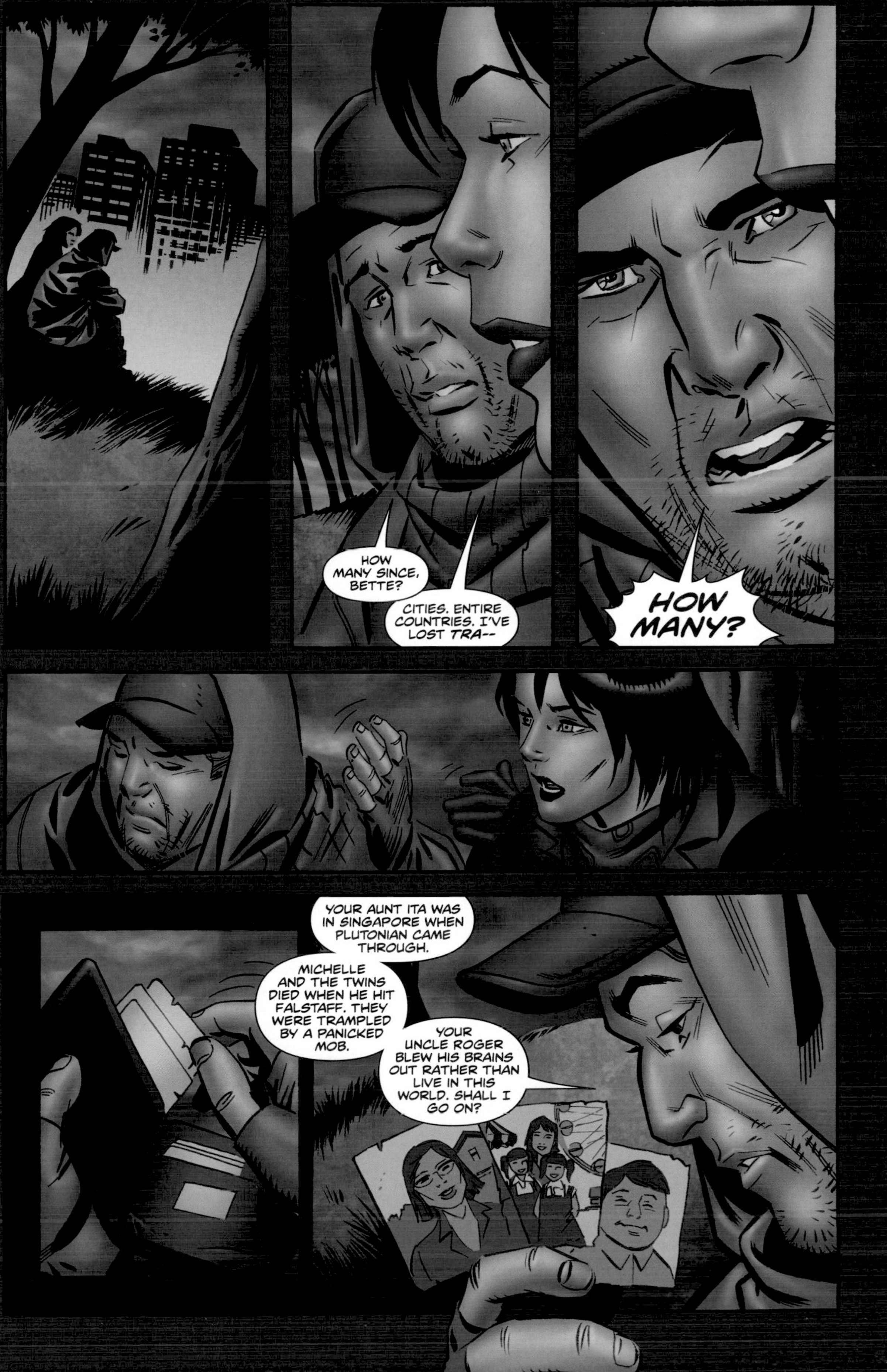
HOW MANY SINCE, BETTE?
CITIES. ENTIRE COUNTRIES. I'VE LOST TRA--
HOW MANY?
YOUR AUNT ITA WAS IN SINGAPORE WHEN PLUTONIAN CAME THROUGH.
MICHELLE AND THE TWINS DIED WHEN HE HIT FALSTAFF. THEY WERE TRAMPLED BY A PANICKED MOB.
YOUR UNCLE ROGER BLEW HIS BRAINS OUT RATHER THAN LIVE IN THIS WORLD. SHALL I GO ON?

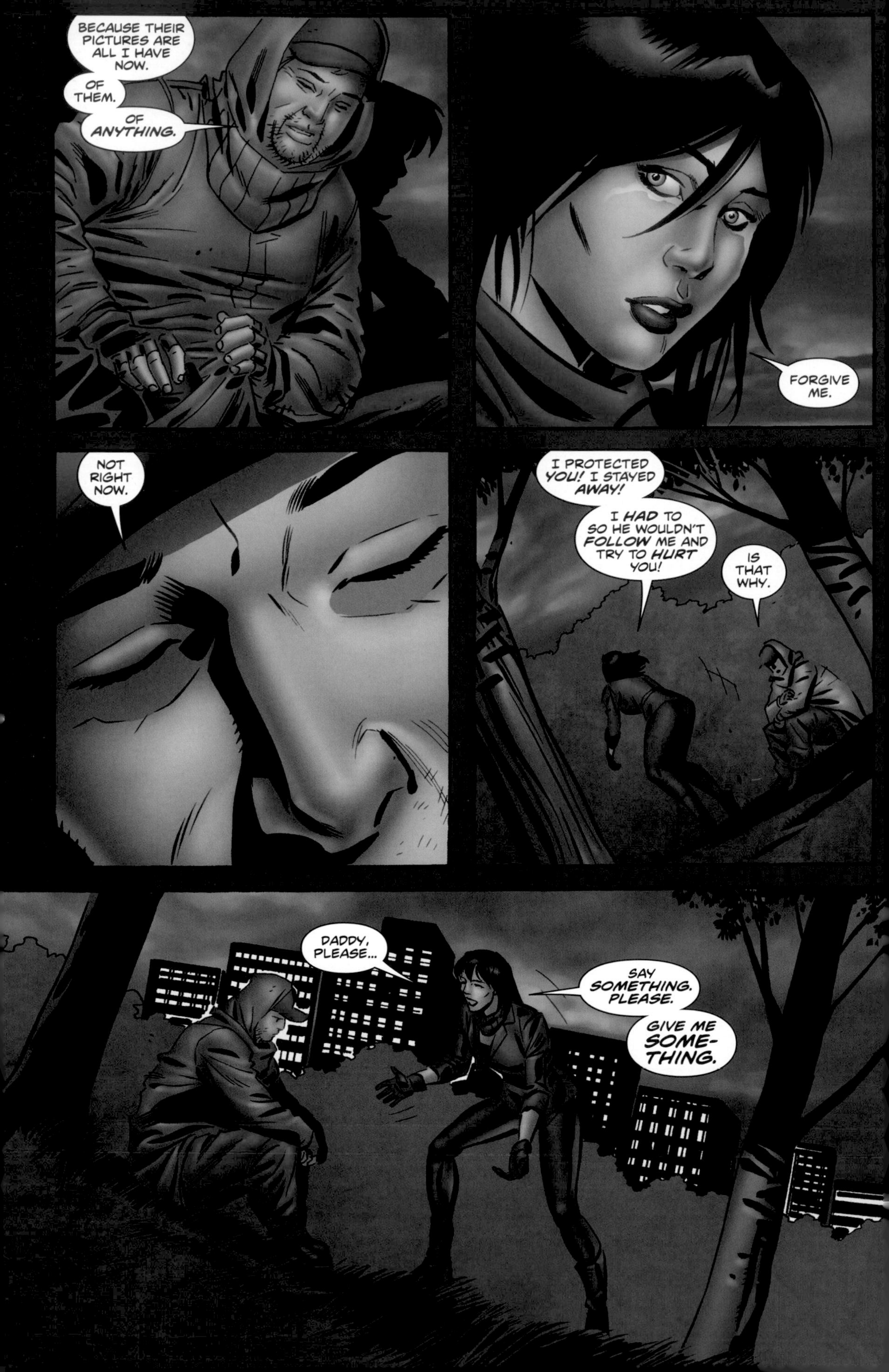
BECAUSE THEIR PICTURES ARE ALL I HAVE NOW.
OF THEM.
OF ANYTHING.
FORGIVE ME.
NOT RIGHT NOW.
I PROTECTED YOU! I STAYED AWAY!
I HAD TO SO HE WOULDN'T FOLLOW ME AND TRY TO HURT YOU!
IS THAT WHY.
DADDY, PLEASE...
SAY SOMETHING. PLEASE.
GIVE ME SOME-THING.

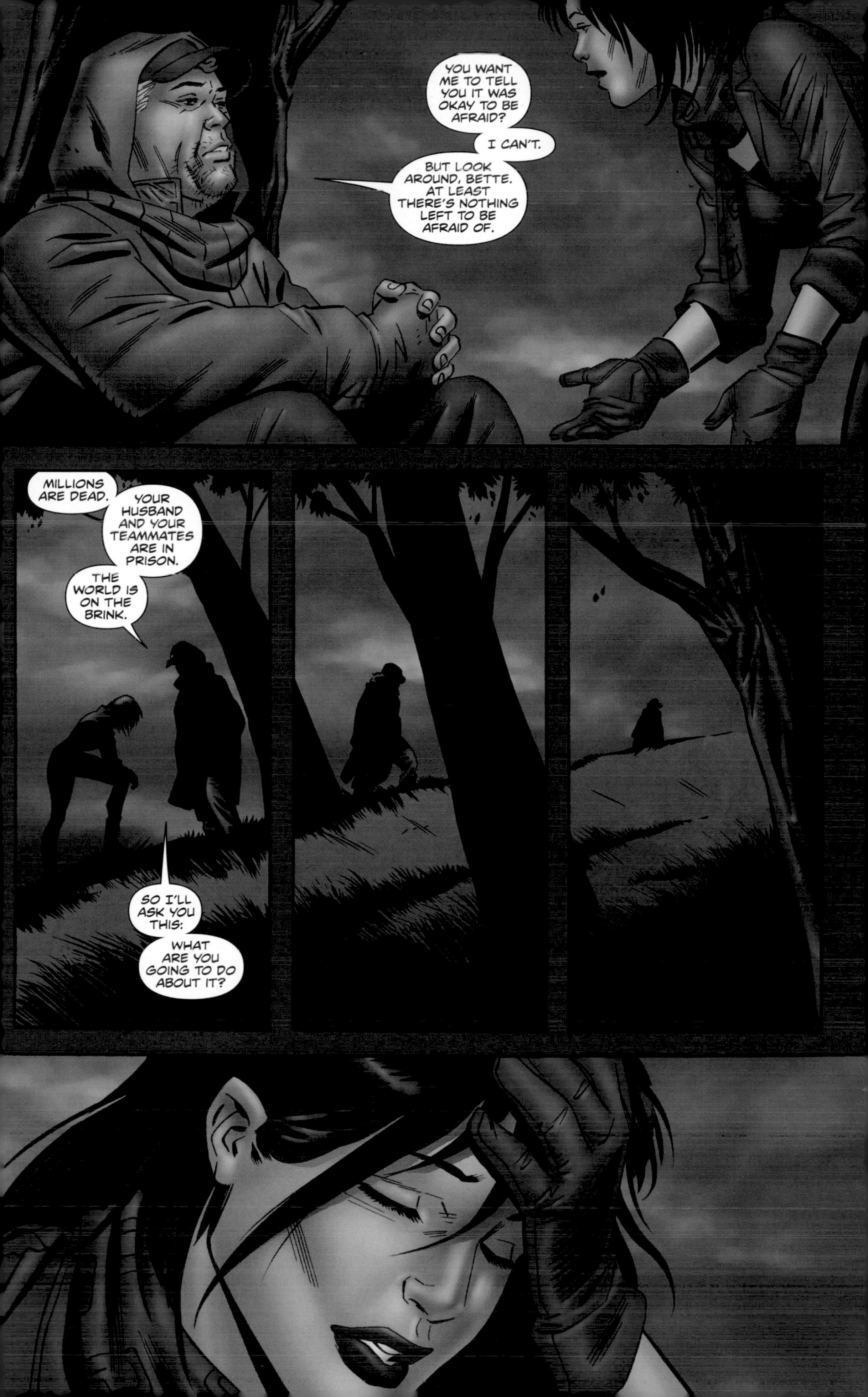
YOU WANT ME TO TELL YOU IT WAS OKAY TO BE AFRAID?
I CAN'T.
BUT LOOK AROUND, BETTE. AT LEAST THERE'S NOTHING LEFT TO BE AFRAID OF.
MILLIONS ARE DEAD.
YOUR HUSBAND AND YOUR TEAMMATES ARE IN PRISON.
THE WORLD IS ON THE BRINK.
SO I'LL ASK YOU THIS:
WHAT ARE YOU GOING TO DO ABOUT IT?

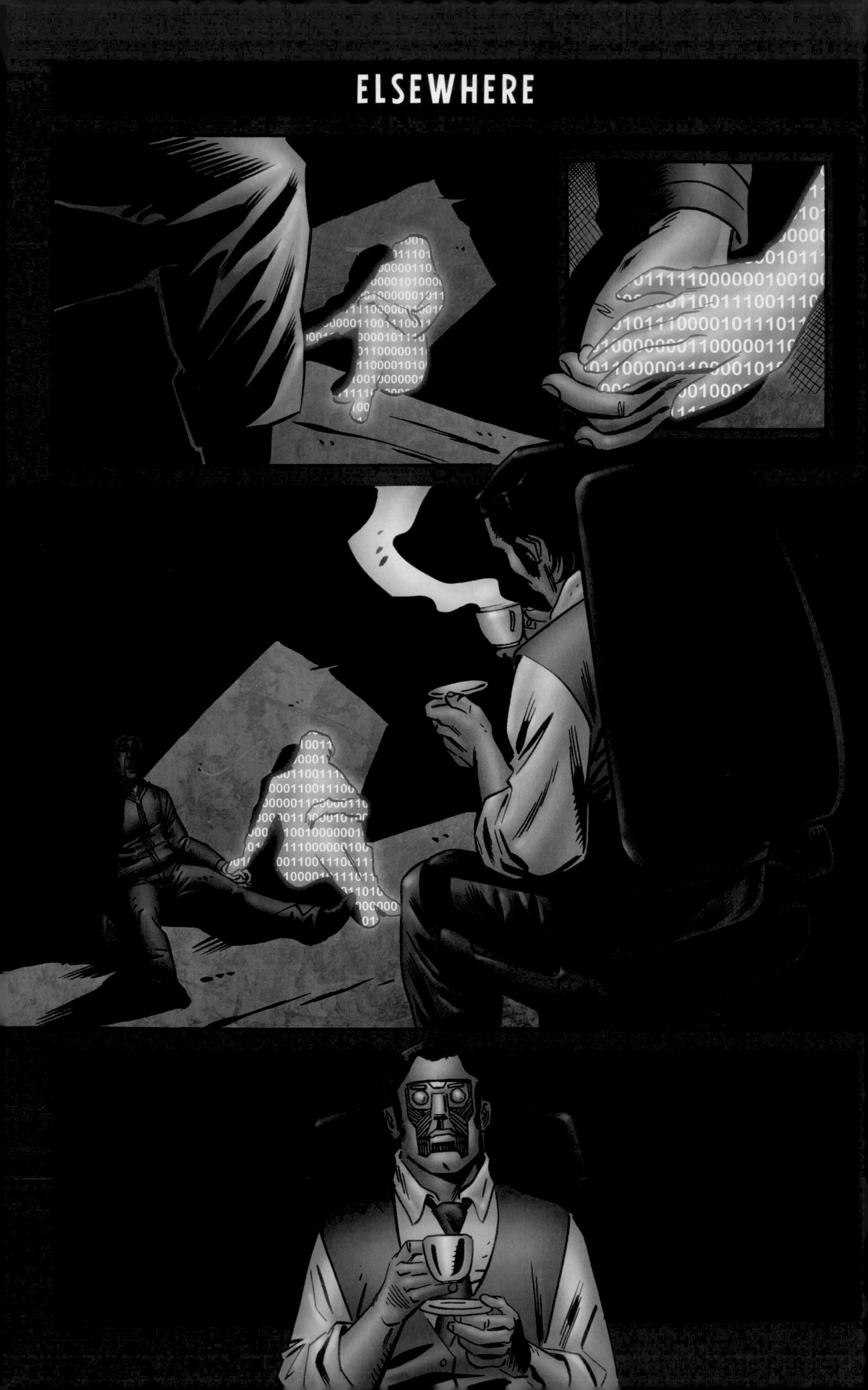
ELSEWHERE

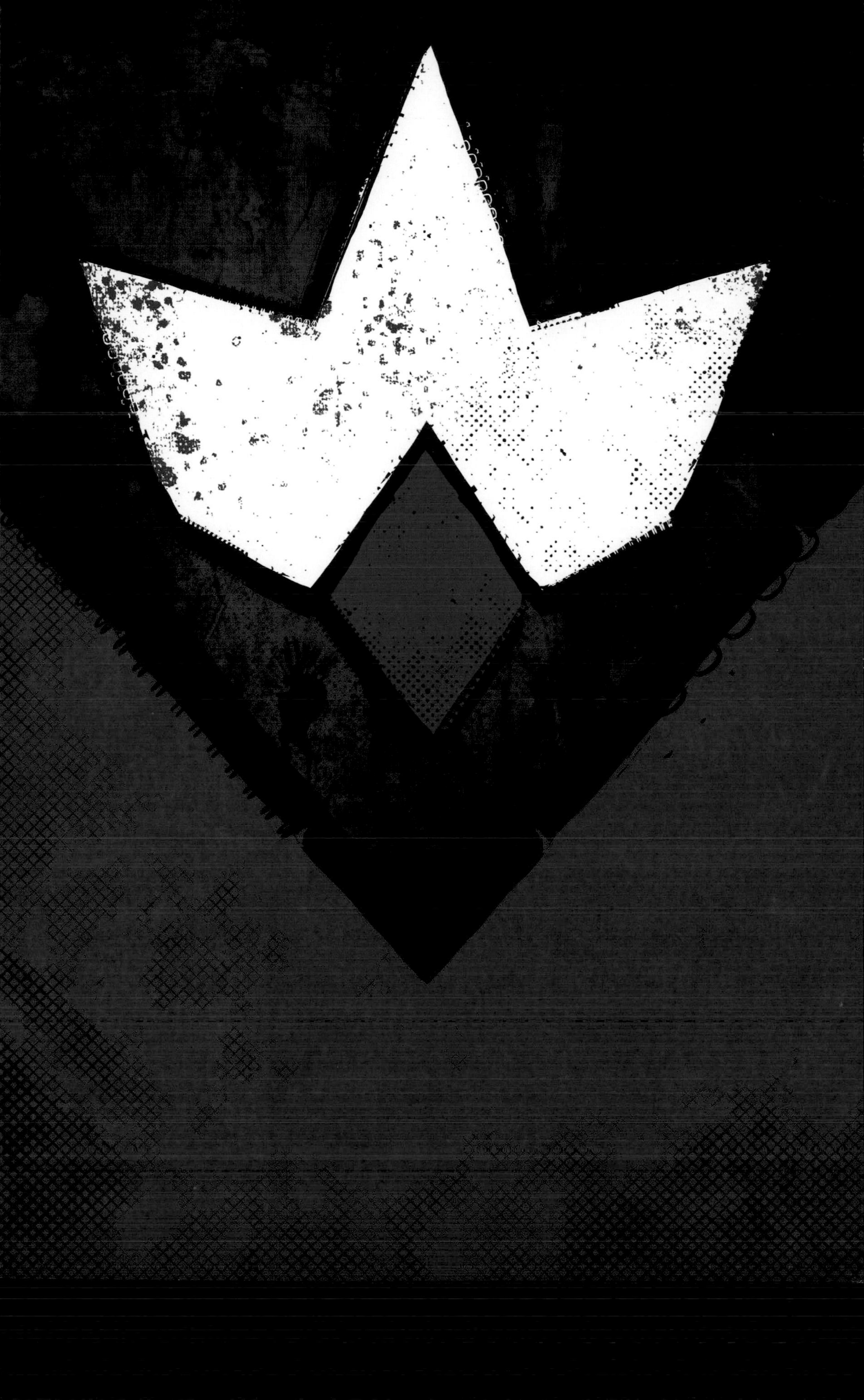

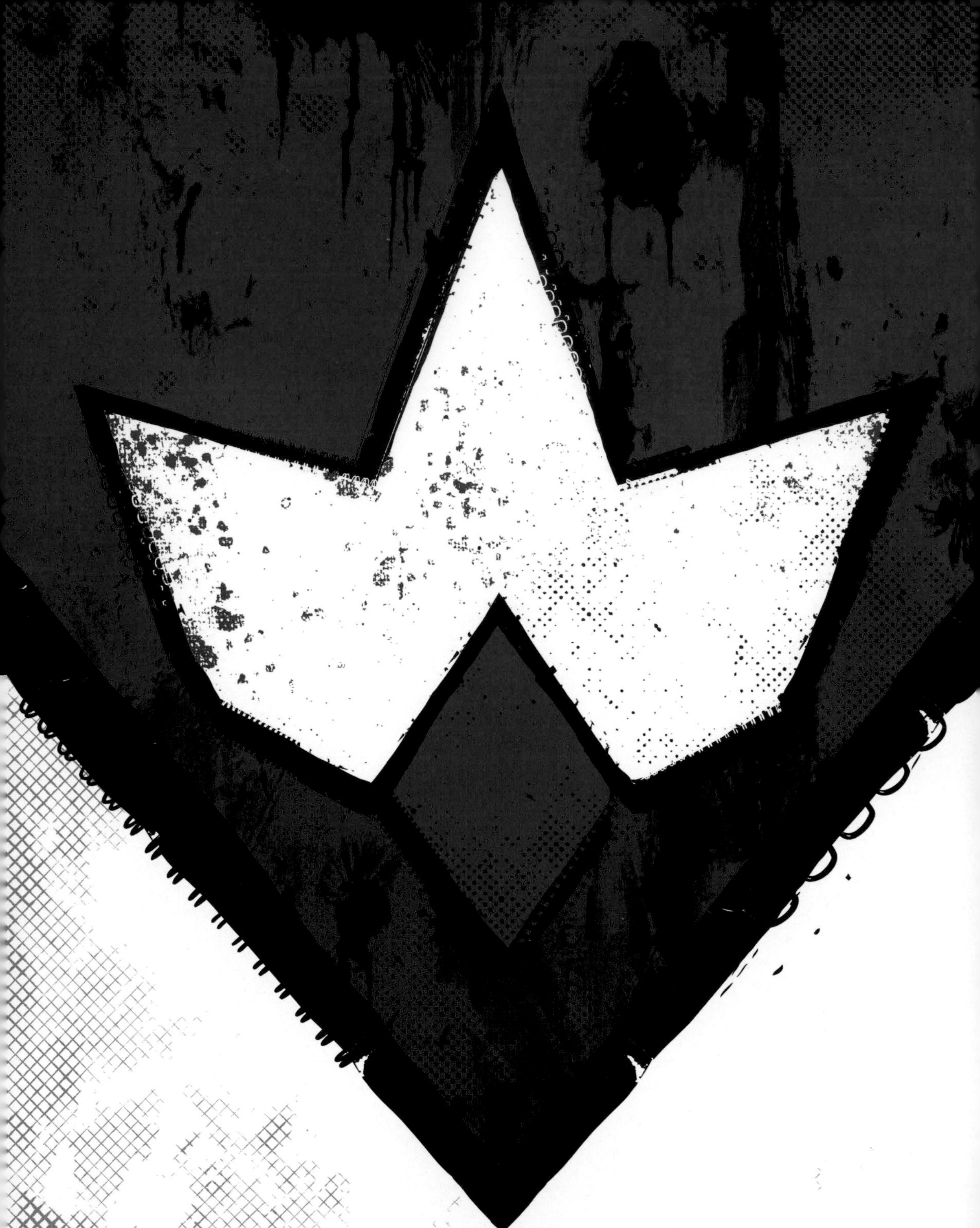

CHAPTER 14

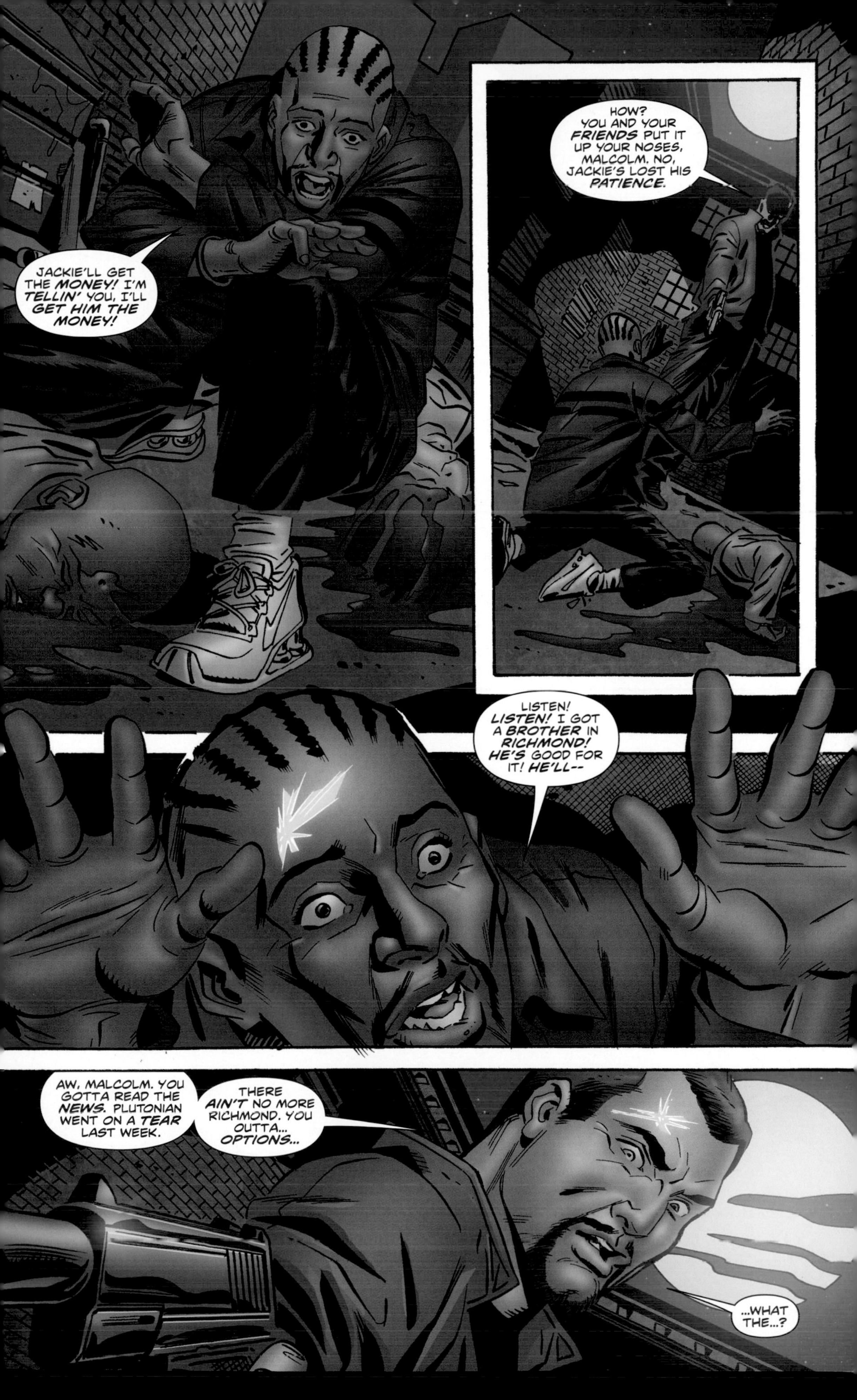
JACKIE'LL GET THE MONEY! I'M TELLIN' YOU, I'LL GET HIM THE MONEY!
HOW? YOU AND YOUR FRIENDS PUT IT UP YOUR NOSES, MALCOLM. NO, JACKIE'S LOST HIS PATIENCE.
LISTEN! LISTEN! I GOT A BROTHER IN RICHMOND! HE'S GOOD FOR IT! HE'LL--
AW, MALCOLM. YOU GOTTA READ THE NEWS. PLUTONIAN WENT ON A TEAR LAST WEEK.
THERE AIN'T NO MORE RICHMOND. YOU OUTTA... OPTIONS...
...WHAT THE...?

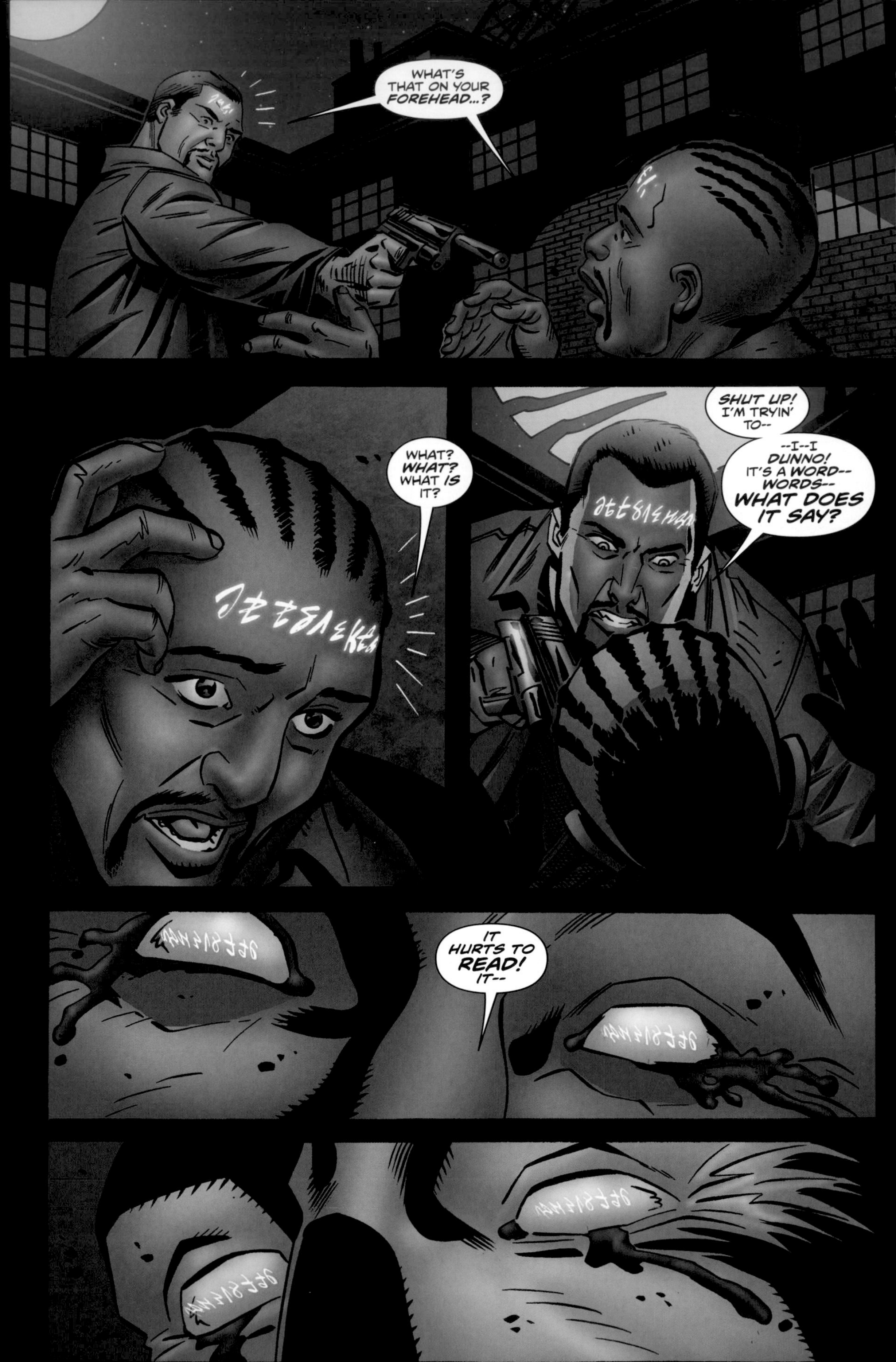
WHAT'S THAT ON YOUR FOREHEAD...?
WHAT? WHAT? WHAT IS IT?
SHUT UP! I'M TRYIN' TO--
--I--I DUNNO! IT'S A WORD-- WORDS-- WHAT DOES IT SAY?
IT HURTS TO READ! IT--

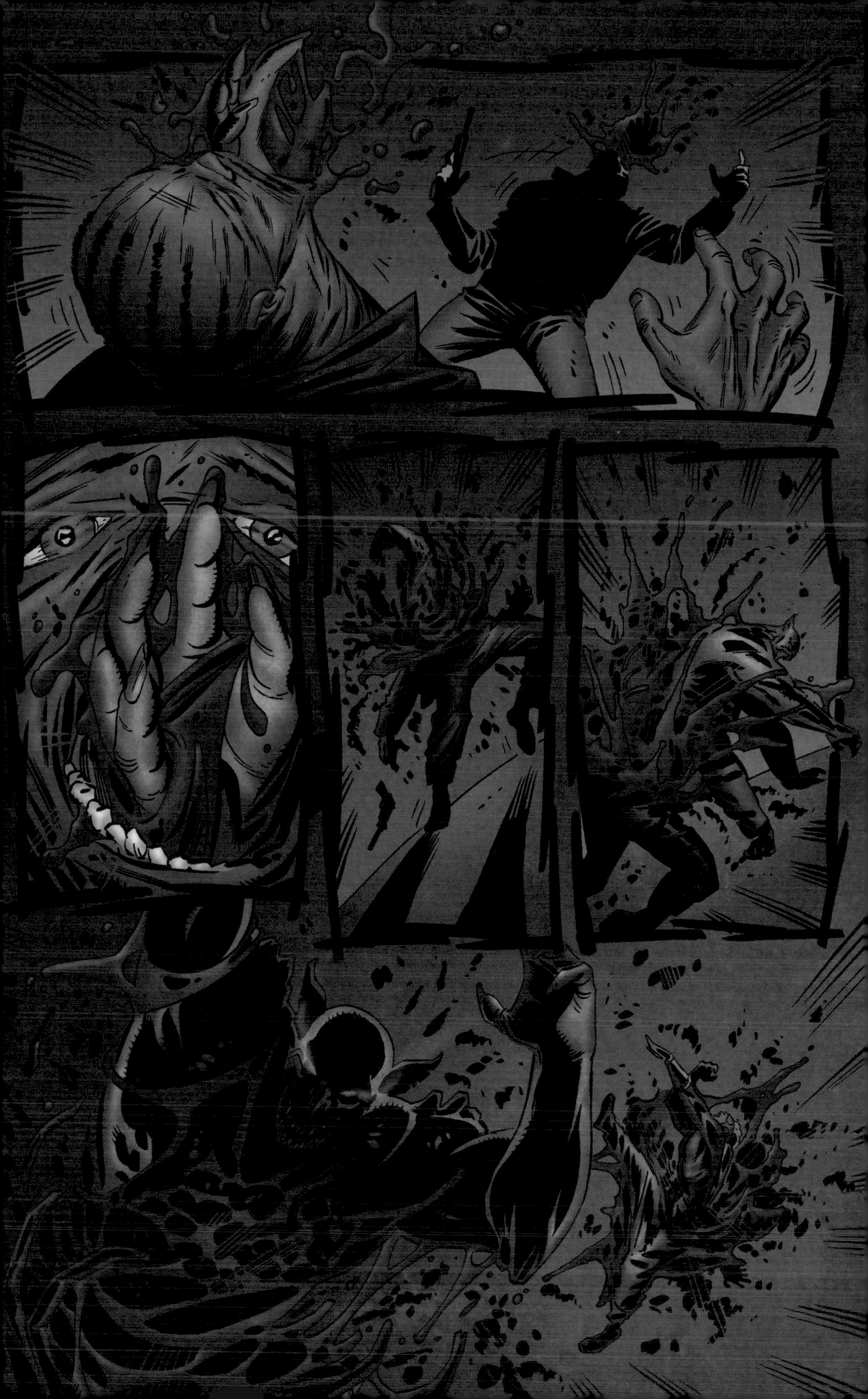

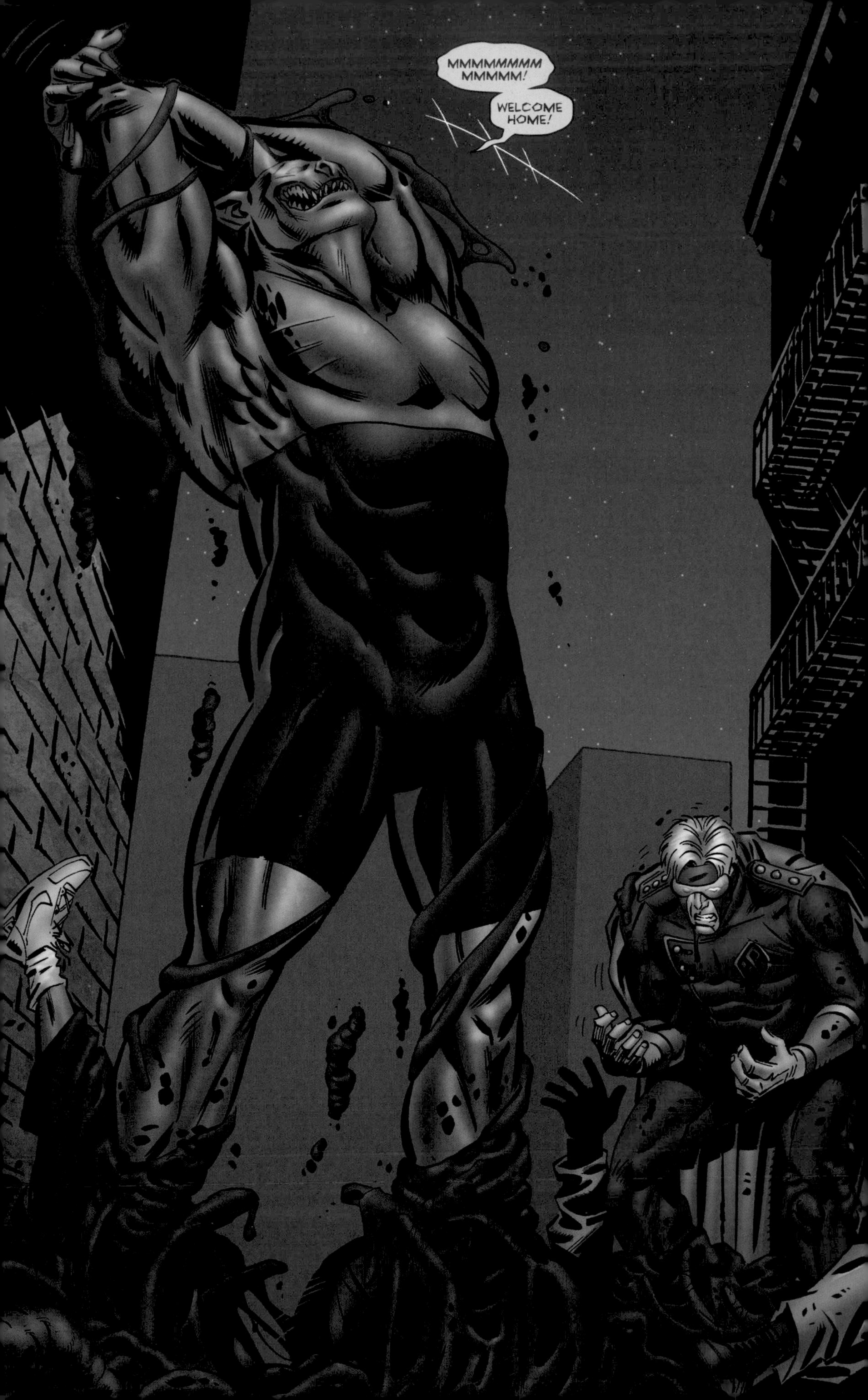
MMMMMMMMM MMMMM!
WELCOME HOME!

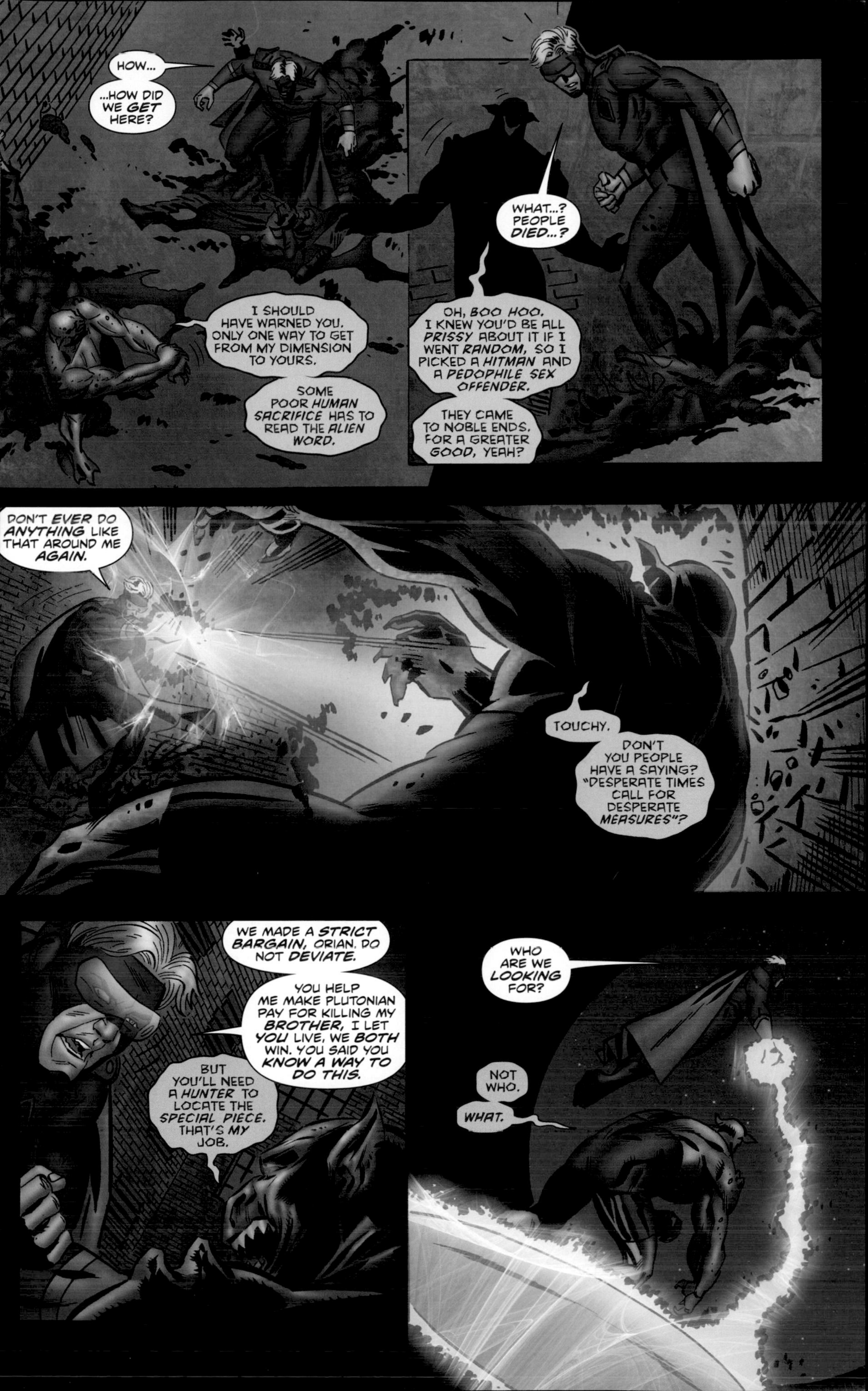
HOW...
...HOW DID WE GET HERE?
WHAT...? PEOPLE DIED...?
I SHOULD HAVE WARNED YOU. ONLY ONE WAY TO GET FROM MY DIMENSION TO YOURS.
SOME POOR HUMAN SACRIFICE HAS TO READ THE ALIEN WORD.
OH, BOO HOO. I KNEW YOU'D BE ALL PRISSY ABOUT IT IF I WENT RANDOM, SO I PICKED A HITMAN AND A PEDOPHILE SEX OFFENDER.
THEY CAME TO NOBLE ENDS, FOR A GREATER GOOD, YEAH?
DON'T EVER DO ANYTHING LIKE THAT AROUND ME AGAIN.
TOUCHY.
DON'T YOU PEOPLE HAVE A SAYING? "DESPERATE TIMES CALL FOR DESPERATE MEASURES"?
WE MADE A STRICT BARGAIN, ORIAN. DO NOT DEVIATE.
YOU HELP ME MAKE PLUTONIAN PAY FOR KILLING MY BROTHER, I LET YOU LIVE, WE BOTH WIN. YOU SAID YOU KNOW A WAY TO DO THIS.
BUT YOU'LL NEED A HUNTER TO LOCATE THE SPECIAL PIECE. THAT'S MY JOB.
WHO ARE WE LOOKING FOR?
NOT WHO.
WHAT.

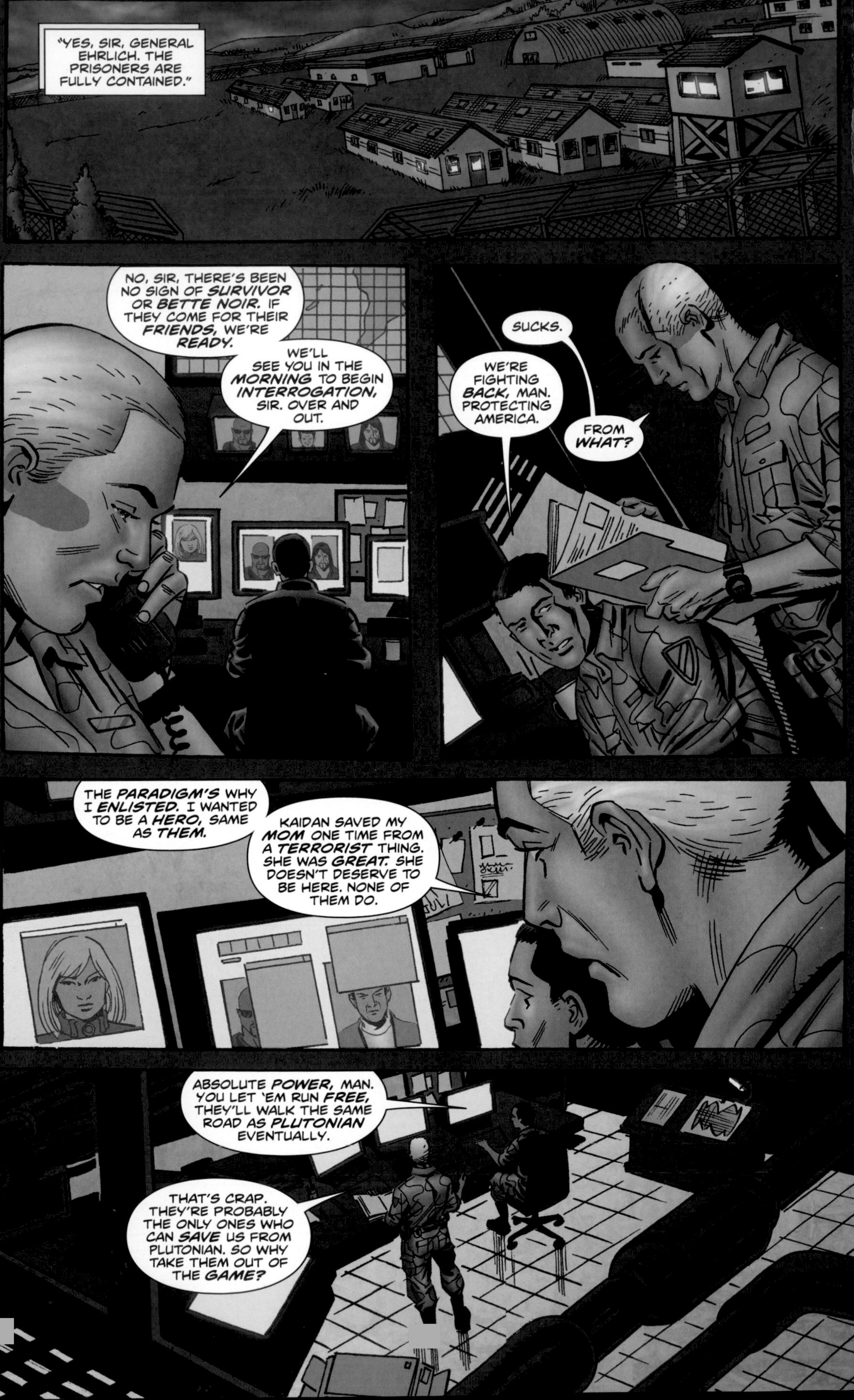
"YES, SIR, GENERAL EHRLICH. THE PRISONERS ARE FULLY CONTAINED."
NO, SIR, THERE'S BEEN NO SIGN OF SURVIVOR OR BETTE NOIR. IF THEY COME FOR THEIR FRIENDS, WE'RE READY.
WE'LL SEE YOU IN THE MORNING TO BEGIN INTERROGATION, SIR. OVER AND OUT.
SUCKS.
WE'RE FIGHTING BACK, MAN. PROTECTING AMERICA.
FROM WHAT?
THE PARADIGM'S WHY I ENLISTED. I WANTED TO BE A HERO, SAME AS THEM.
KAIDAN SAVED MY MOM ONE TIME FROM A TERRORIST THING. SHE WAS GREAT. SHE DOESN'T DESERVE TO BE HERE. NONE OF THEM DO.
ABSOLUTE POWER, MAN. YOU LET 'EM RUN FREE, THEY'LL WALK THE SAME ROAD AS PLUTONIAN EVENTUALLY.
THAT'S CRAP. THEY'RE PROBABLY THE ONLY ONES WHO CAN SAVE US FROM PLUTONIAN. SO WHY TAKE THEM OUT OF THE GAME?

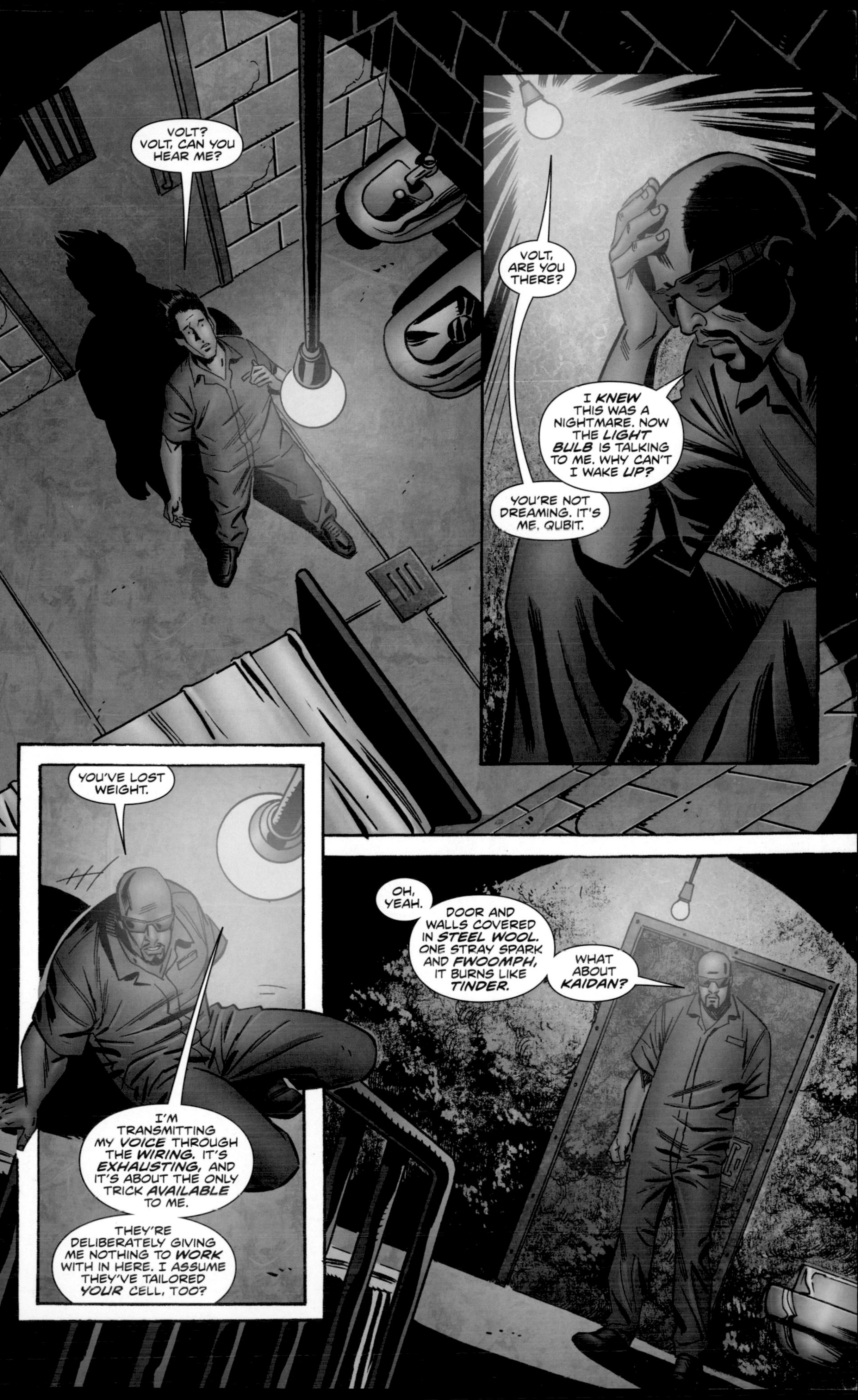
VOLT? VOLT, CAN YOU HEAR ME?
VOLT, ARE YOU THERE?
I KNEW THIS WAS A NIGHTMARE. NOW THE LIGHT BULB IS TALKING TO ME. WHY CAN'T I WAKE UP?
YOU'RE NOT DREAMING. IT'S ME. QUBIT.
YOU'VE LOST WEIGHT.
I'M TRANSMITTING MY VOICE THROUGH THE WIRING. IT'S EXHAUSTING, AND IT'S ABOUT THE ONLY TRICK AVAILABLE TO ME.
THEY'RE DELIBERATELY GIVING ME NOTHING TO WORK WITH IN HERE. I ASSUME THEY'VE TAILORED YOUR CELL, TOO?
OH, YEAH.
DOOR AND WALLS COVERED IN STEEL WOOL. ONE STRAY SPARK AND FWOOMPH, IT BURNS LIKE TINDER.
WHAT ABOUT KAIDAN?

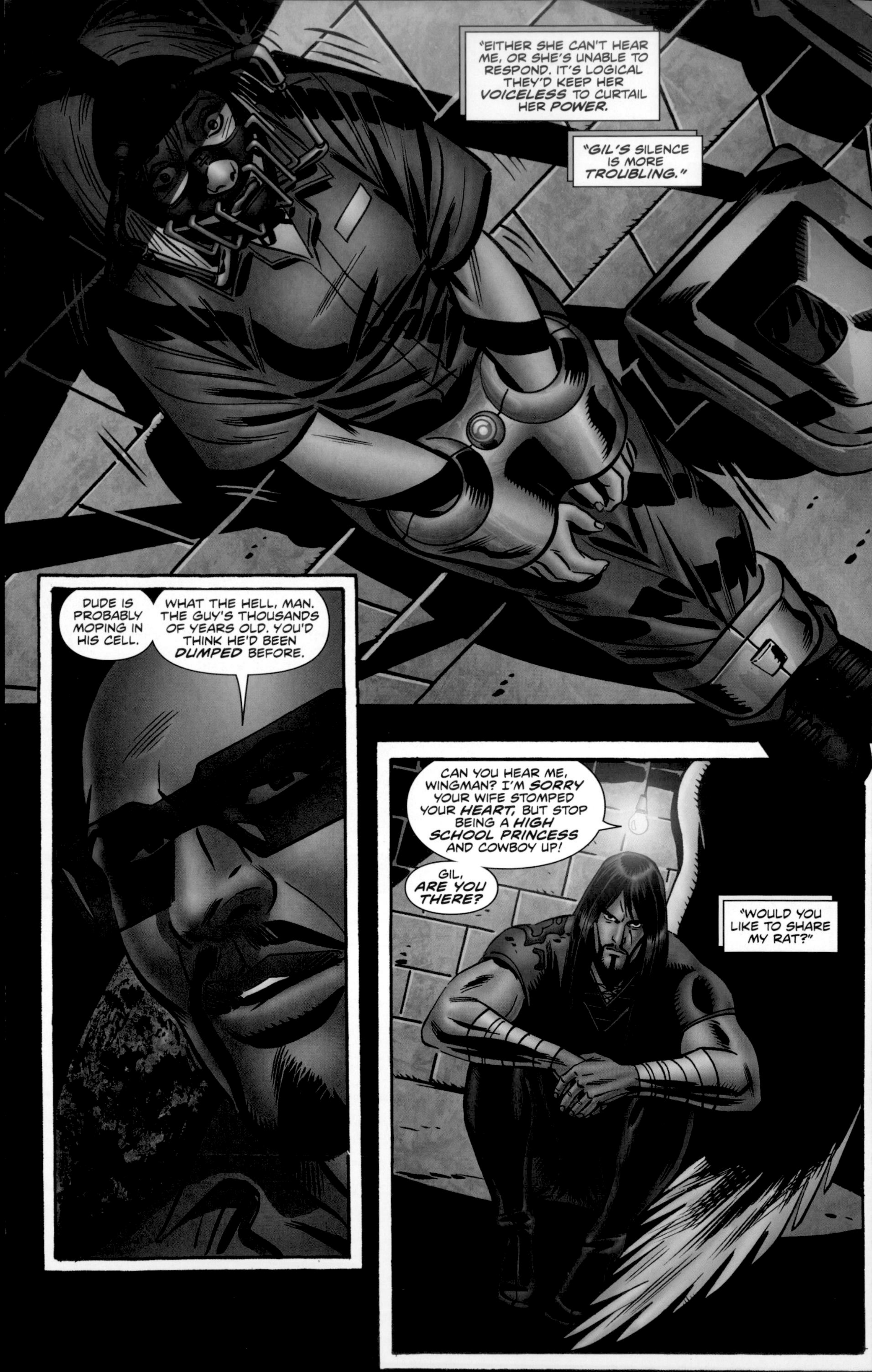
"EITHER SHE CAN'T HEAR ME, OR SHE'S UNABLE TO RESPOND. IT'S LOGICAL THEY'D KEEP HER VOICELESS TO CURTAIL HER POWER.
"GIL'S SILENCE IS MORE TROUBLING."
DUDE IS PROBABLY MOPING IN HIS CELL.
WHAT THE HELL, MAN. THE GUY'S THOUSANDS OF YEARS OLD. YOU'D THINK HE'D BEEN DUMPED BEFORE.
CAN YOU HEAR ME, WINGMAN? I'M SORRY YOUR WIFE STOMPED YOUR HEART, BUT STOP BEING A HIGH SCHOOL PRINCESS AND COWBOY UP!
GIL, ARE YOU THERE?
"WOULD YOU LIKE TO SHARE MY RAT?"

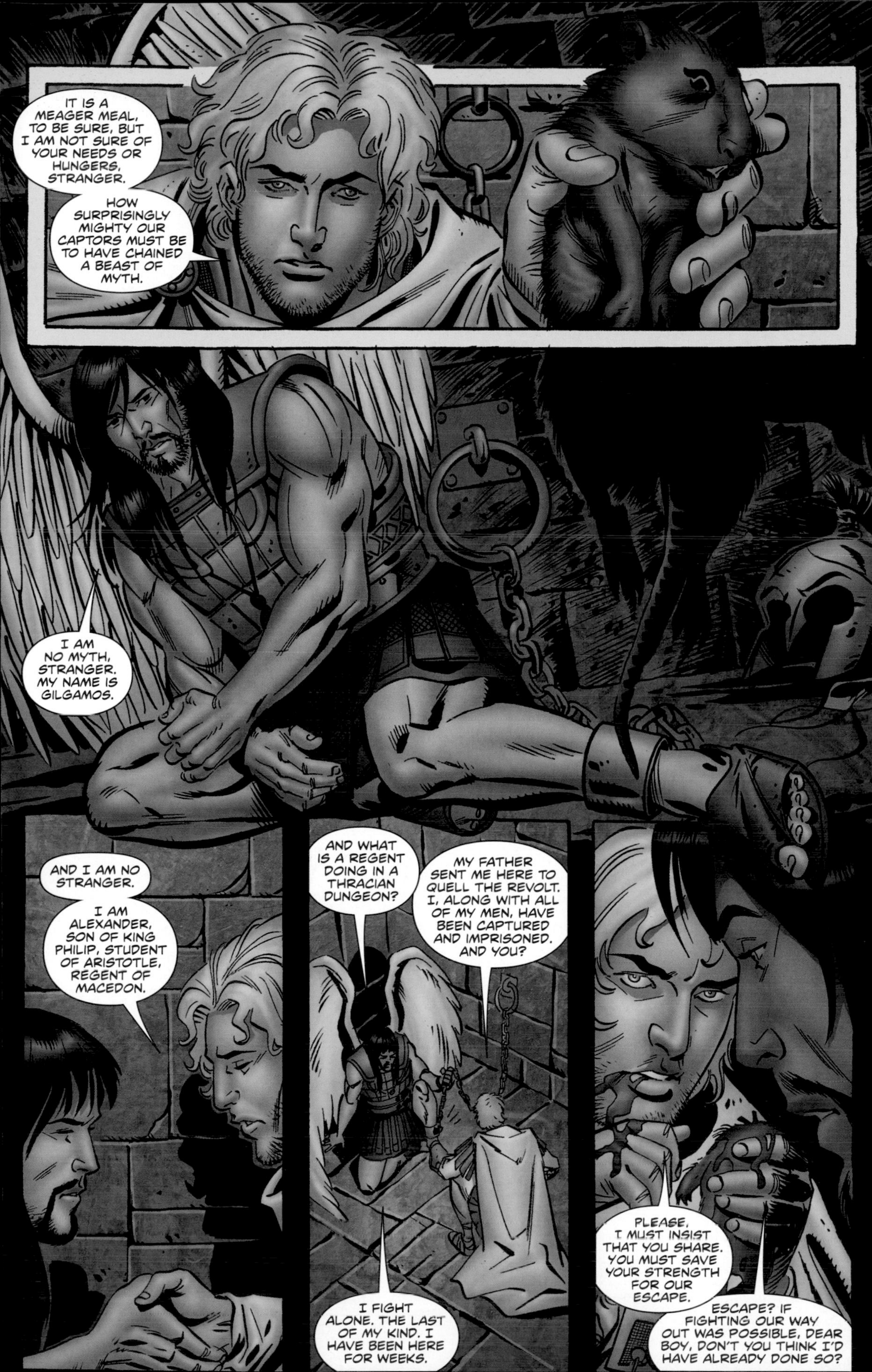
IT IS A MEAGER MEAL, TO BE SURE, BUT I AM NOT SURE OF YOUR NEEDS OR HUNGERS, STRANGER.
HOW SURPRISINGLY MIGHTY OUR CAPTORS MUST BE TO HAVE CHAINED A BEAST OF MYTH.
I AM NO MYTH, STRANGER. MY NAME IS GILGAMOS.
AND I AM NO STRANGER.
I AM ALEXANDER, SON OF KING PHILIP, STUDENT OF ARISTOTLE, REGENT OF MACEDON.
AND WHAT IS A REGENT DOING IN A THRACIAN DUNGEON?
MY FATHER SENT ME HERE TO QUELL THE REVOLT. I, ALONG WITH ALL OF MY MEN, HAVE BEEN CAPTURED AND IMPRISONED. AND YOU?
I FIGHT ALONE. THE LAST OF MY KIND. I HAVE BEEN HERE FOR WEEKS.
PLEASE, I MUST INSIST THAT YOU SHARE. YOU MUST SAVE YOUR STRENGTH FOR OUR ESCAPE.
ESCAPE? IF FIGHTING OUR WAY OUT WAS POSSIBLE, DEAR BOY, DON'T YOU THINK I'D HAVE ALREADY DONE SO?

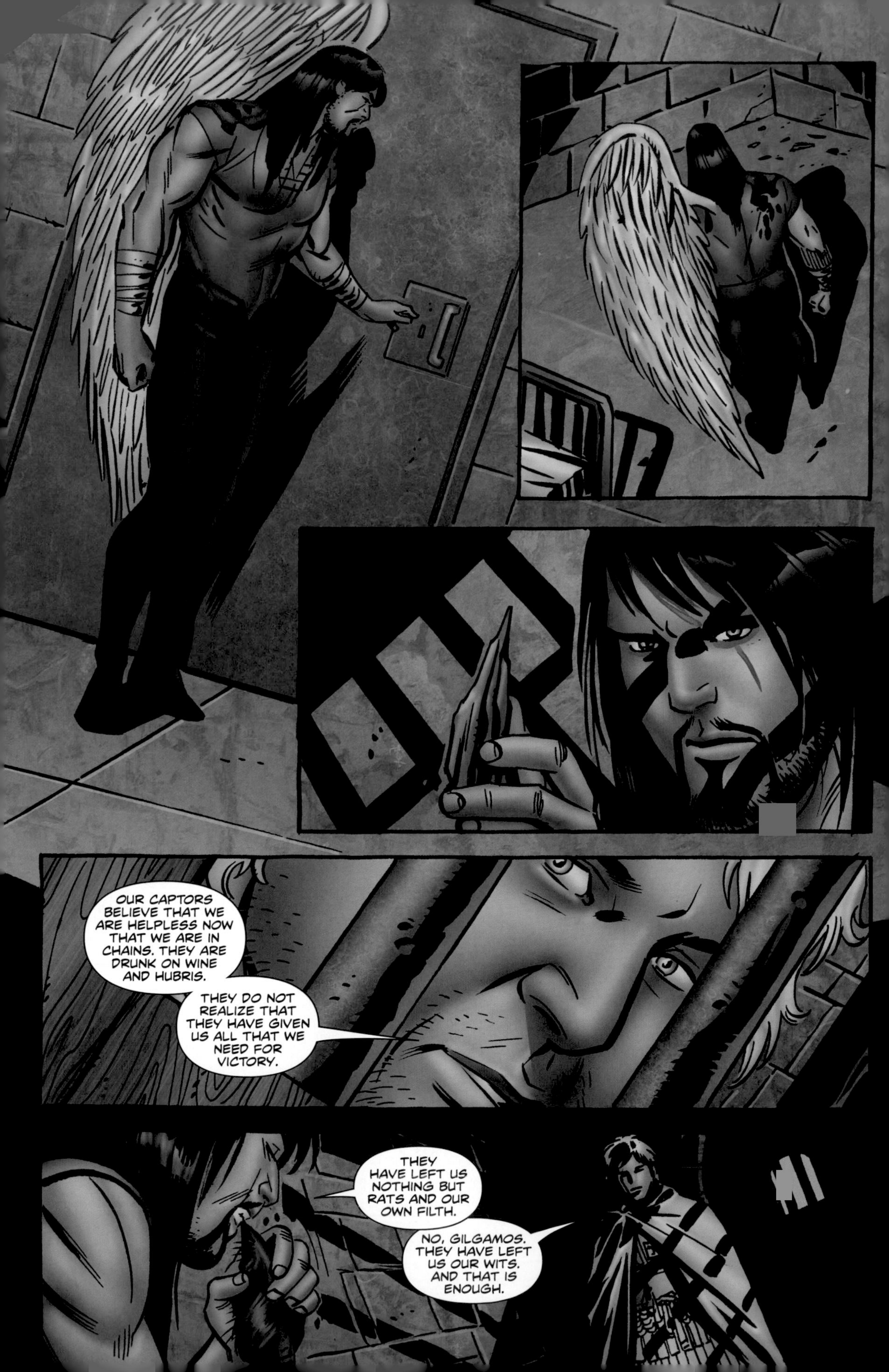
OUR CAPTORS BELIEVE THAT WE ARE HELPLESS NOW THAT WE ARE IN CHAINS. THEY ARE DRUNK ON WINE AND HUBRIS.
THEY DO NOT REALIZE THAT THEY HAVE GIVEN US ALL THAT WE NEED FOR VICTORY.
THEY HAVE LEFT US NOTHING BUT RATS AND OUR OWN FILTH.
NO, GILGAMOS. THEY HAVE LEFT US OUR WITS. AND THAT IS ENOUGH.

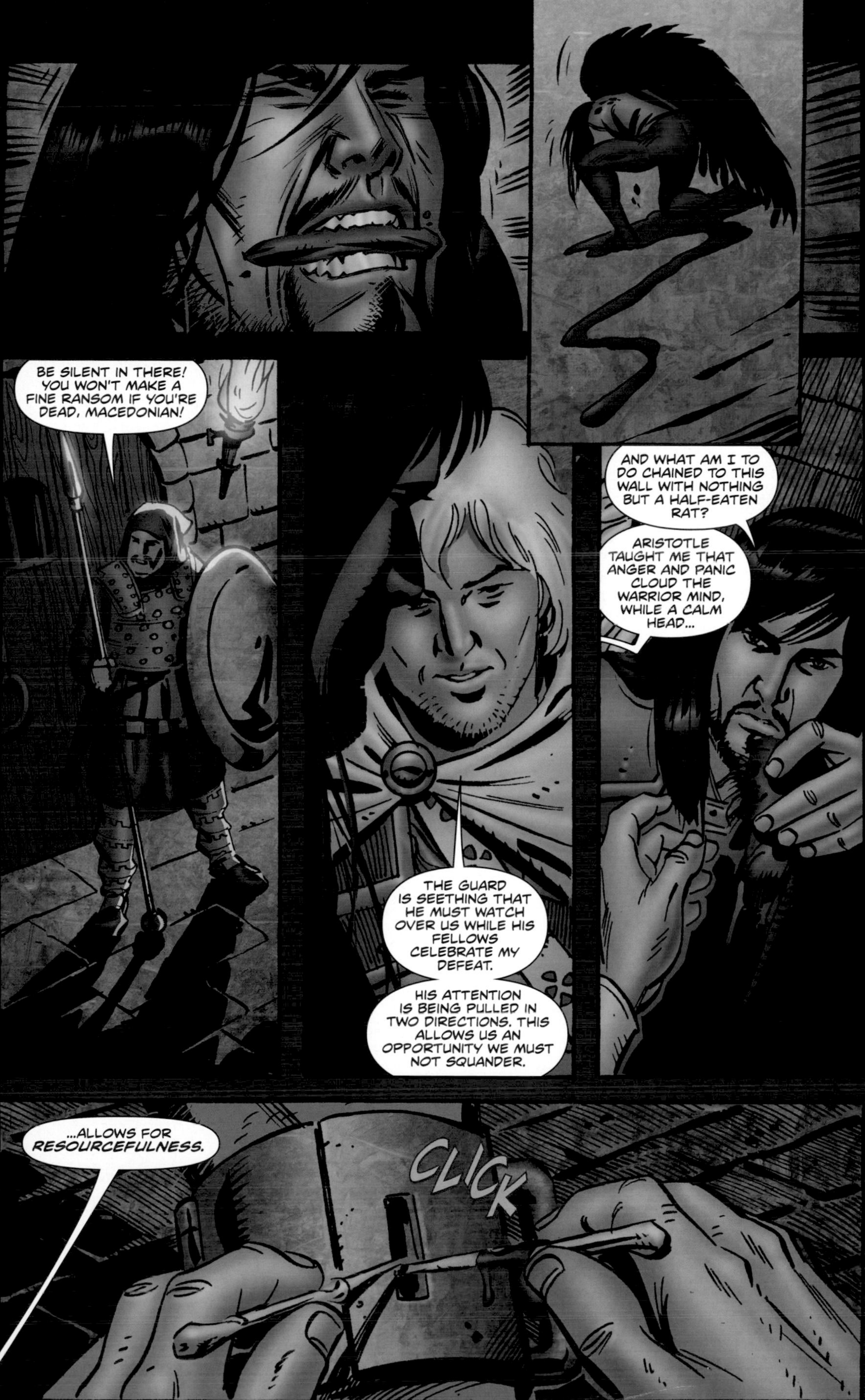
BE SILENT IN THERE! YOU WON'T MAKE A FINE RANSOM IF YOU'RE DEAD, MACEDONIAN!
THE GUARD IS SEETHING THAT HE MUST WATCH OVER US WHILE HIS FELLOWS CELEBRATE MY DEFEAT.
HIS ATTENTION IS BEING PULLED IN TWO DIRECTIONS. THIS ALLOWS US AN OPPORTUNITY WE MUST NOT SQUANDER.
AND WHAT AM I TO DO CHAINED TO THIS WALL WITH NOTHING BUT A HALF-EATEN RAT?
ARISTOTLE TAUGHT ME THAT ANGER AND PANIC CLOUD THE WARRIOR MIND, WHILE A CALM HEAD...
...ALLOWS FOR *RESOURCEFULNESS.*
CLICK

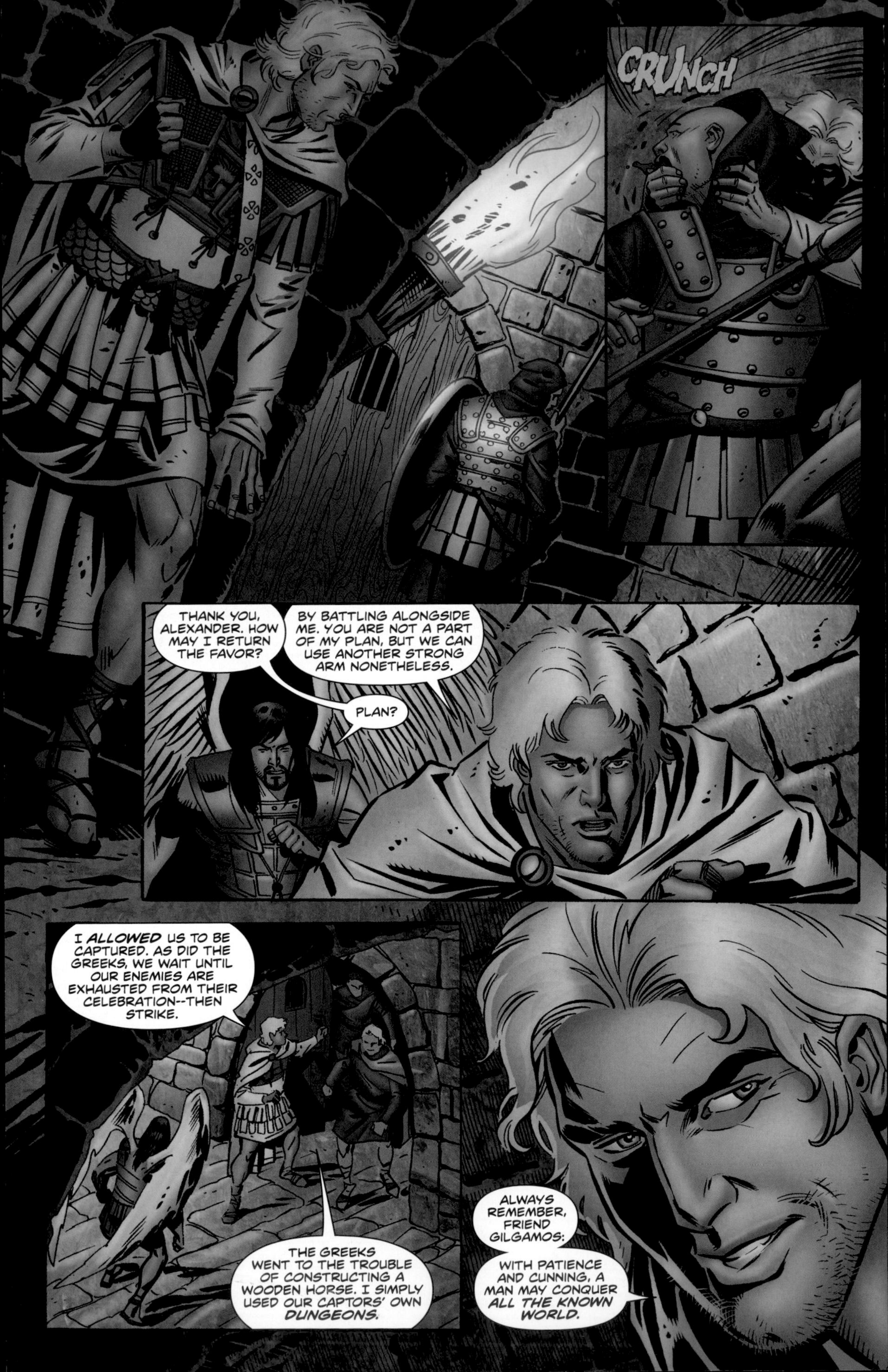
CRUNCH
THANK YOU, ALEXANDER. HOW MAY I RETURN THE FAVOR?
BY BATTLING ALONGSIDE ME. YOU ARE NOT A PART OF MY PLAN, BUT WE CAN USE ANOTHER STRONG ARM NONETHELESS.
PLAN?
I ALLOWED US TO BE CAPTURED. AS DID THE GREEKS, WE WAIT UNTIL OUR ENEMIES ARE EXHAUSTED FROM THEIR CELEBRATION--THEN STRIKE.
THE GREEKS WENT TO THE TROUBLE OF CONSTRUCTING A WOODEN HORSE. I SIMPLY USED OUR CAPTORS' OWN DUNGEONS.
ALWAYS REMEMBER, FRIEND GILGAMOS:
WITH PATIENCE AND CUNNING, A MAN MAY CONQUER ALL THE KNOWN WORLD.

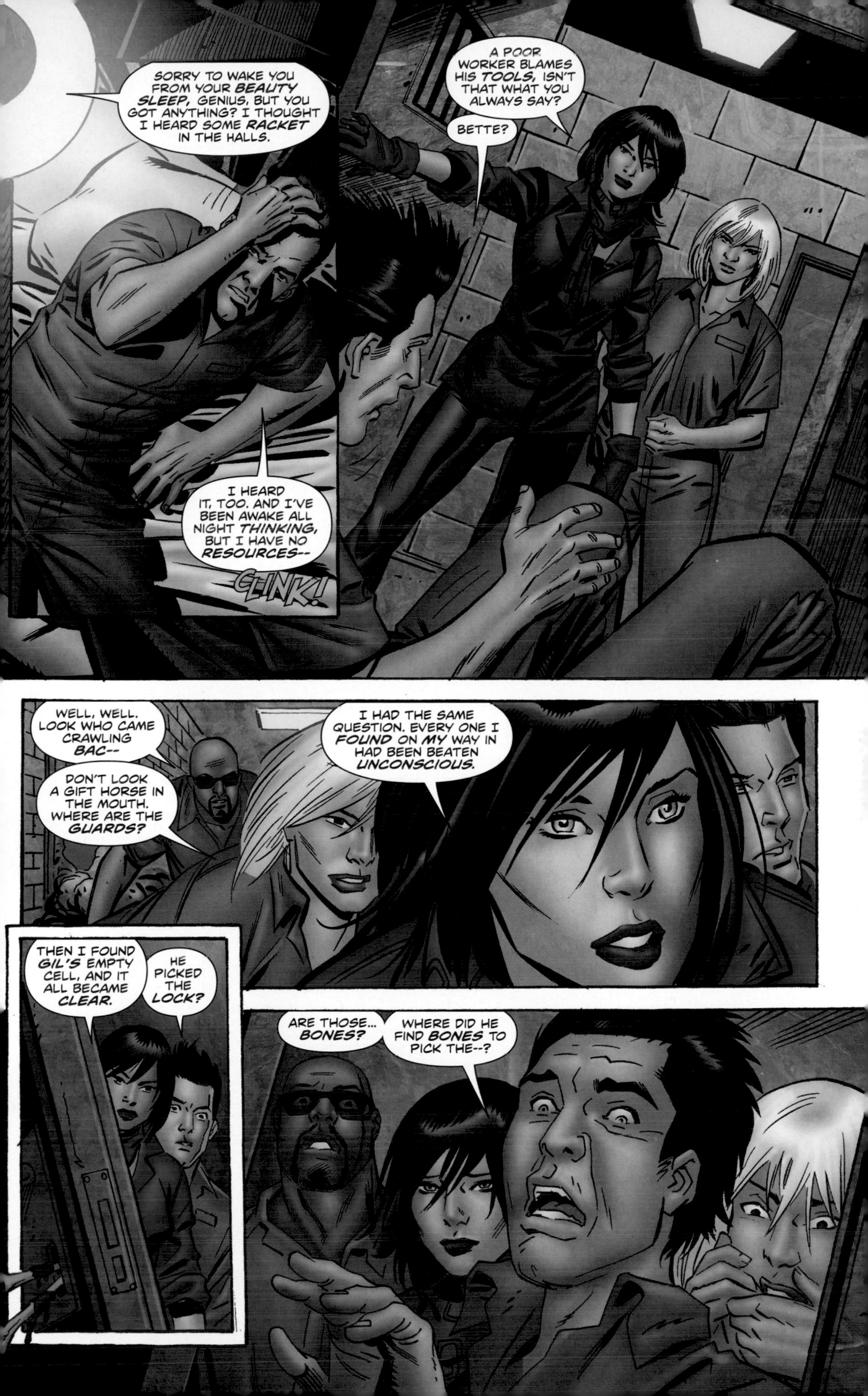
SORRY TO WAKE YOU FROM YOUR BEAUTY SLEEP, GENIUS, BUT YOU GOT ANYTHING? I THOUGHT I HEARD SOME RACKET IN THE HALLS.
A POOR WORKER BLAMES HIS TOOLS, ISN'T THAT WHAT YOU ALWAYS SAY?
BETTE?
I HEARD IT, TOO. AND I'VE BEEN AWAKE ALL NIGHT THINKING, BUT I HAVE NO RESOURCES--
CLINK!
WELL, WELL. LOOK WHO CAME CRAWLING BAC--
DON'T LOOK A GIFT HORSE IN THE MOUTH. WHERE ARE THE GUARDS?
I HAD THE SAME QUESTION. EVERY ONE I FOUND ON MY WAY IN HAD BEEN BEATEN UNCONSCIOUS.
THEN I FOUND GIL'S EMPTY CELL, AND IT ALL BECAME CLEAR.
HE PICKED THE LOCK?
ARE THOSE... BONES?
WHERE DID HE FIND BONES TO PICK THE--?

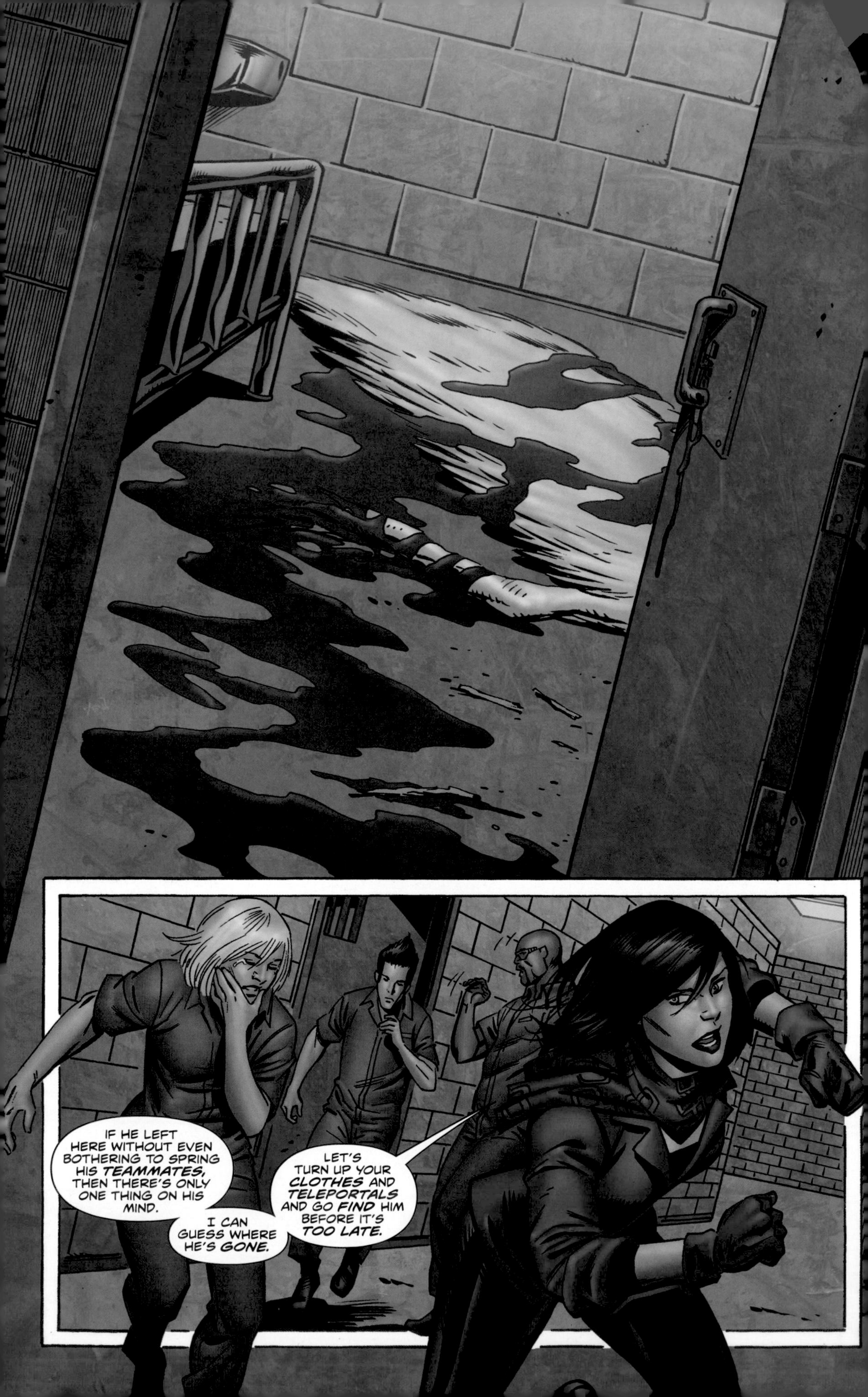
IF HE LEFT HERE WITHOUT EVEN BOTHERING TO SPRING HIS TEAMMATES, THEN THERE'S ONLY ONE THING ON HIS MIND.
I CAN GUESS WHERE HE'S GONE.
LET'S TURN UP YOUR CLOTHES AND TELEPORTALS AND GO FIND HIM BEFORE IT'S TOO LATE.

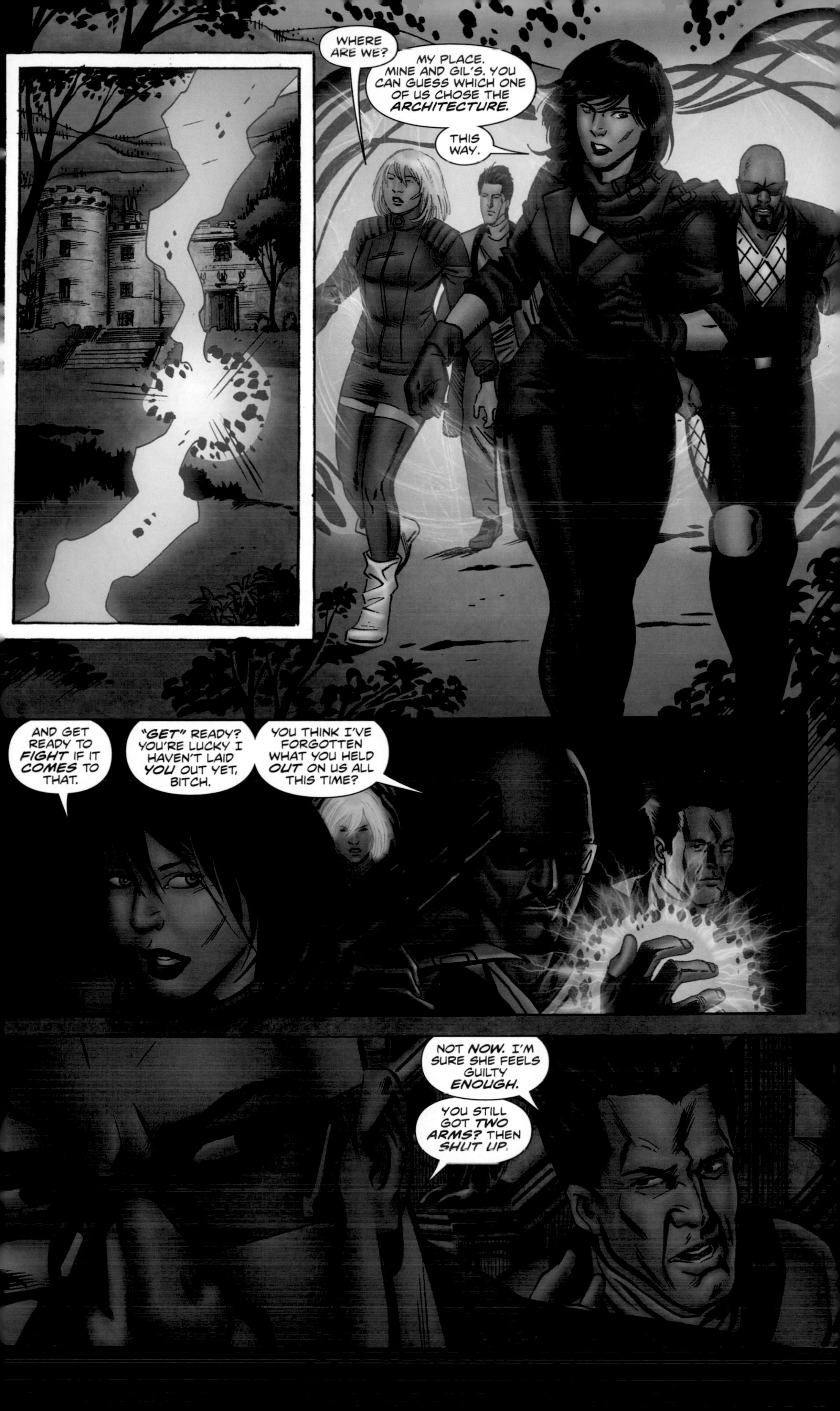
WHERE ARE WE?
MY PLACE. MINE AND GIL'S. YOU CAN GUESS WHICH ONE OF US CHOSE THE ARCHITECTURE.
THIS WAY.
AND GET READY TO FIGHT IF IT COMES TO THAT.
"GET" READY? YOU'RE LUCKY I HAVEN'T LAID YOU OUT YET, BITCH.
YOU THINK I'VE FORGOTTEN WHAT YOU HELD OUT ON US ALL THIS TIME?
NOT NOW. I'M SURE SHE FEELS GUILTY ENOUGH.
YOU STILL GOT TWO ARMS? THEN SHUT UP.

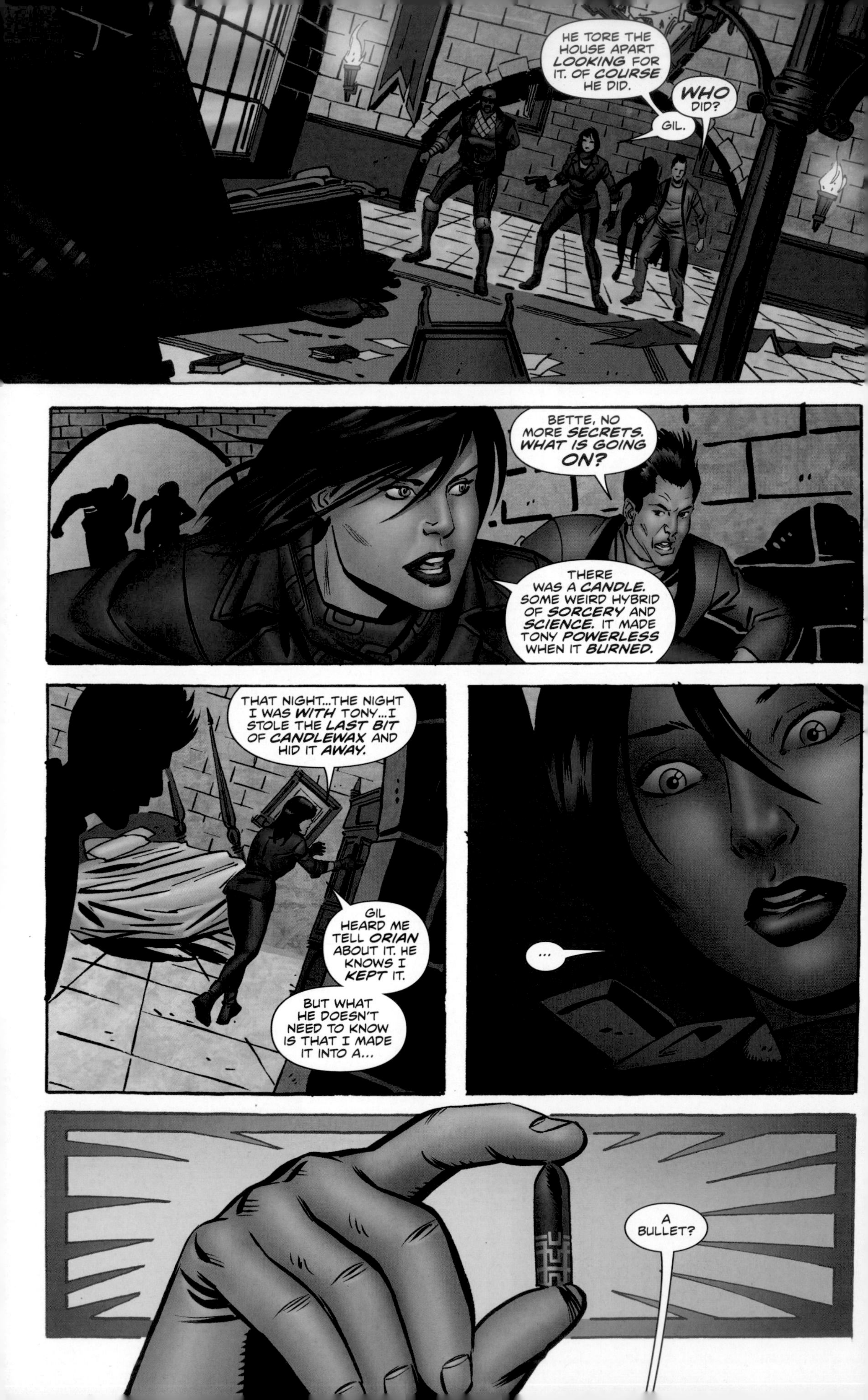
HE TORE THE HOUSE APART LOOKING FOR IT. OF COURSE HE DID.
WHO DID?
GIL.
BETTE, NO MORE SECRETS. WHAT IS GOING ON?
THERE WAS A CANDLE. SOME WEIRD HYBRID OF SORCERY AND SCIENCE. IT MADE TONY POWERLESS WHEN IT BURNED.
THAT NIGHT...THE NIGHT I WAS WITH TONY...I STOLE THE LAST BIT OF CANDLEWAX AND HID IT AWAY.
GIL HEARD ME TELL ORIAN ABOUT IT. HE KNOWS I KEPT IT.
BUT WHAT HE DOESN'T NEED TO KNOW IS THAT I MADE IT INTO A...
...
A BULLET?

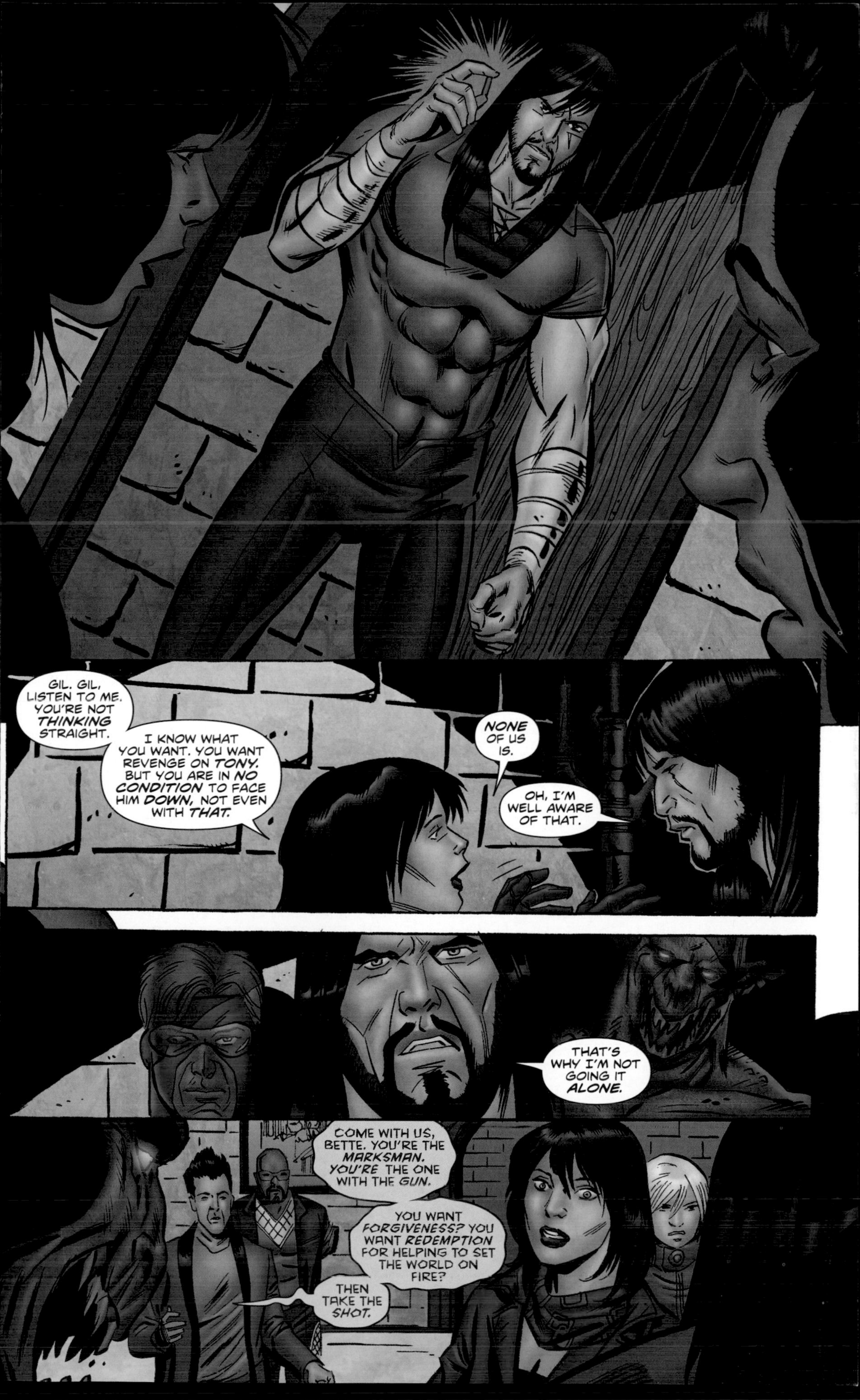
GIL. GIL, LISTEN TO ME. YOU'RE NOT THINKING STRAIGHT.
I KNOW WHAT YOU WANT. YOU WANT REVENGE ON TONY. BUT YOU ARE IN NO CONDITION TO FACE HIM DOWN, NOT EVEN WITH THAT.
NONE OF US IS.
OH, I'M WELL AWARE OF THAT.
THAT'S WHY I'M NOT GOING IT ALONE.
COME WITH US, BETTE. YOU'RE THE MARKSMAN. YOU'RE THE ONE WITH THE GUN.
YOU WANT FORGIVENESS? YOU WANT REDEMPTION FOR HELPING TO SET THE WORLD ON FIRE?
THEN TAKE THE SHOT.

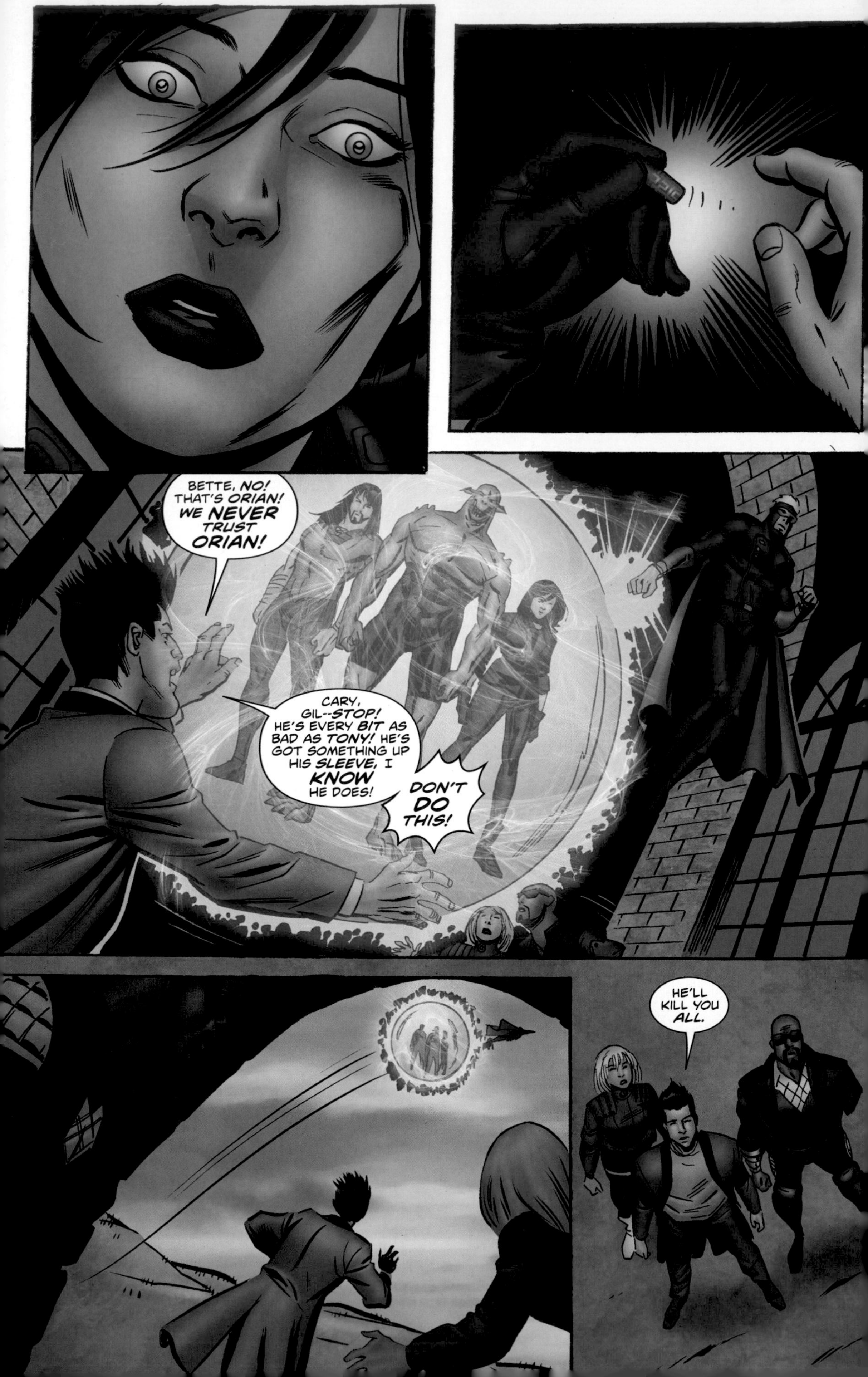
BETTE, NO! THAT'S ORIAN! WE NEVER TRUST ORIAN!
CARY, GIL--STOP! HE'S EVERY BIT AS BAD AS TONY! HE'S GOT SOMETHING UP HIS SLEEVE, I KNOW HE DOES!
DON'T DO THIS!
HE'LL KILL YOU ALL.

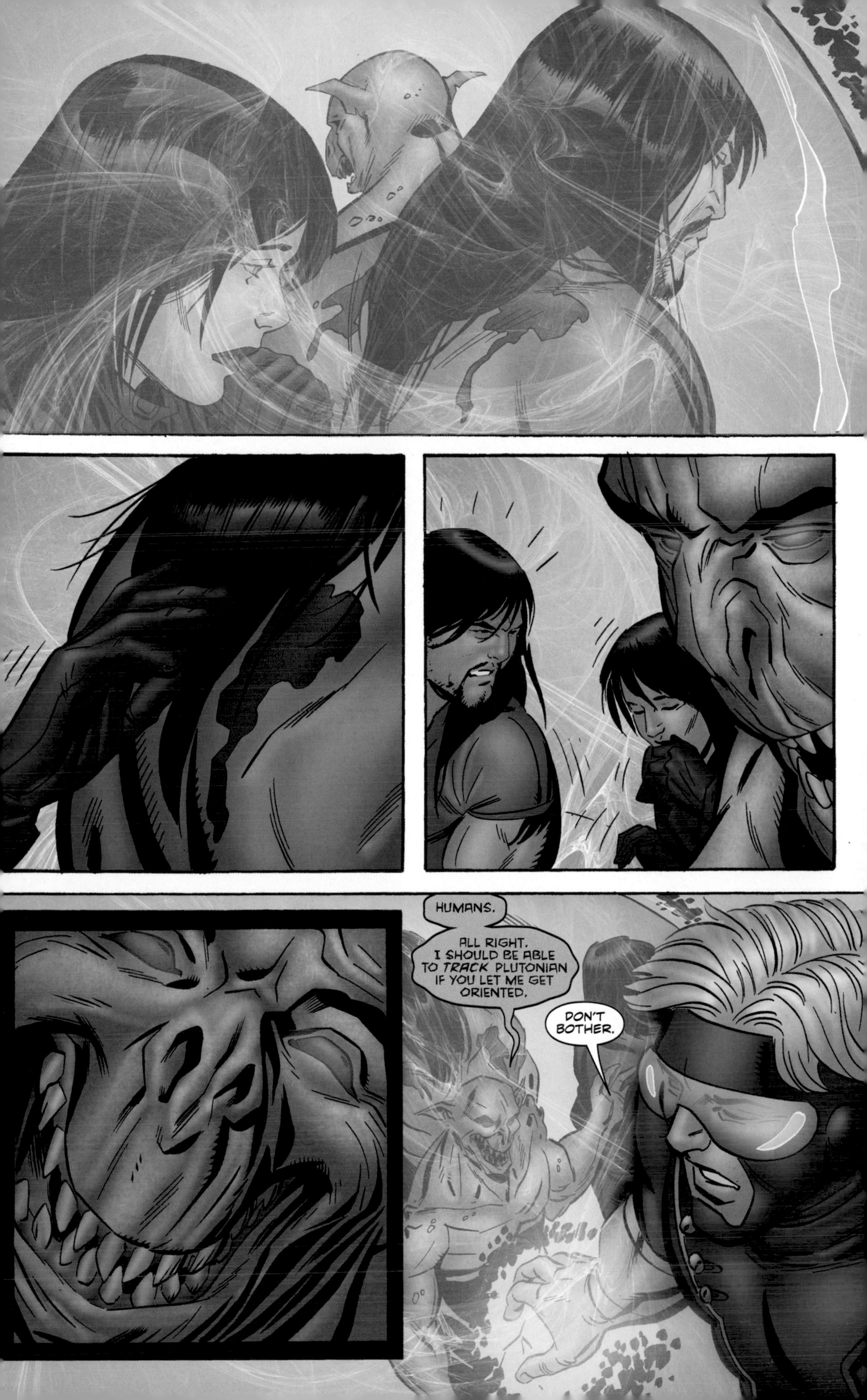
HUMANS.
ALL RIGHT. I SHOULD BE ABLE TO TRACK PLUTONIAN IF YOU LET ME GET ORIENTED.
DON'T BOTHER.

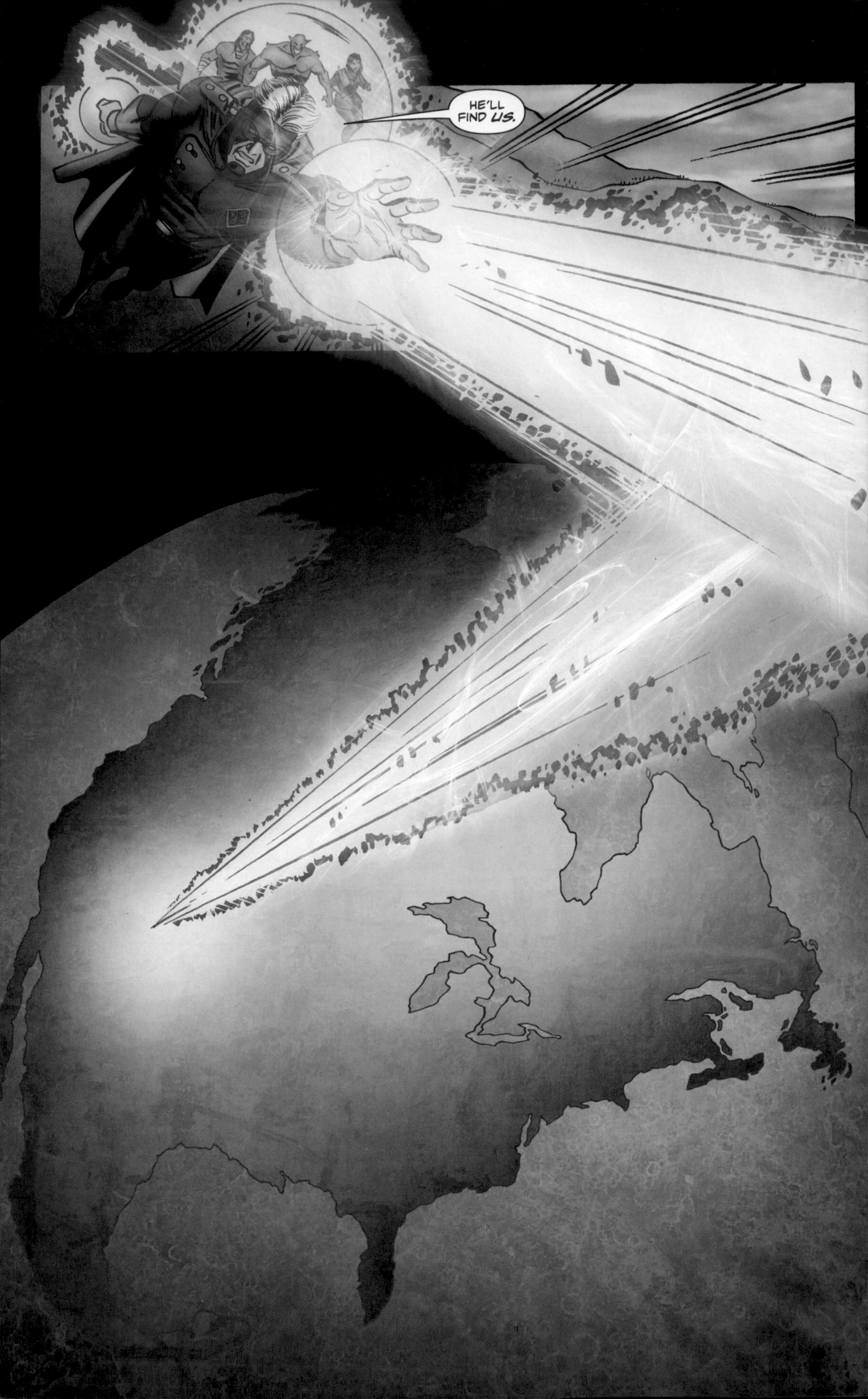
HE'LL FIND US.

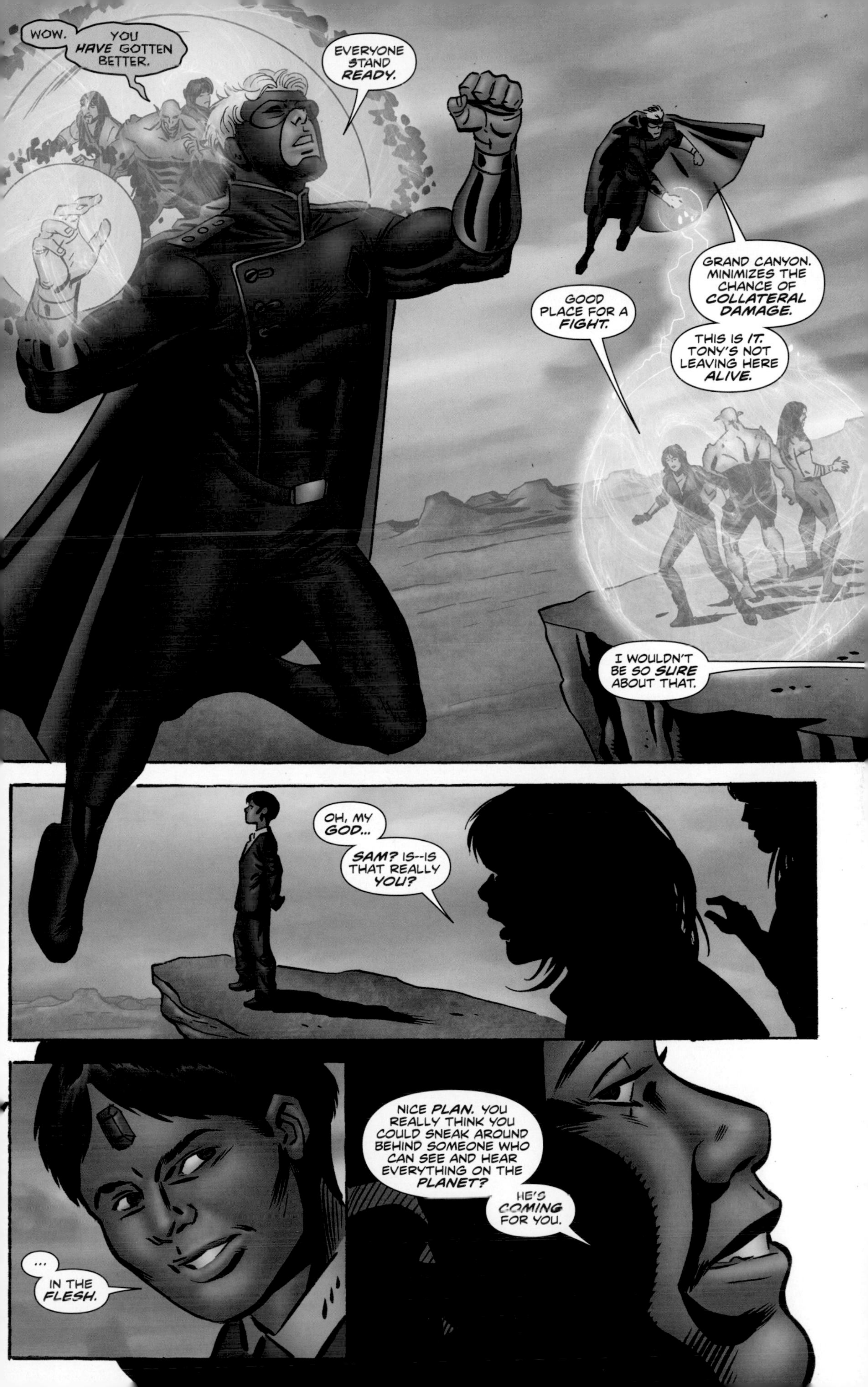
WOW. YOU HAVE GOTTEN BETTER.
EVERYONE STAND READY.
GOOD PLACE FOR A FIGHT.
GRAND CANYON. MINIMIZES THE CHANCE OF COLLATERAL DAMAGE.
THIS IS IT. TONY'S NOT LEAVING HERE ALIVE.
I WOULDN'T BE SO SURE ABOUT THAT.
OH, MY GOD...
SAM? IS--IS THAT REALLY YOU?
... IN THE FLESH.
NICE PLAN. YOU REALLY THINK YOU COULD SNEAK AROUND BEHIND SOMEONE WHO CAN SEE AND HEAR EVERYTHING ON THE PLANET?
HE'S COMING FOR YOU.

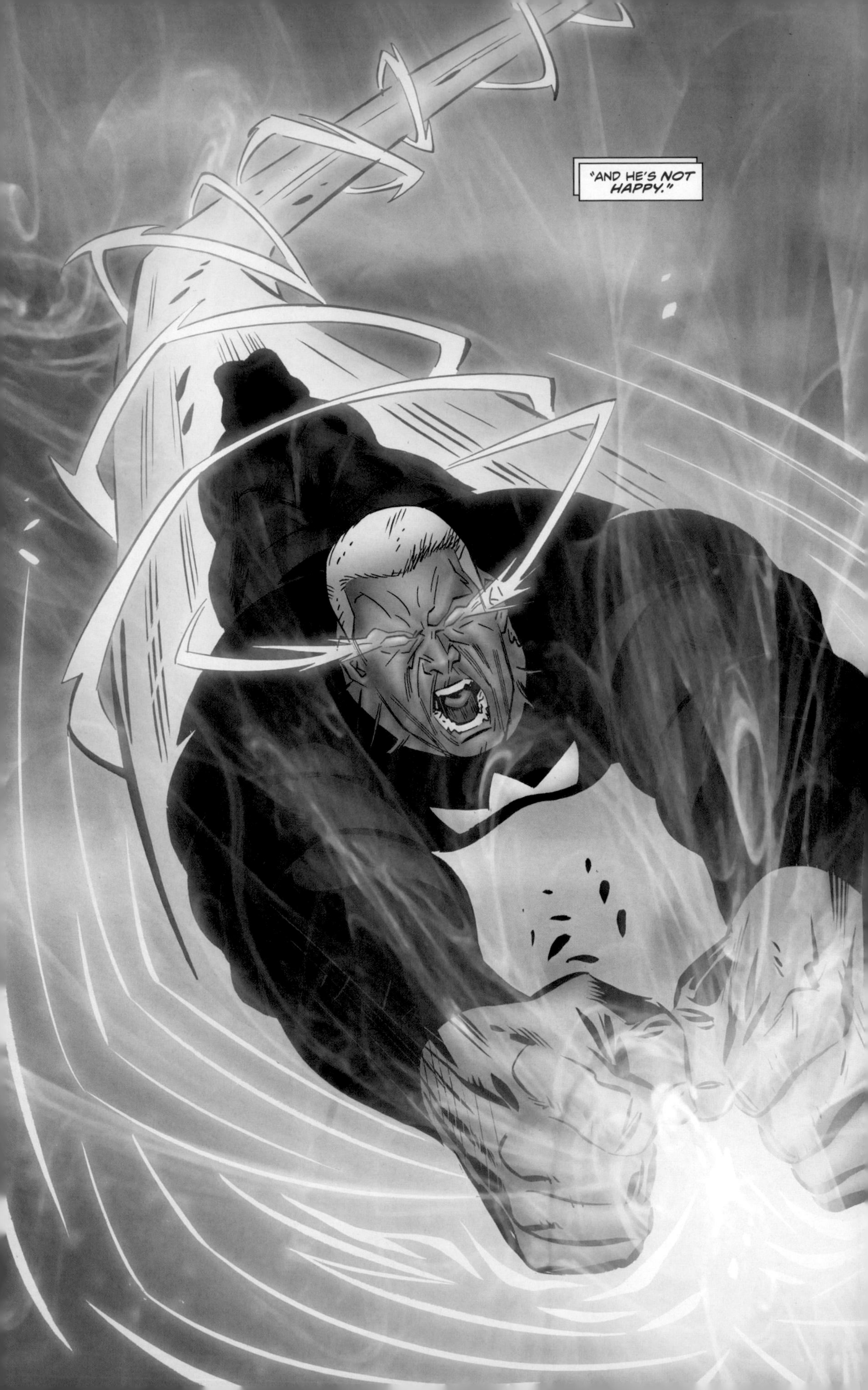
"AND HE'S NOT HAPPY."

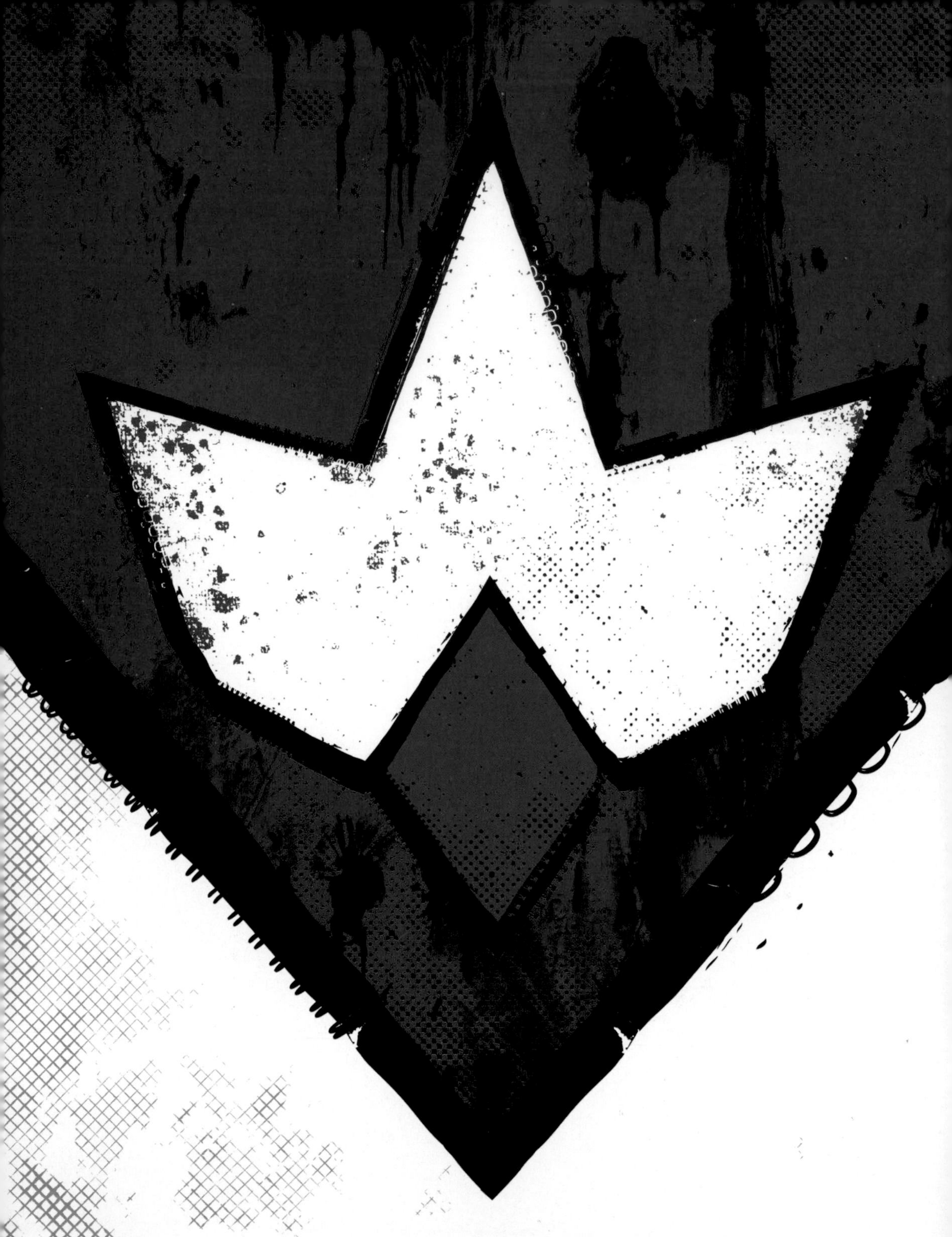

CHAPTER 15

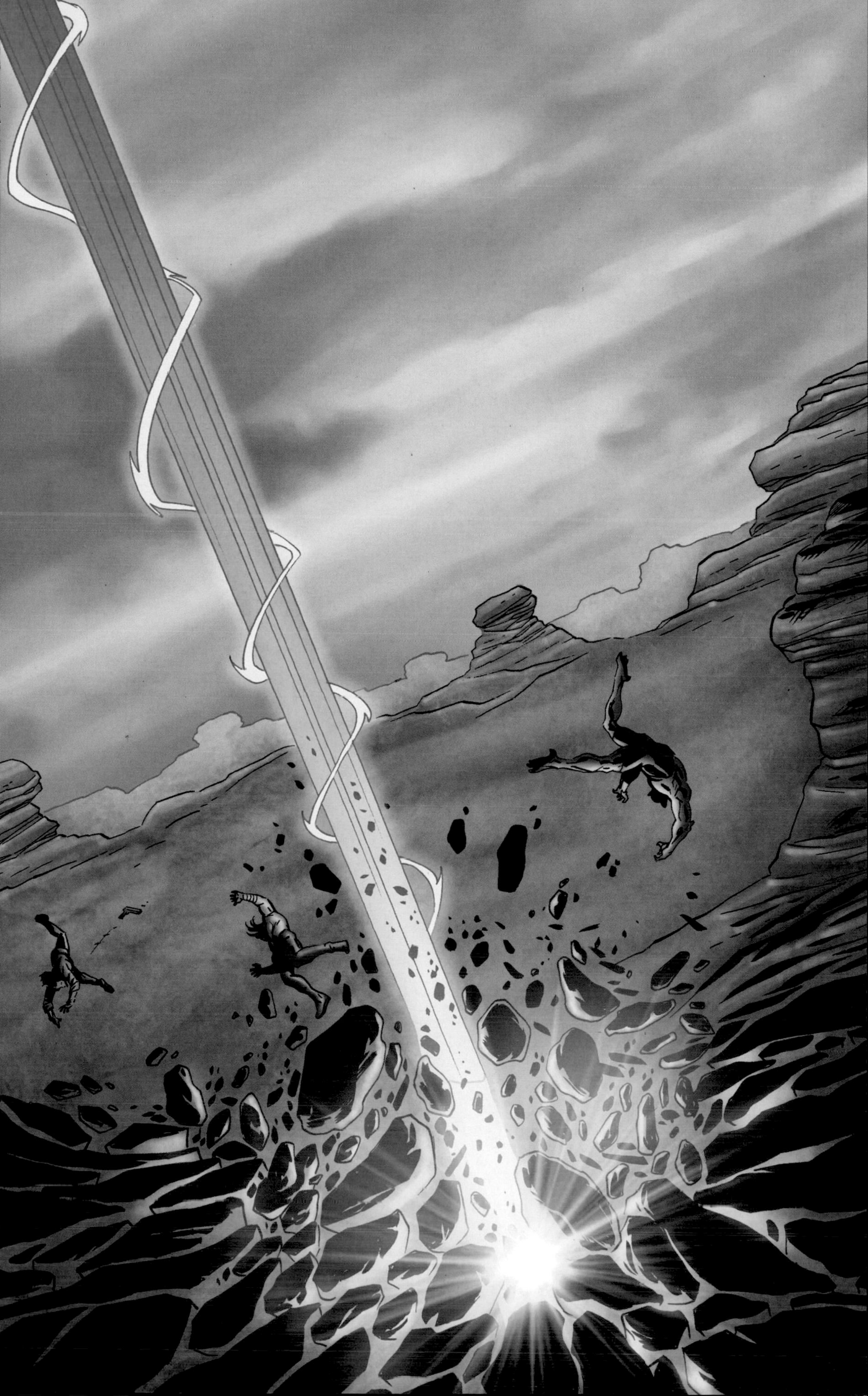

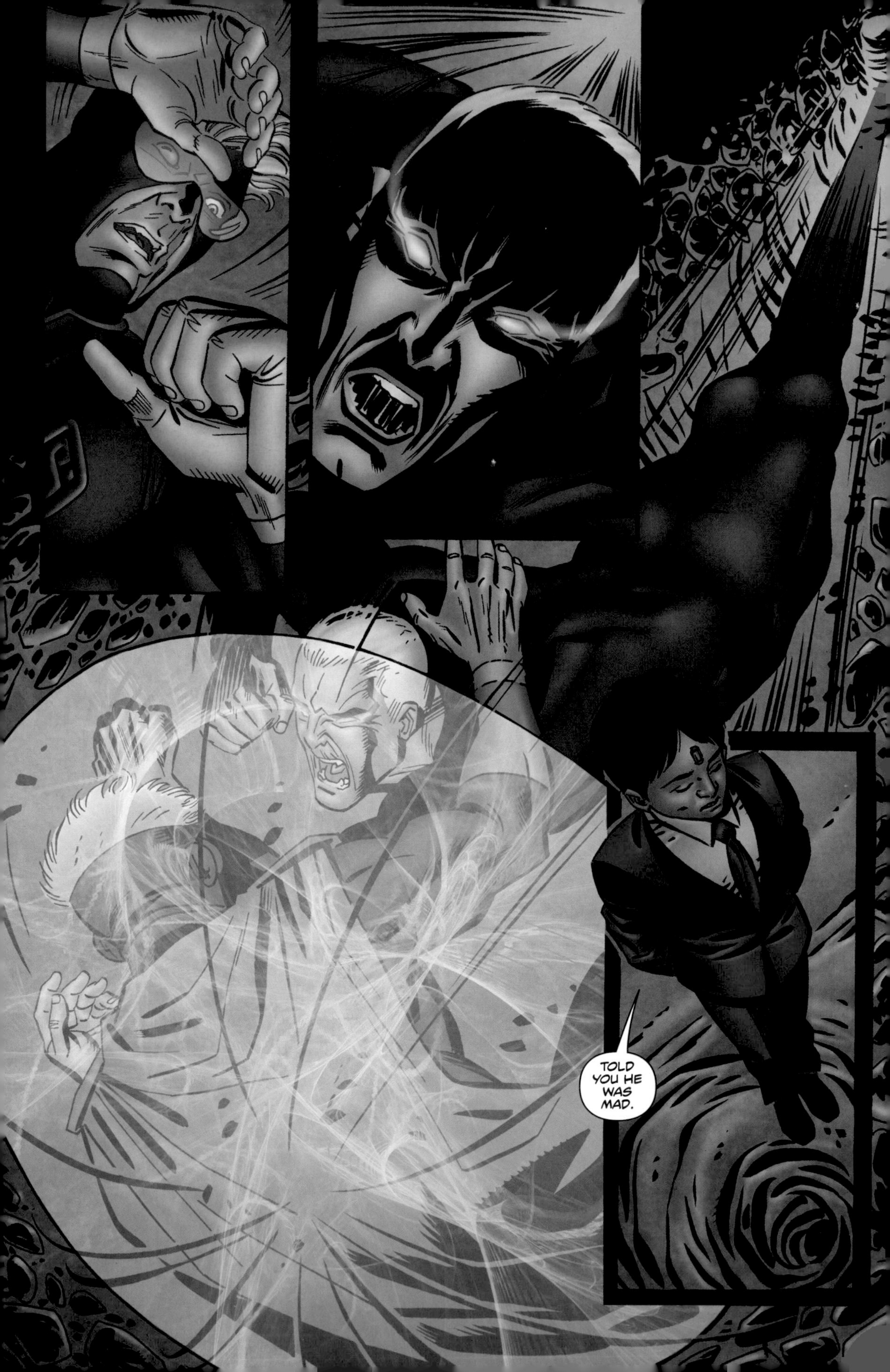
TOLD YOU HE WAS MAD.

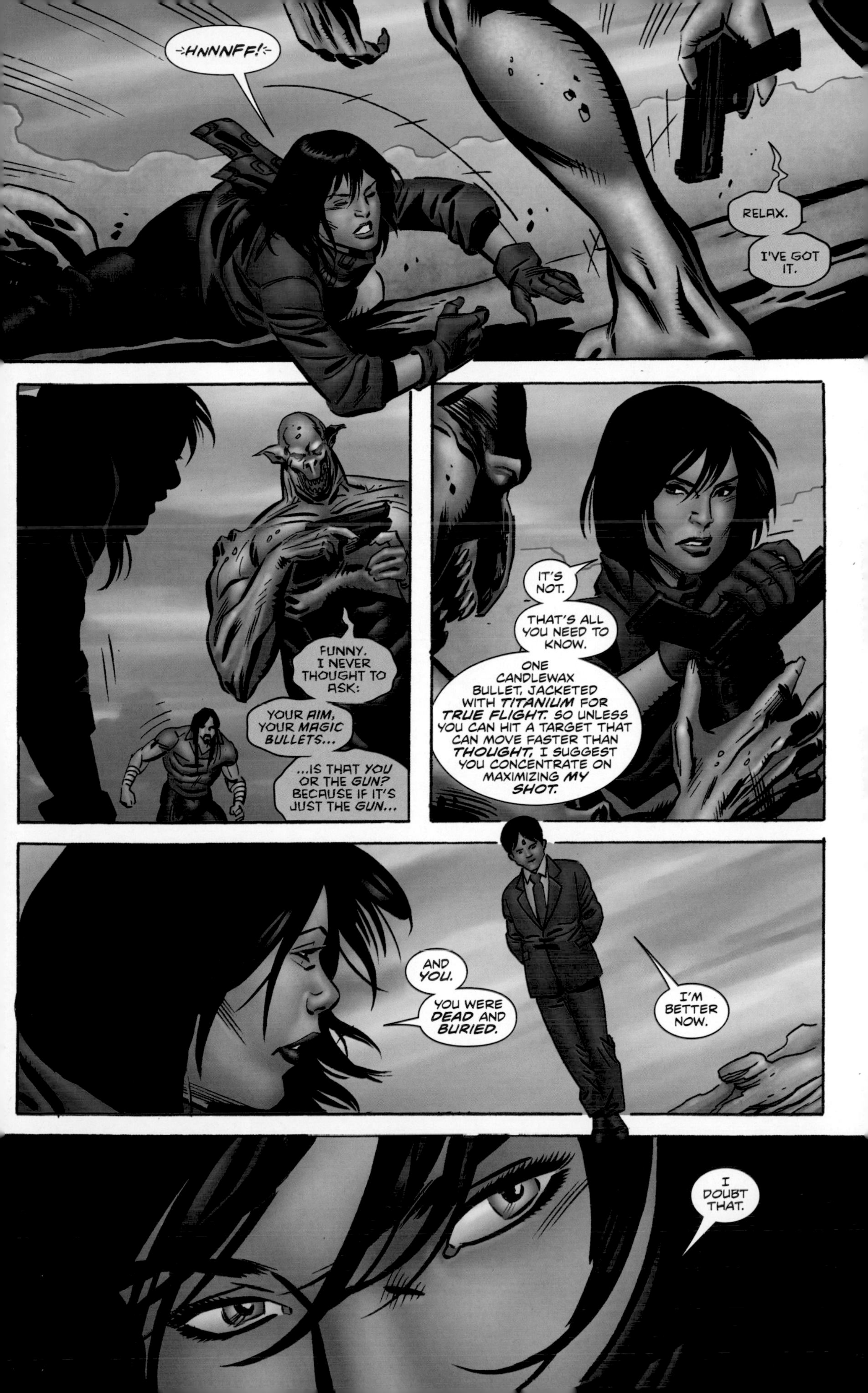

-HNNNFF!-
RELAX.
I'VE GOT IT.
FUNNY. I NEVER THOUGHT TO ASK:
YOUR AIM, YOUR MAGIC BULLETS...
...IS THAT YOU OR THE GUN? BECAUSE IF IT'S JUST THE GUN...
IT'S NOT.
THAT'S ALL YOU NEED TO KNOW.
ONE CANDLEWAX BULLET, JACKETED WITH TITANIUM FOR TRUE FLIGHT. SO UNLESS YOU CAN HIT A TARGET THAT CAN MOVE FASTER THAN THOUGHT, I SUGGEST YOU CONCENTRATE ON MAXIMIZING MY SHOT.
AND YOU.
YOU WERE DEAD AND BURIED.
I'M BETTER NOW.
I DOUBT THAT.

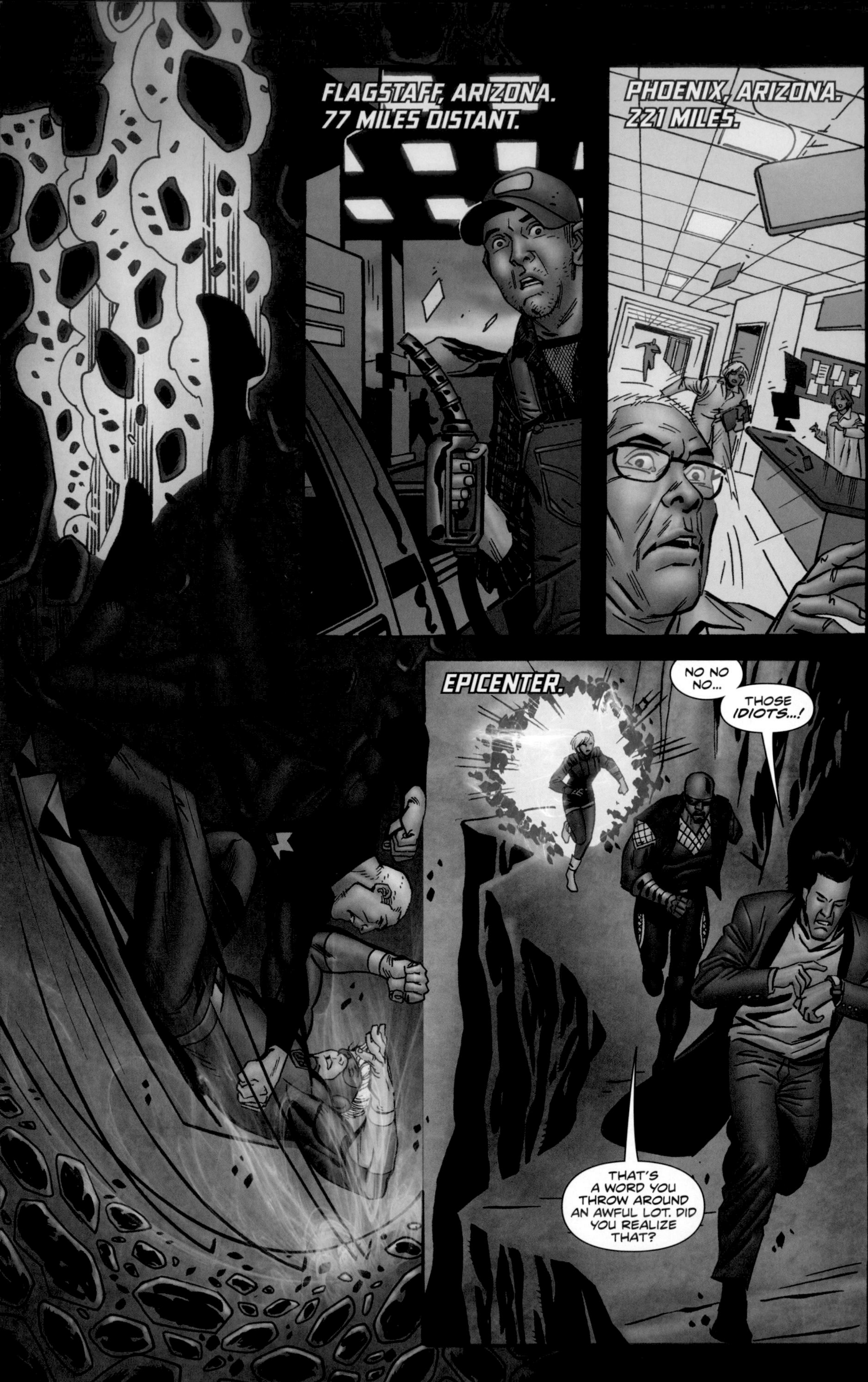
FLAGSTAFF, ARIZONA. 77 MILES DISTANT.
PHOENIX, ARIZONA. 221 MILES.
EPICENTER.
NO NO NO...
THOSE IDIOTS...!
THAT'S A WORD YOU THROW AROUND AN AWFUL LOT. DID YOU REALIZE THAT?

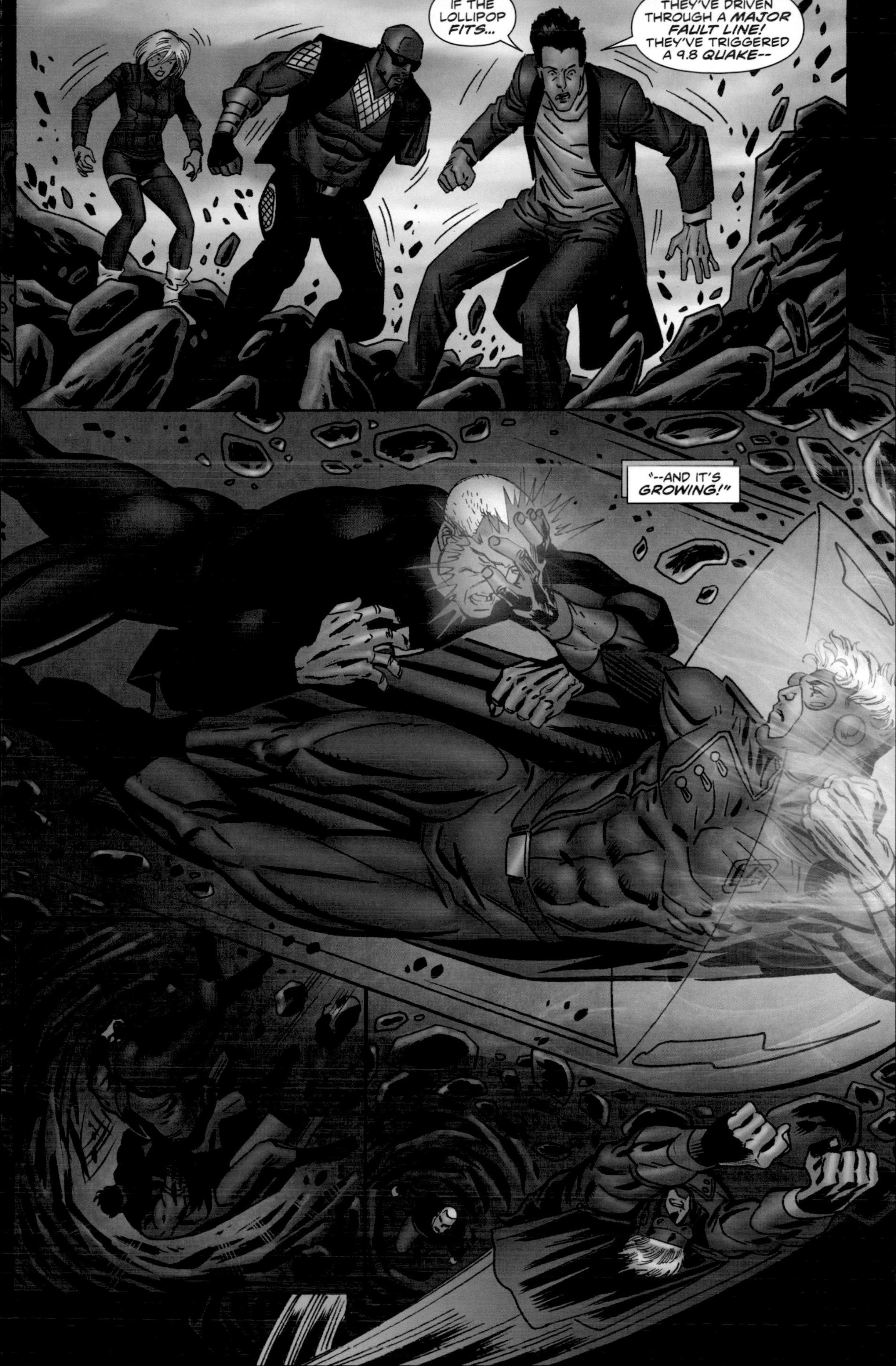

IF THE LOLLIPOP FITS...
THEY'VE DRIVEN THROUGH A MAJOR FAULT LINE! THEY'VE TRIGGERED A 9.8 QUAKE--
"--AND IT'S GROWING!"

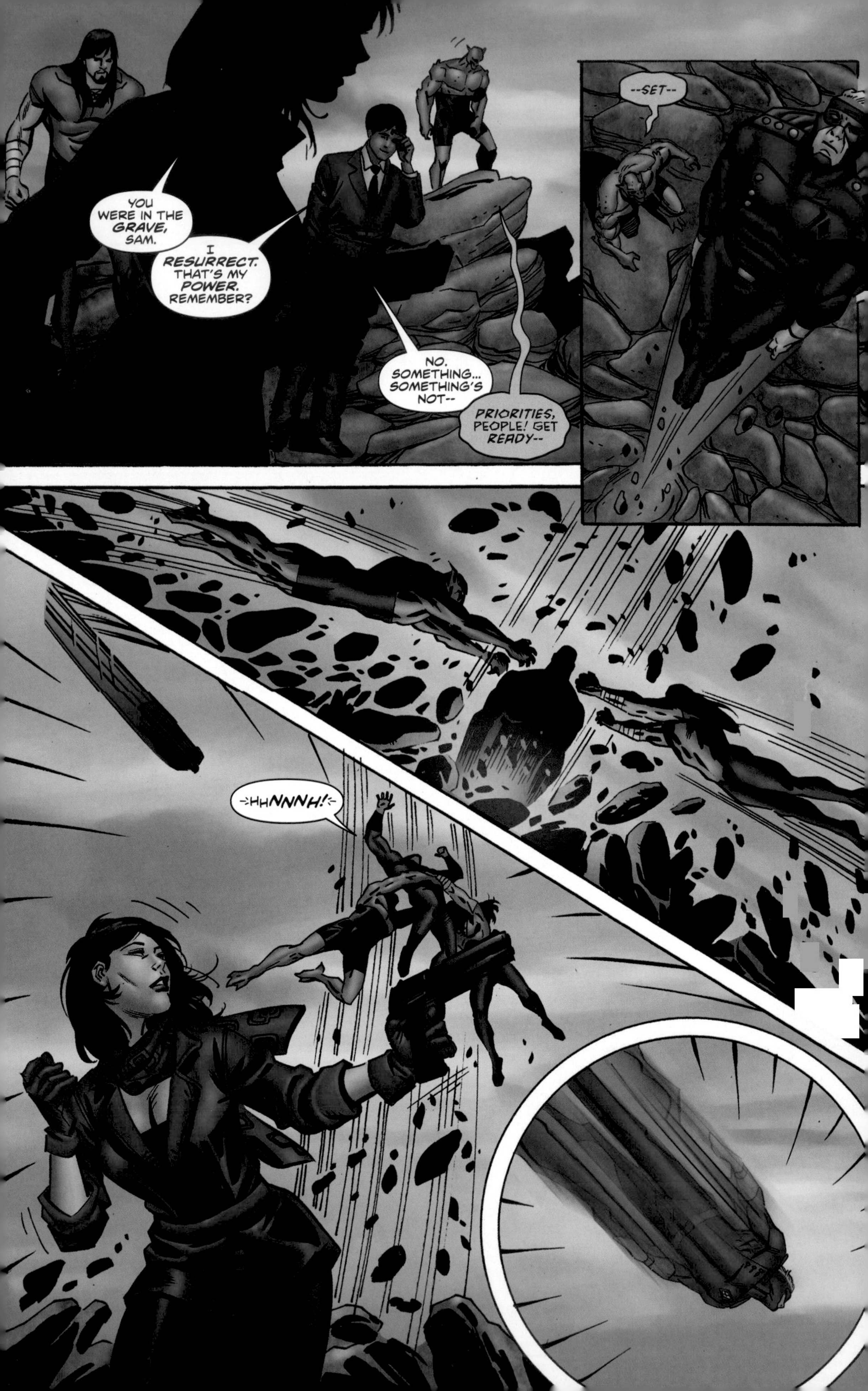
YOU WERE IN THE GRAVE, SAM.
I RESURRECT. THAT'S MY POWER. REMEMBER?
NO. SOMETHING... SOMETHING'S NOT--
PRIORITIES, PEOPLE! GET READY--
--SET--
HHNNNH!

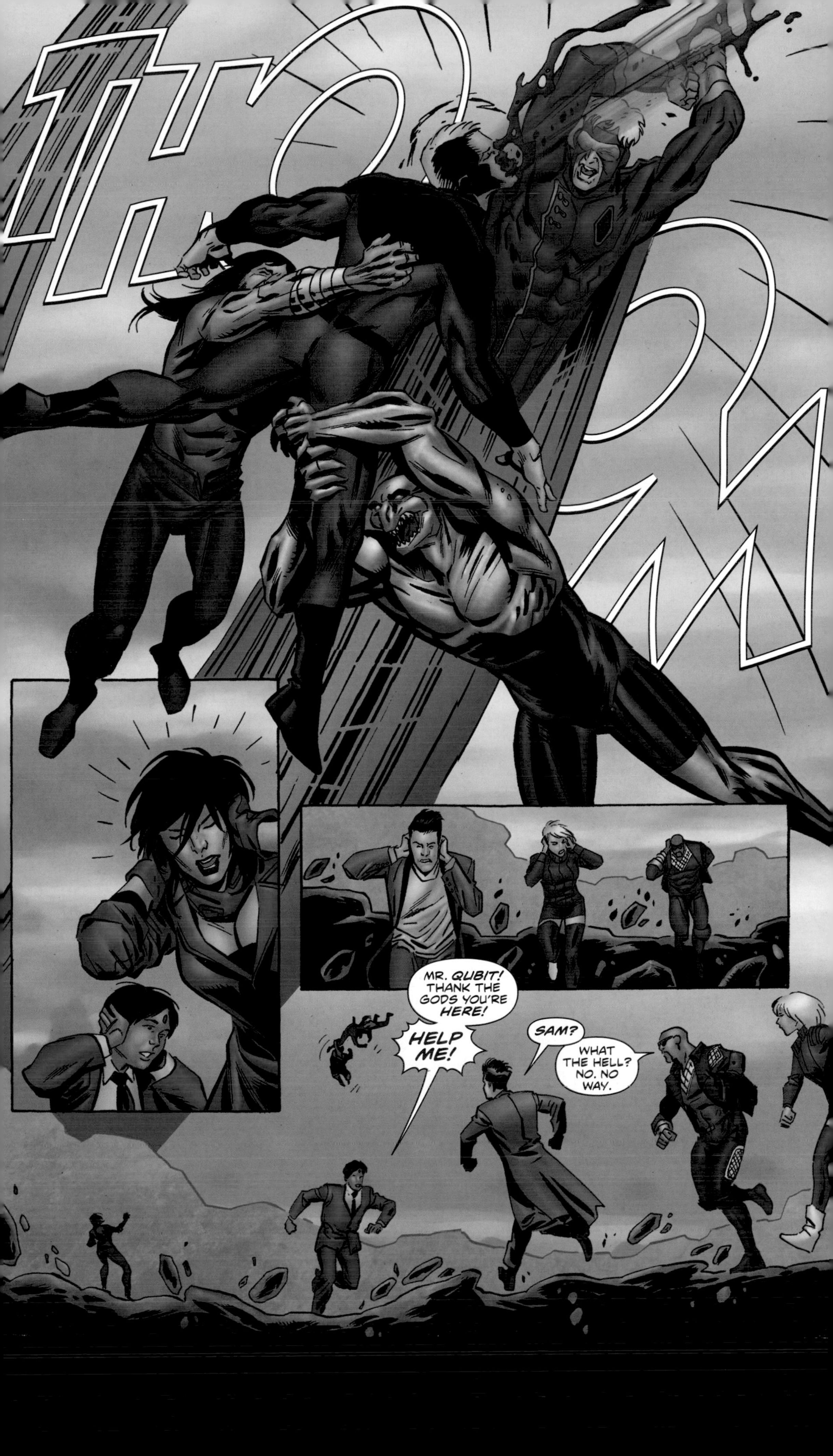
THOOOM
MR. QUBIT! THANK THE GODS YOU'RE HERE!
HELP ME!
SAM?
WHAT THE HELL? NO. NO WAY.

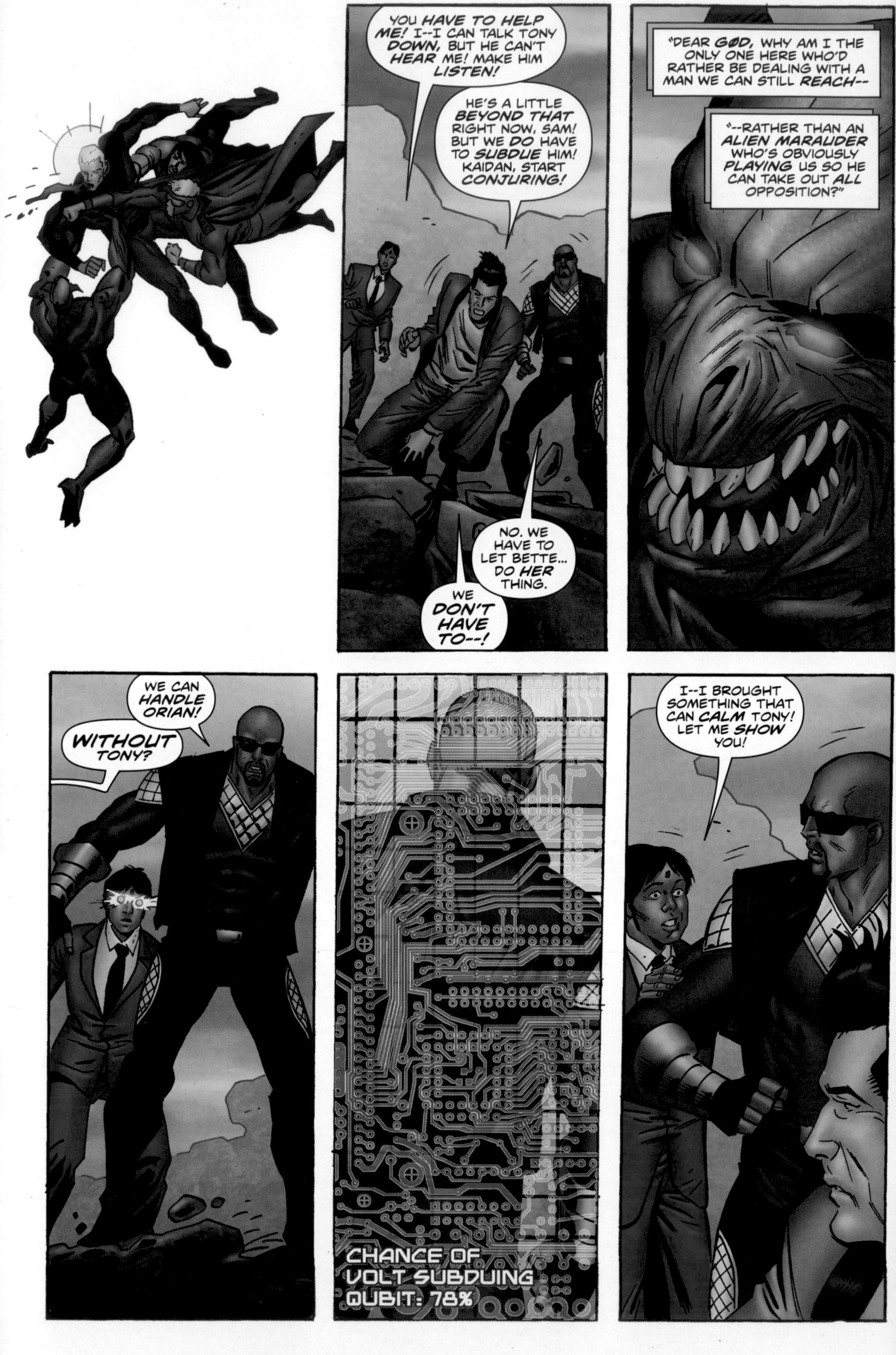
YOU HAVE TO HELP ME! I--I CAN TALK TONY DOWN, BUT HE CAN'T HEAR ME! MAKE HIM LISTEN!
HE'S A LITTLE BEYOND THAT RIGHT NOW, SAM! BUT WE DO HAVE TO SUBDUE HIM! KAIDAN, START CONJURING!
NO. WE HAVE TO LET BETTE... DO HER THING.
WE DON'T HAVE TO--!
"DEAR GØD, WHY AM I THE ONLY ONE HERE WHO'D RATHER BE DEALING WITH A MAN WE CAN STILL REACH--
"--RATHER THAN AN ALIEN MARAUDER WHO'S OBVIOUSLY PLAYING US SO HE CAN TAKE OUT ALL OPPOSITION?"
WE CAN HANDLE ORIAN!
WITHOUT TONY?
CHANCE OF VOLT SUBDUING QUBIT: 78%
I--I BROUGHT SOMETHING THAT CAN CALM TONY! LET ME SHOW YOU!

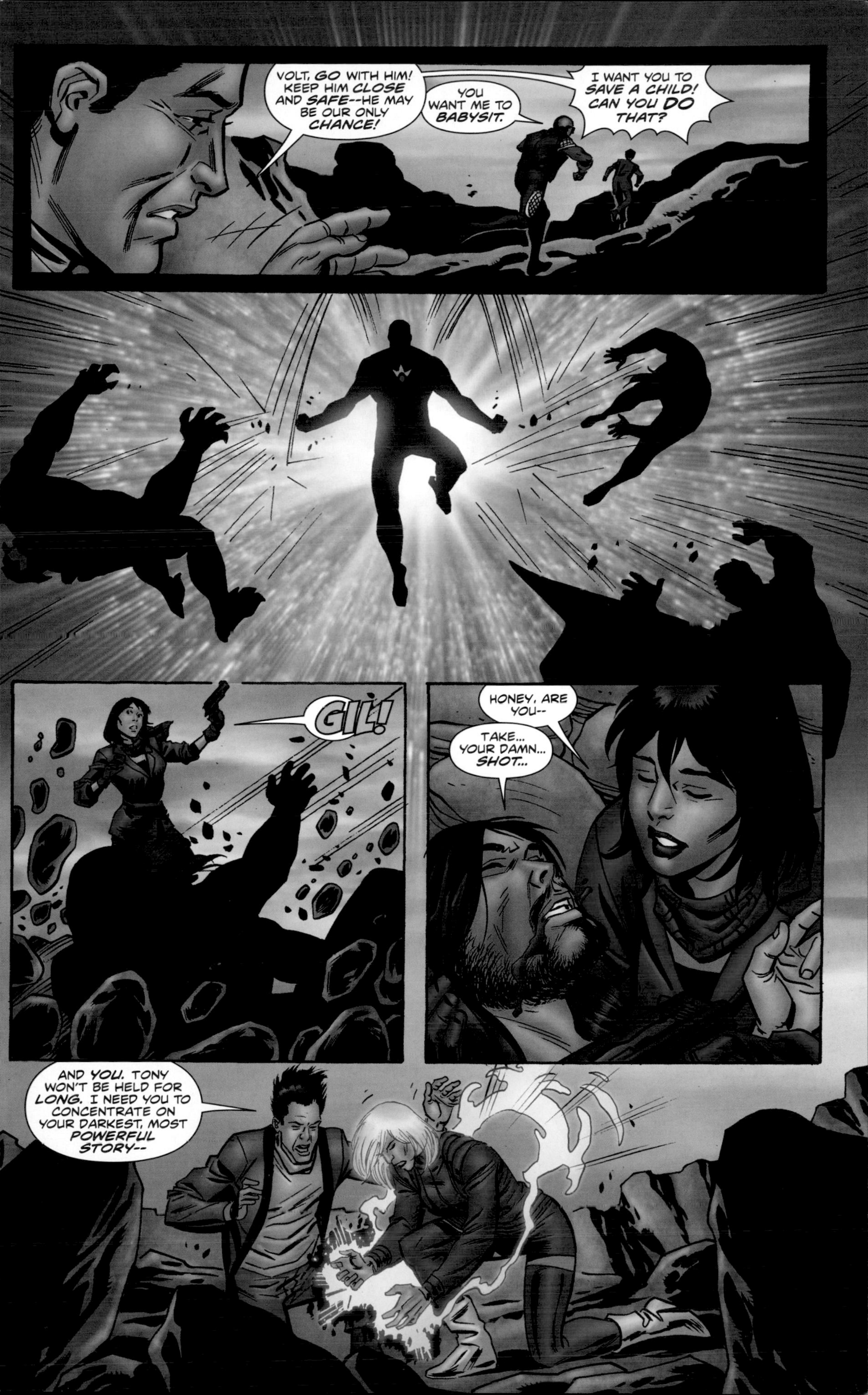
VOLT, GO WITH HIM! KEEP HIM CLOSE AND SAFE--HE MAY BE OUR ONLY CHANCE!
YOU WANT ME TO BABYSIT.
I WANT YOU TO SAVE A CHILD! CAN YOU DO THAT?
GIL!
HONEY, ARE YOU--
TAKE... YOUR DAMN... SHOT...
AND YOU. TONY WON'T BE HELD FOR LONG. I NEED YOU TO CONCENTRATE ON YOUR DARKEST, MOST POWERFUL STORY--

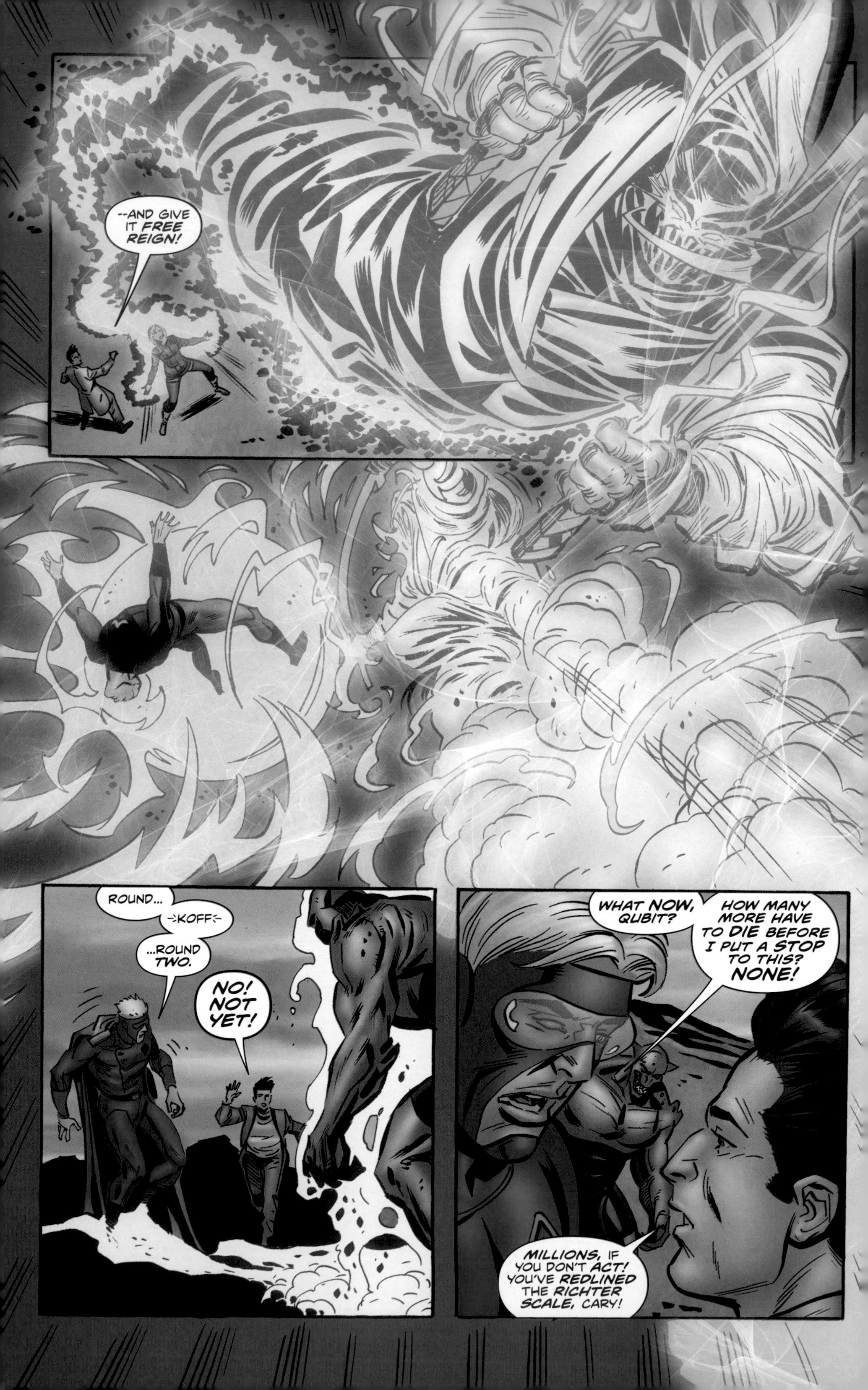
--AND GIVE IT FREE REIGN!
ROUND...
-KOFF-
...ROUND TWO.
NO! NOT YET!
WHAT NOW, QUBIT?
HOW MANY MORE HAVE TO DIE BEFORE I PUT A STOP TO THIS? NONE!
MILLIONS, IF YOU DON'T ACT! YOU'VE REDLINED THE RICHTER SCALE, CARY!

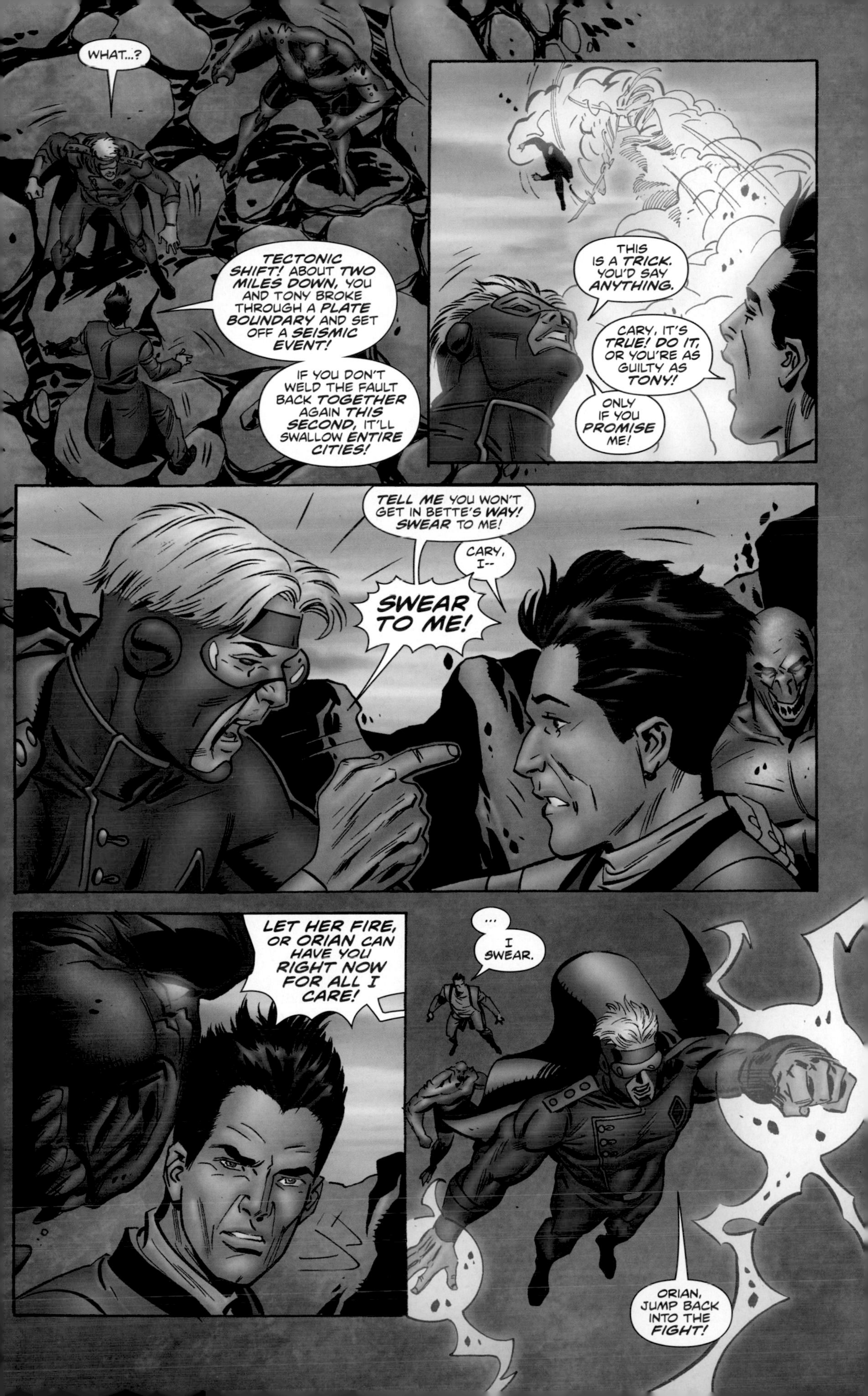
WHAT...?
TECTONIC SHIFT! ABOUT TWO MILES DOWN, YOU AND TONY BROKE THROUGH A PLATE BOUNDARY AND SET OFF A SEISMIC EVENT!
IF YOU DON'T WELD THE FAULT BACK TOGETHER AGAIN THIS SECOND, IT'LL SWALLOW ENTIRE CITIES!
THIS IS A TRICK. YOU'D SAY ANYTHING.
CARY, IT'S TRUE! DO IT, OR YOU'RE AS GUILTY AS TONY!
ONLY IF YOU PROMISE ME!
TELL ME YOU WON'T GET IN BETTE'S WAY! SWEAR TO ME!
CARY, I--
SWEAR TO ME!
LET HER FIRE, OR ORIAN CAN HAVE YOU RIGHT NOW FOR ALL I CARE!
...
I SWEAR.
ORIAN, JUMP BACK INTO THE FIGHT!

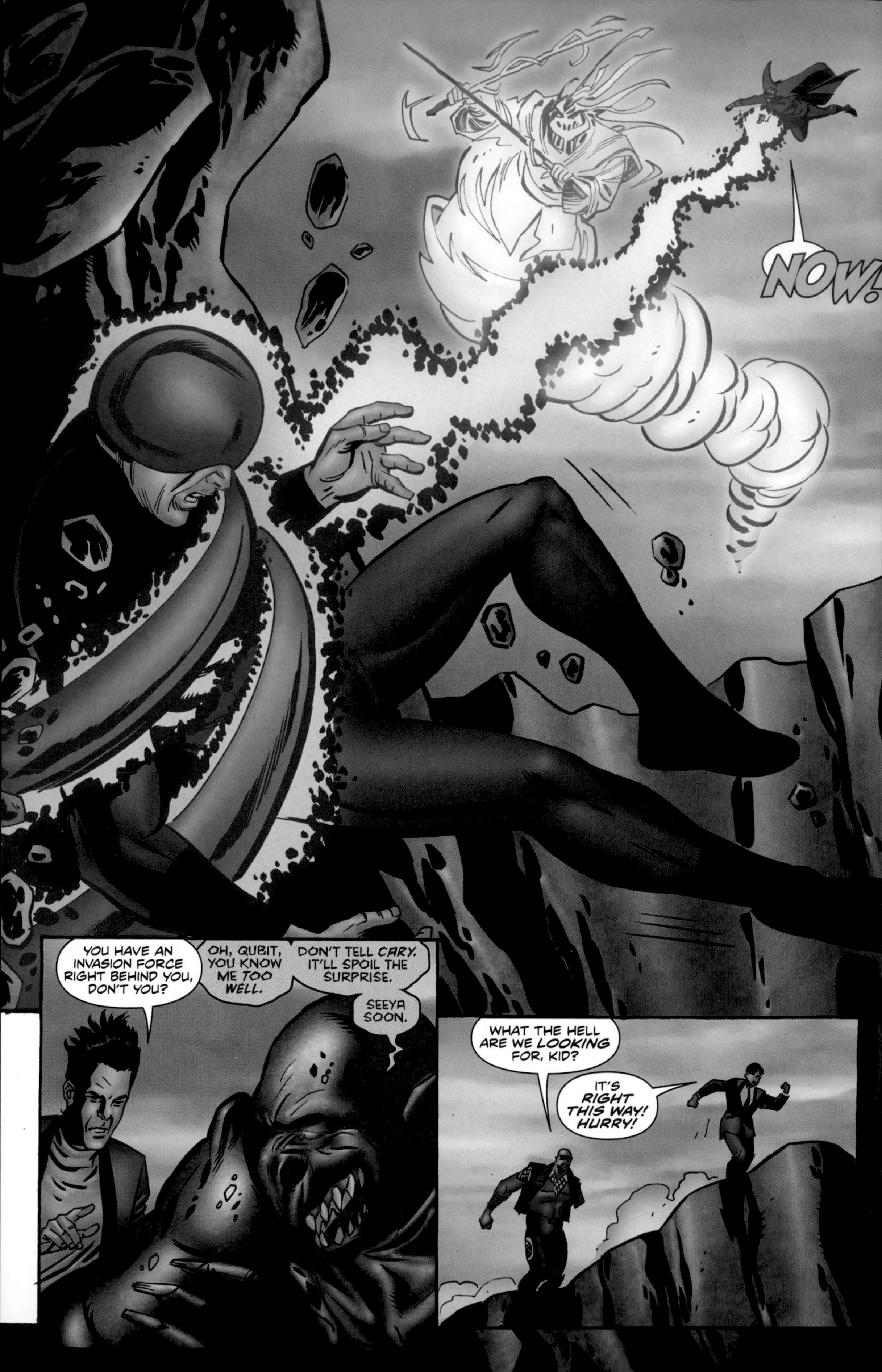
NOW!
YOU HAVE AN INVASION FORCE RIGHT BEHIND YOU, DON'T YOU?
OH, QUBIT, YOU KNOW ME TOO WELL.
DON'T TELL CARY. IT'LL SPOIL THE SURPRISE.
SEEYA SOON.
WHAT THE HELL ARE WE LOOKING FOR, KID?
IT'S RIGHT THIS WAY! HURRY!

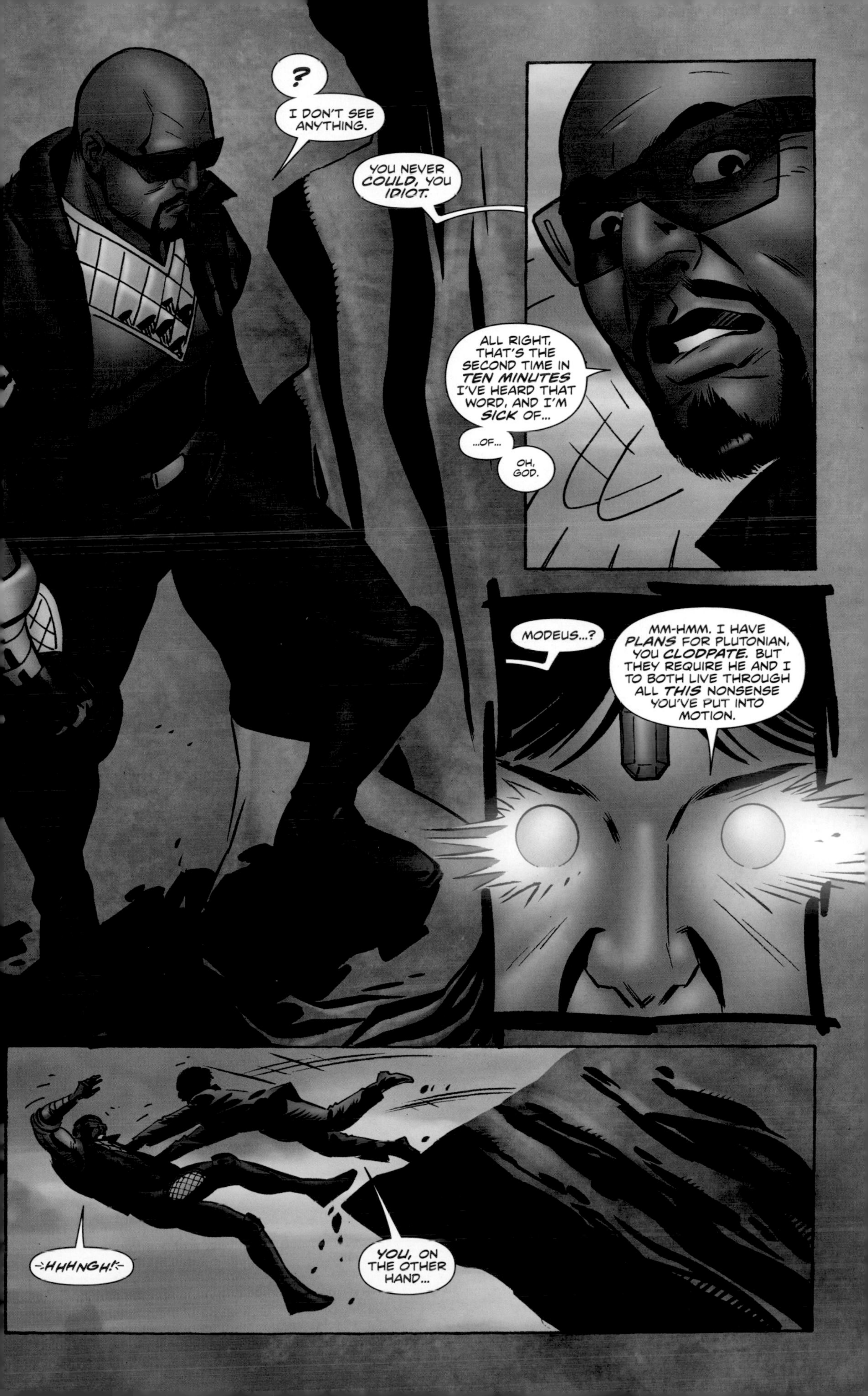
?
I DON'T SEE ANYTHING.
YOU NEVER COULD, YOU IDIOT.
ALL RIGHT, THAT'S THE SECOND TIME IN TEN MINUTES I'VE HEARD THAT WORD, AND I'M SICK OF...
...OF...
OH, GOD.
MODEUS...?
MM-HMM. I HAVE PLANS FOR PLUTONIAN, YOU CLODPATE. BUT THEY REQUIRE HE AND I TO BOTH LIVE THROUGH ALL THIS NONSENSE YOU'VE PUT INTO MOTION.
HHHNGH!
YOU, ON THE OTHER HAND...

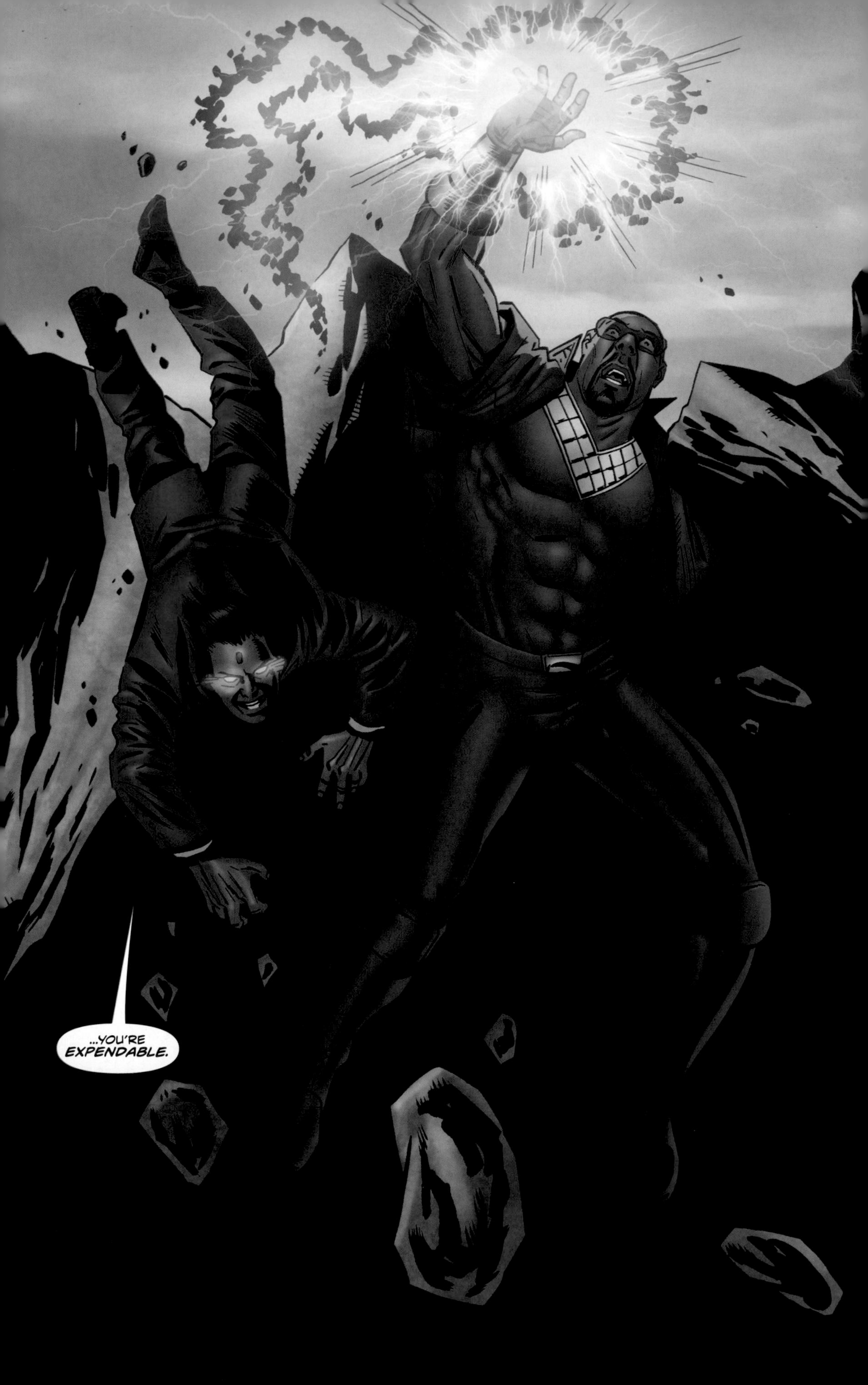
...YOU'RE EXPENDABLE.

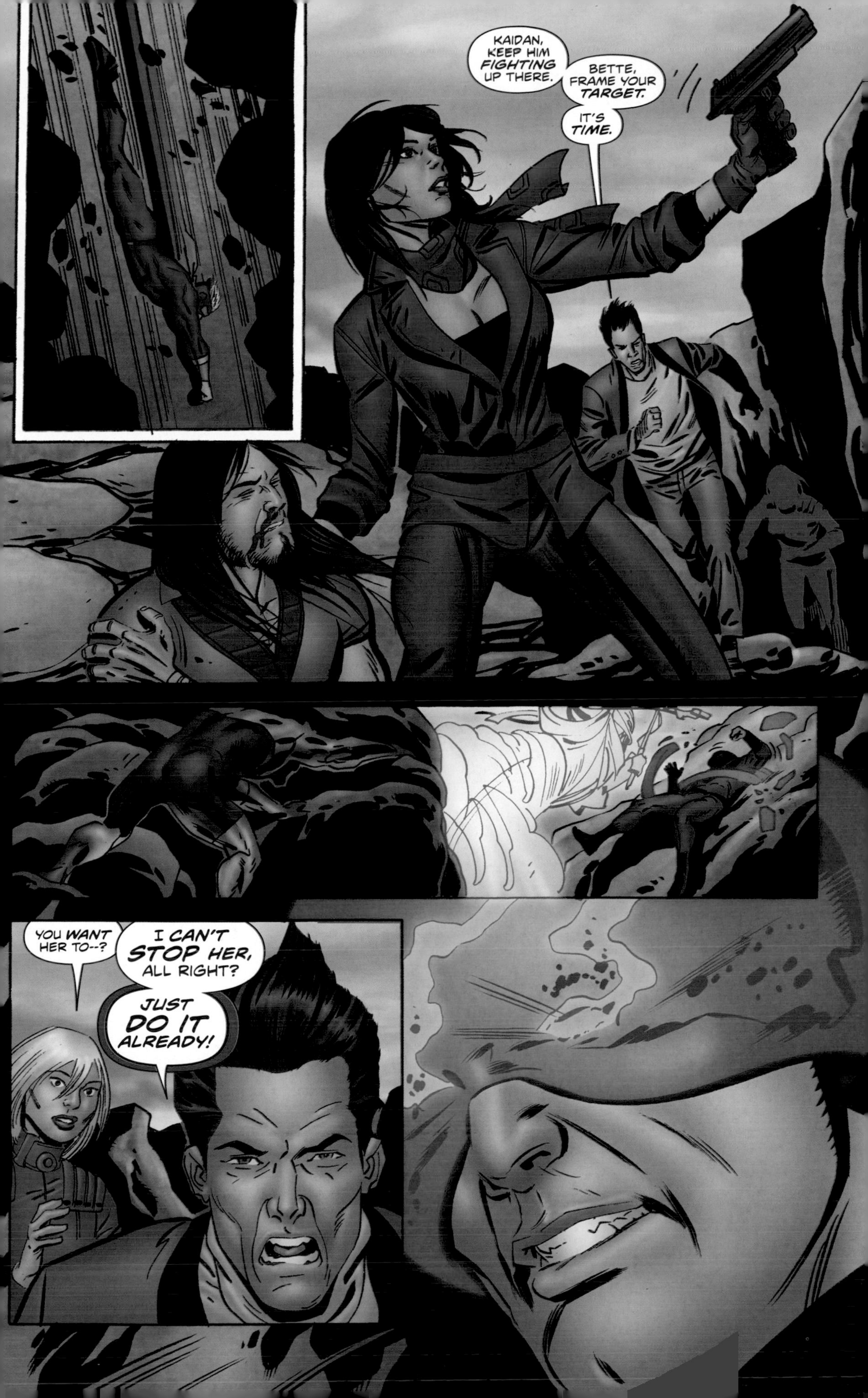
KAIDAN, KEEP HIM FIGHTING UP THERE.
BETTE, FRAME YOUR TARGET.
IT'S TIME.
YOU WANT HER TO--?
I CAN'T STOP HER, ALL RIGHT?
JUST DO IT ALREADY!

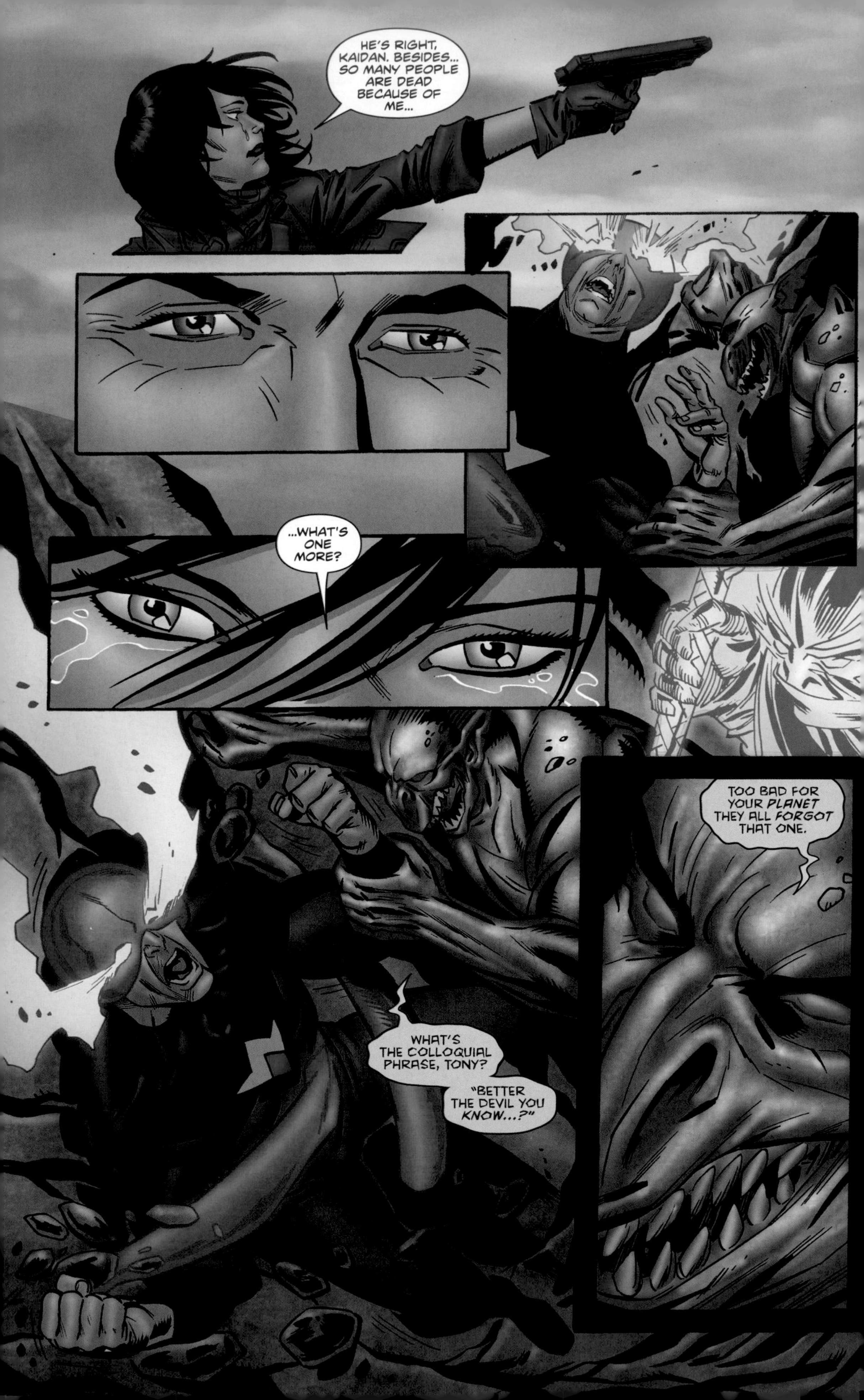
HE'S RIGHT, KAIDAN. BESIDES... SO MANY PEOPLE ARE DEAD BECAUSE OF ME...
...WHAT'S ONE MORE?
TOO BAD FOR YOUR *PLANET* THEY ALL *FORGOT* THAT ONE.
WHAT'S THE COLLOQUIAL PHRASE, TONY?
"BETTER THE DEVIL YOU *KNOW*...?"

TKK
WH--?

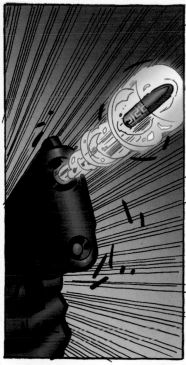

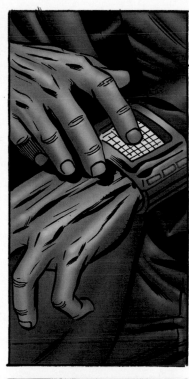

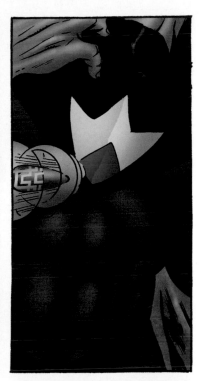

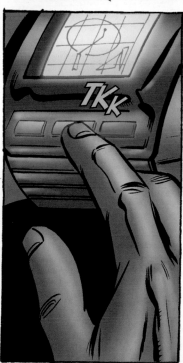

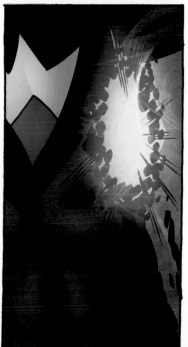

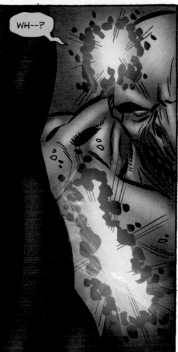

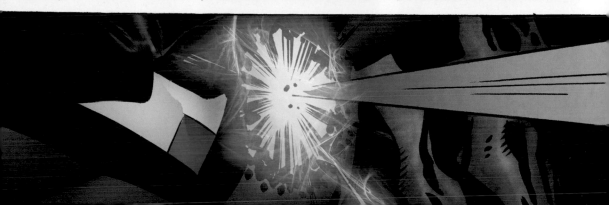

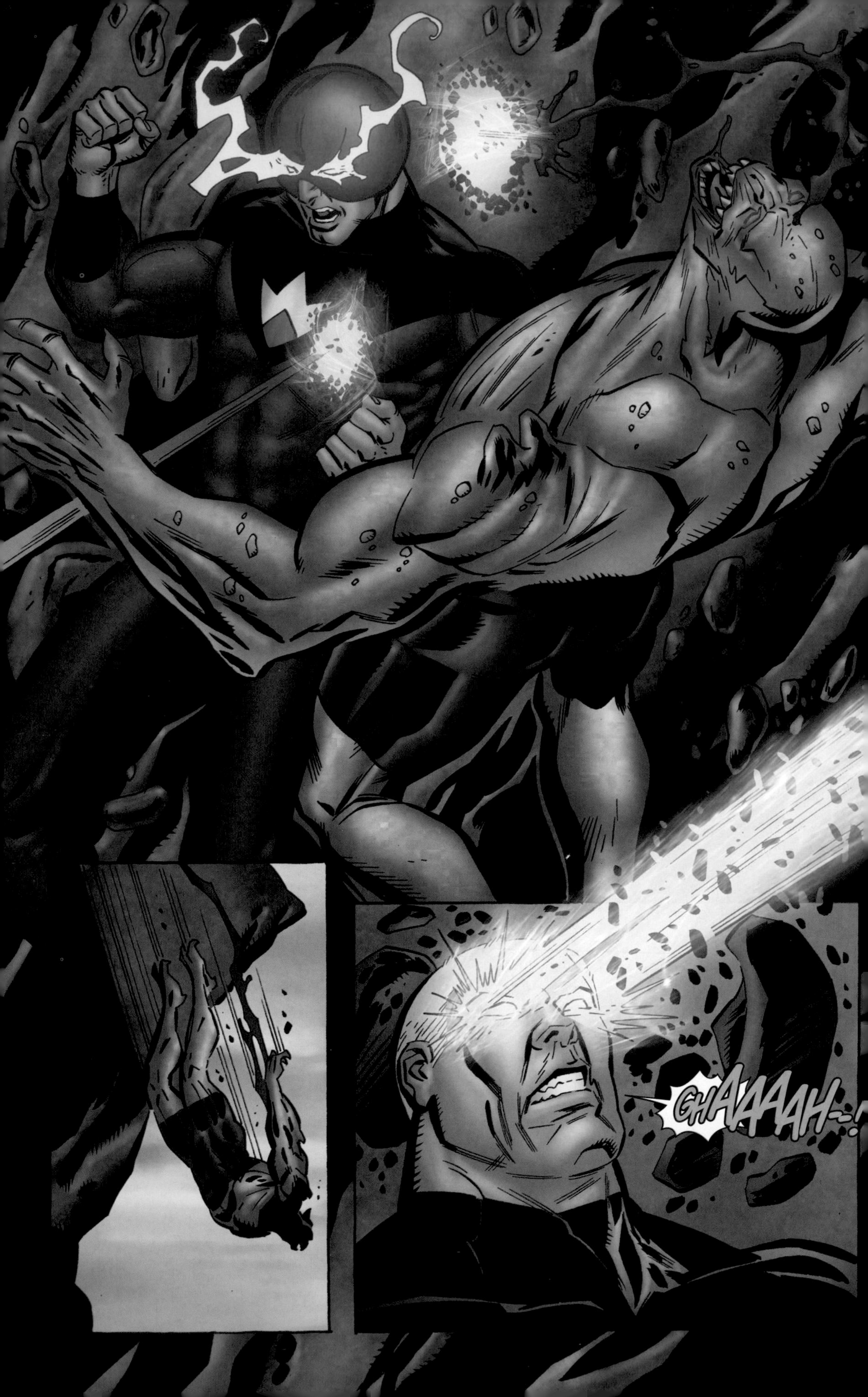
GHAAAAH--!

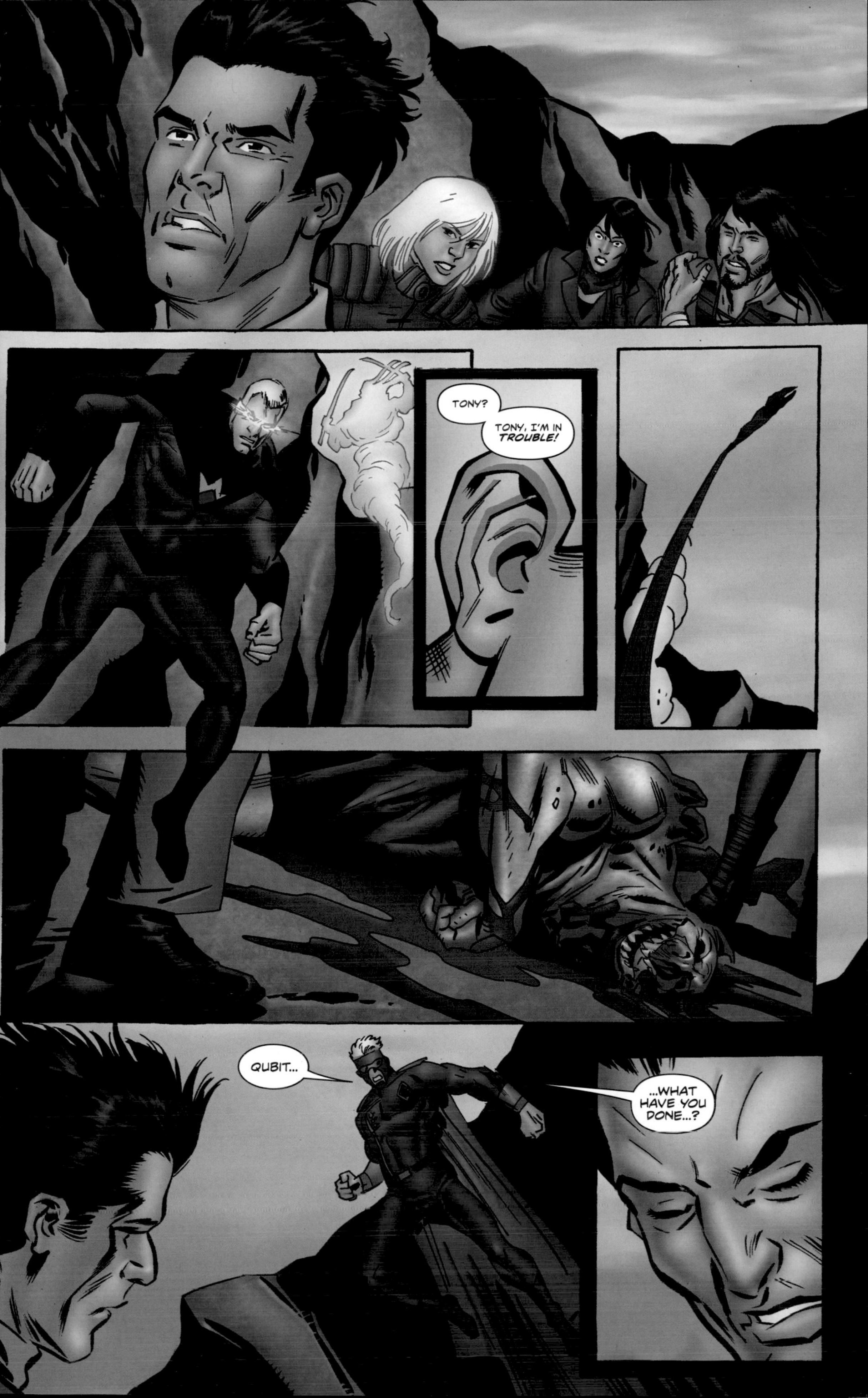
TONY?
TONY, I'M IN TROUBLE!
QUBIT...
...WHAT HAVE YOU DONE...?

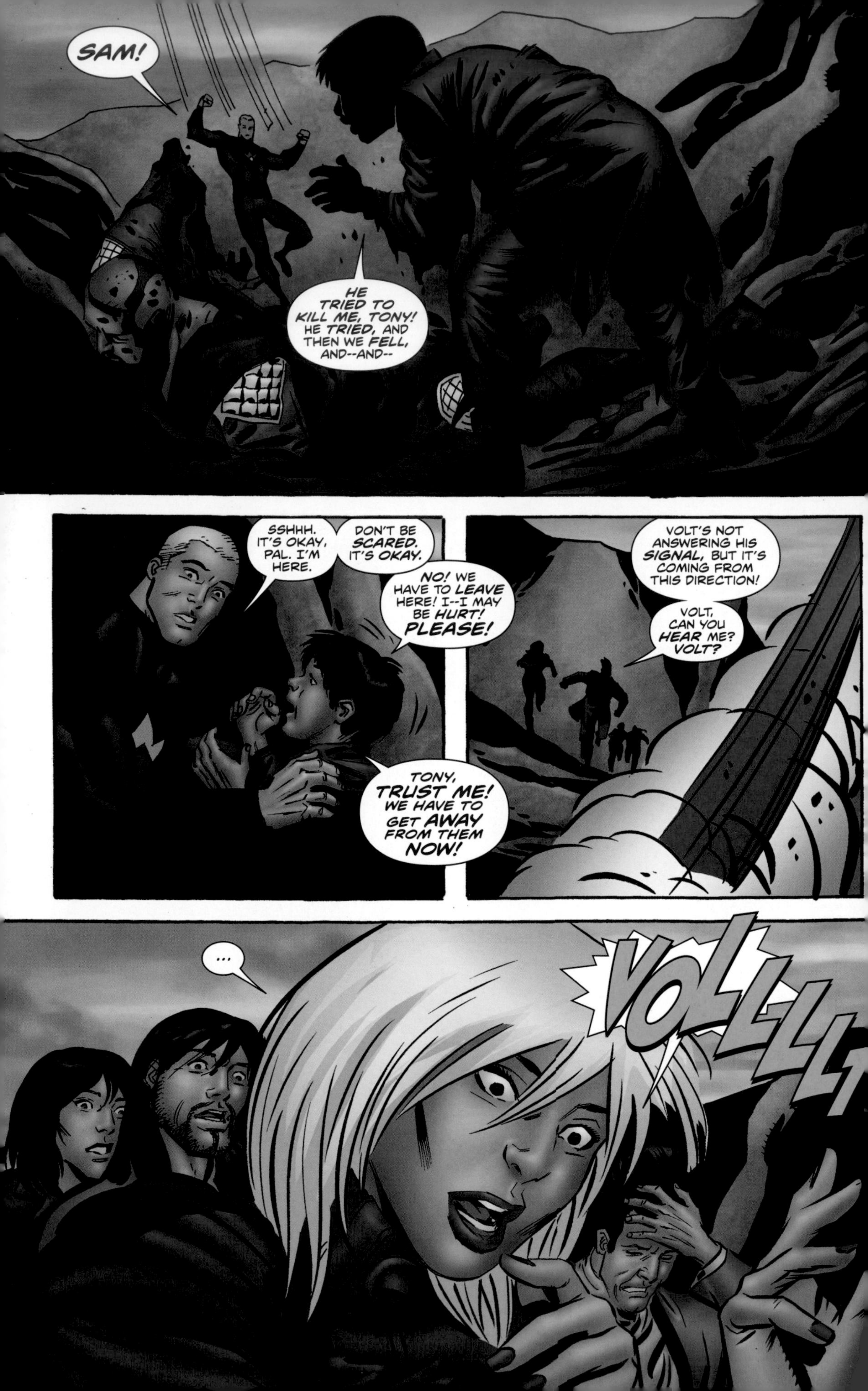
SAM!
HE TRIED TO KILL ME, TONY! HE TRIED, AND THEN WE FELL, AND--AND--
SSHHH. IT'S OKAY, PAL. I'M HERE.
DON'T BE SCARED. IT'S OKAY.
NO! WE HAVE TO LEAVE HERE! I--I MAY BE HURT! PLEASE!
TONY, TRUST ME! WE HAVE TO GET AWAY FROM THEM NOW!
VOLT'S NOT ANSWERING HIS SIGNAL, BUT IT'S COMING FROM THIS DIRECTION!
VOLT, CAN YOU HEAR ME? VOLT?
...
VOLLLLT

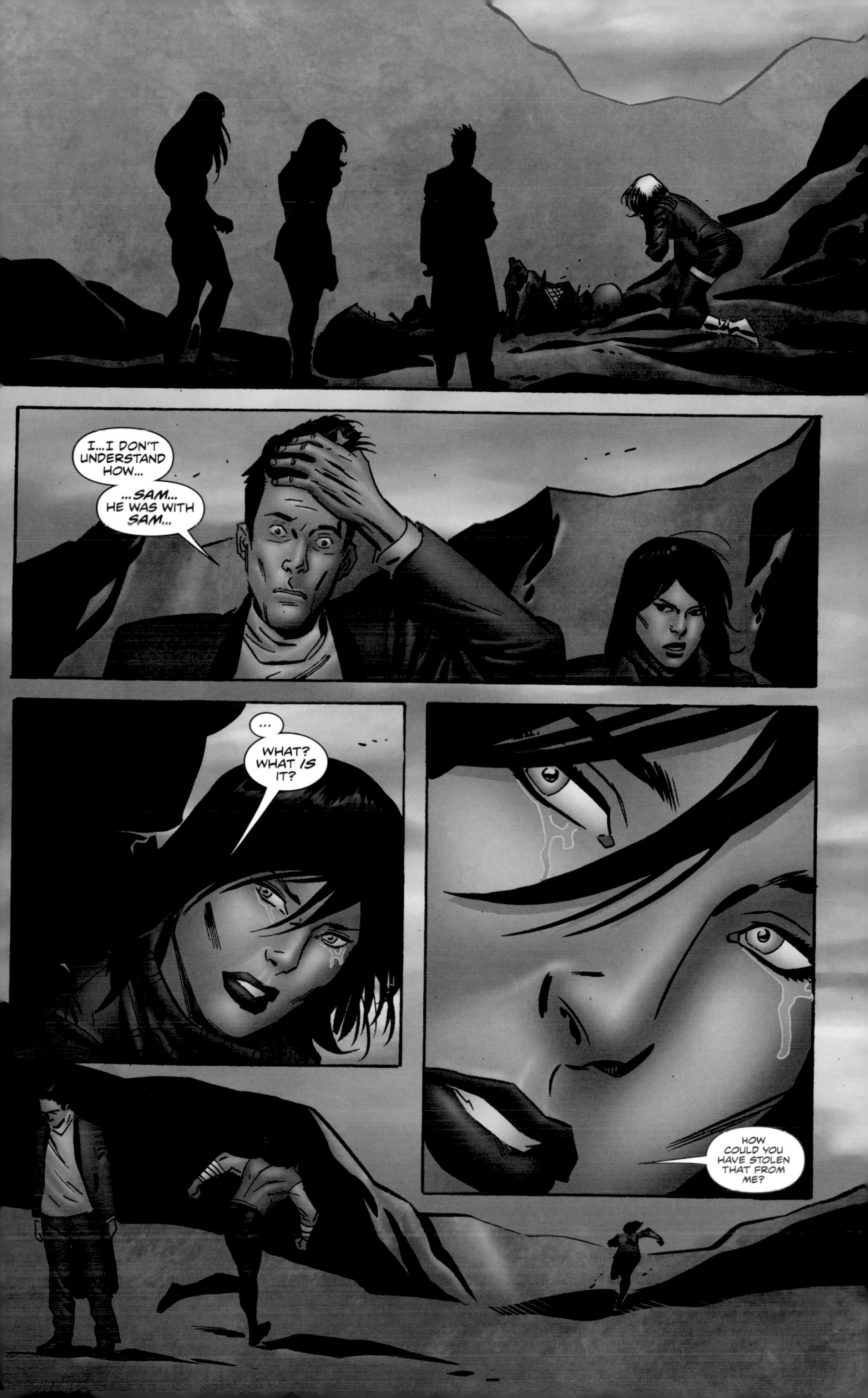
I...I DON'T UNDERSTAND HOW...
...SAM... HE WAS WITH SAM...
...
WHAT? WHAT IS IT?
HOW COULD YOU HAVE STOLEN THAT FROM ME?

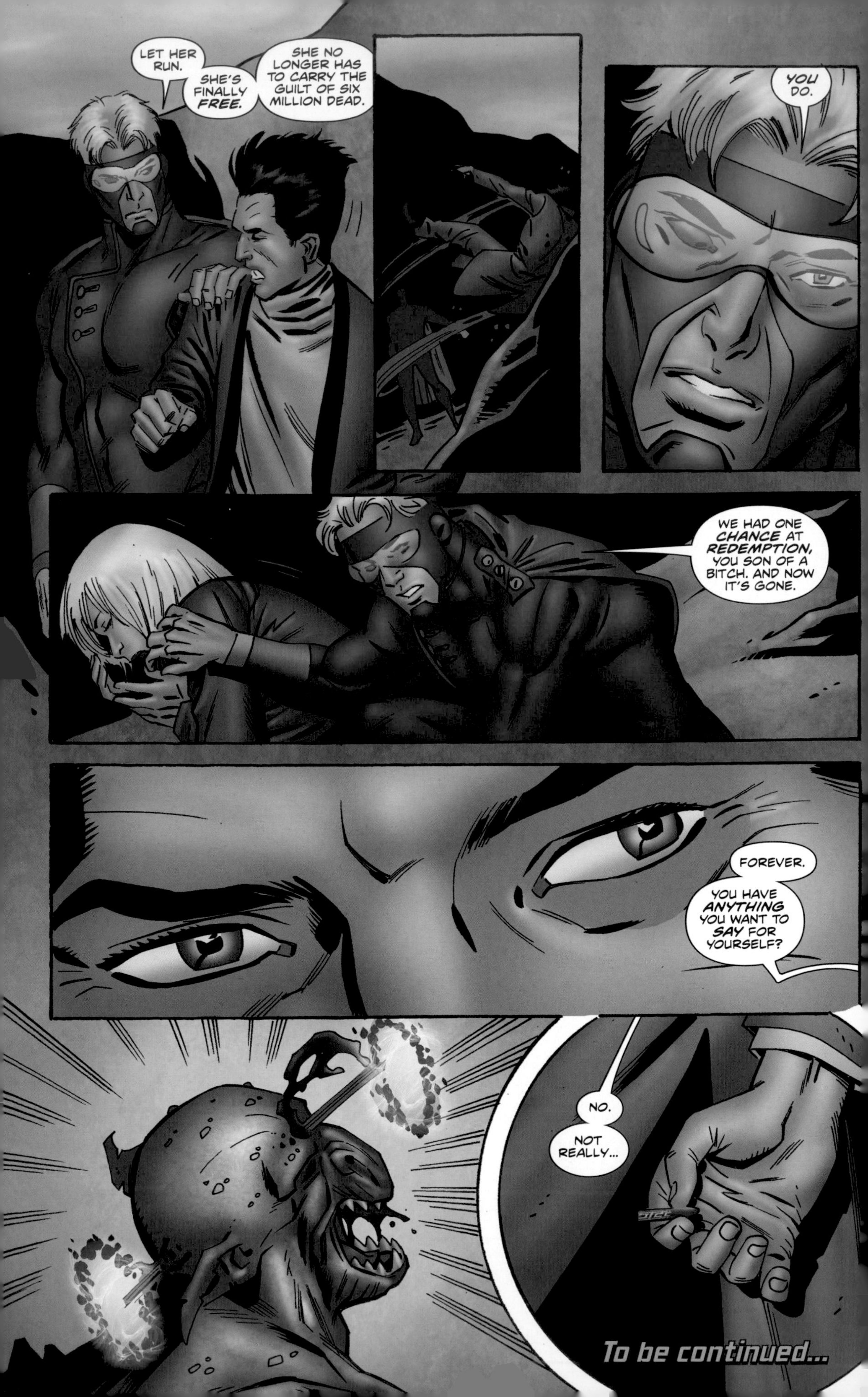
LET HER RUN.
SHE'S FINALLY FREE.
SHE NO LONGER HAS TO CARRY THE GUILT OF SIX MILLION DEAD.
YOU DO.
WE HAD ONE CHANCE AT REDEMPTION, YOU SON OF A BITCH. AND NOW IT'S GONE.
FOREVER.
YOU HAVE ANYTHING YOU WANT TO SAY FOR YOURSELF?
NO.
NOT REALLY...
To be continued...

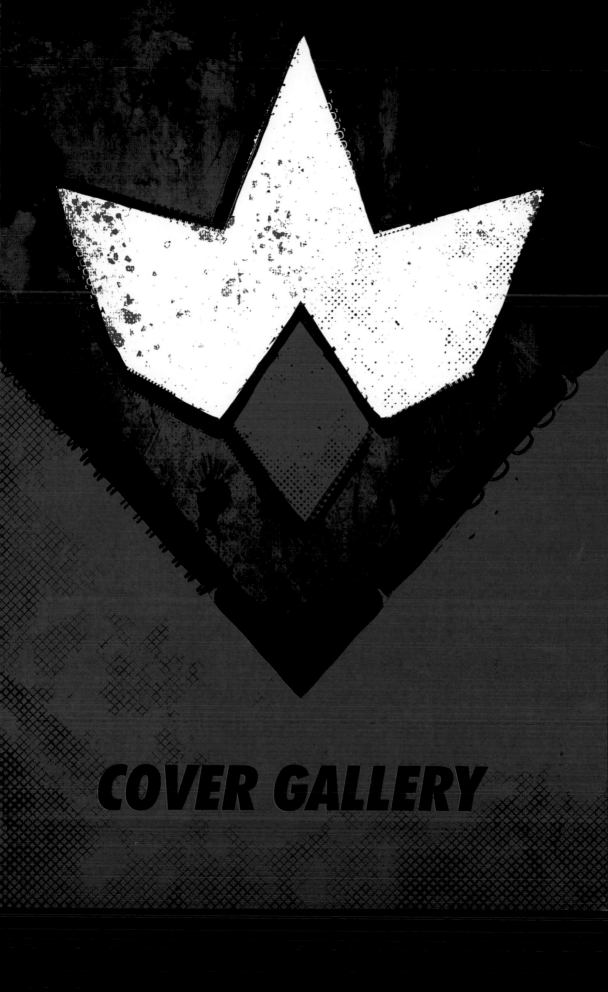

COVER GALLERY

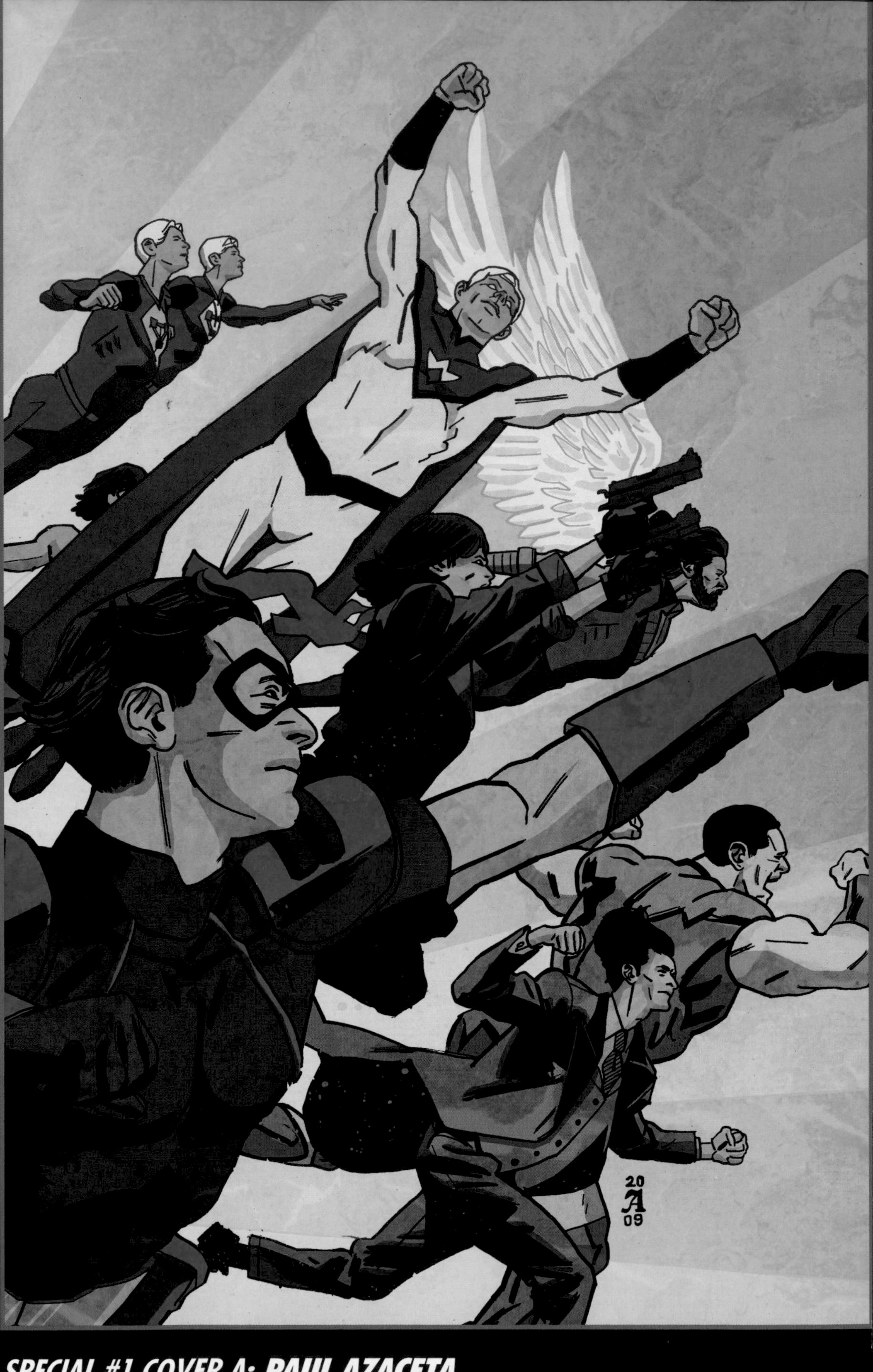

SPECIAL #1 COVER A: PAUL AZACETA
COLORS: ANDREW DALHOUSE

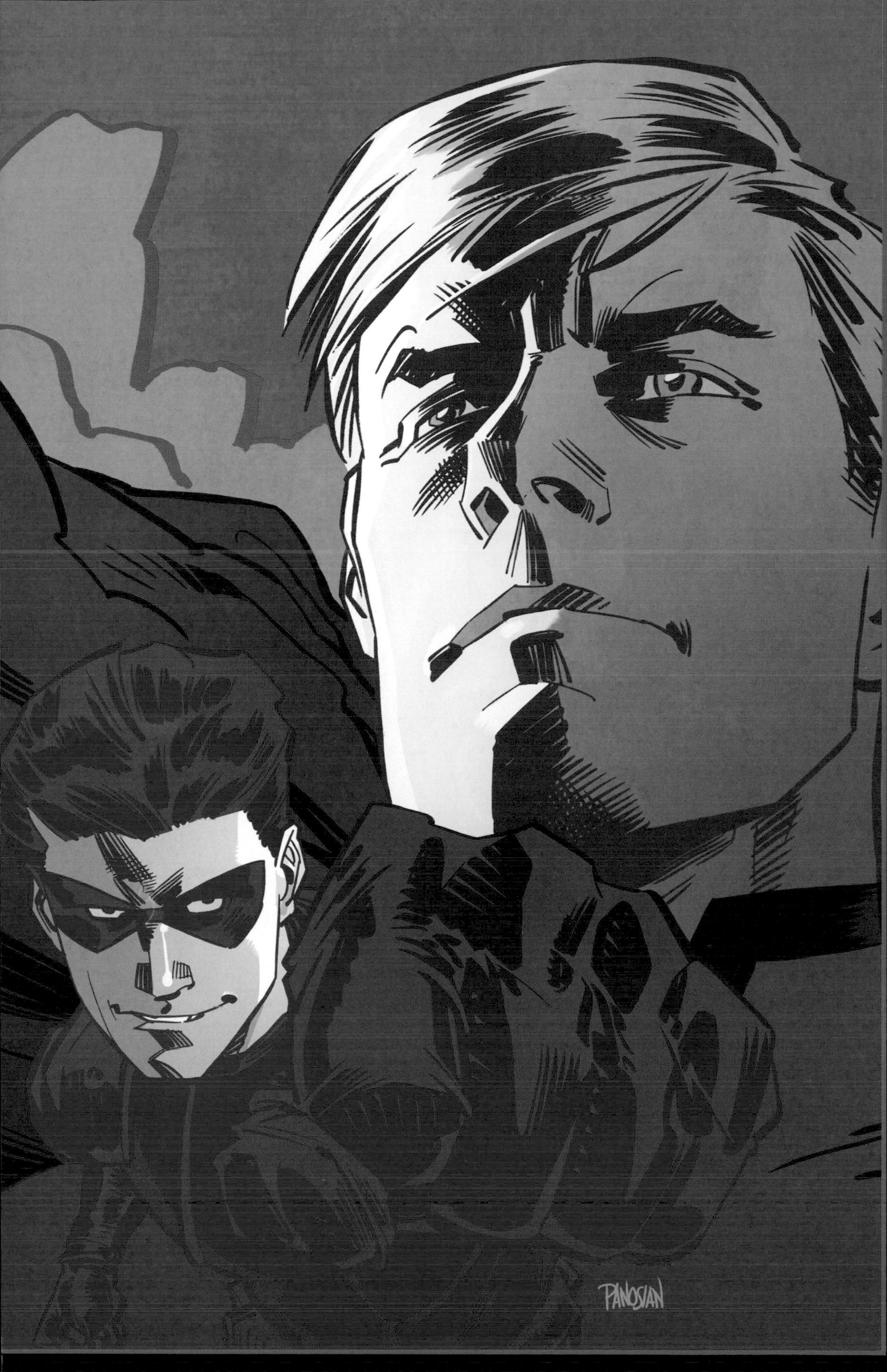
PANOSIAN

SPECIAL #1 COVER B: **DAN PANOSIAN**

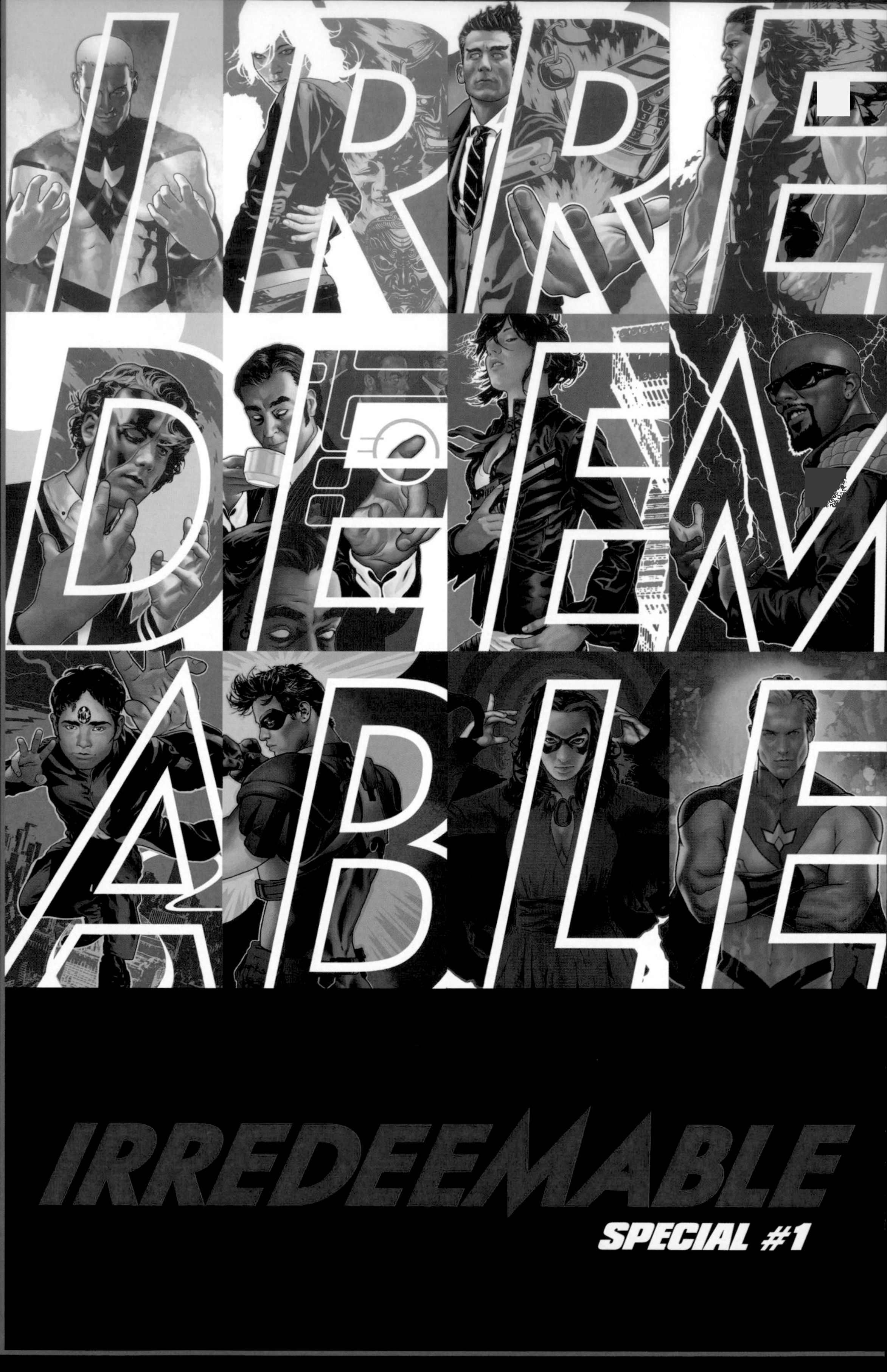
IRREDEEMABLE
SPECIAL #1

SPECIAL #1 COVER C: JEFFREY SPOKES

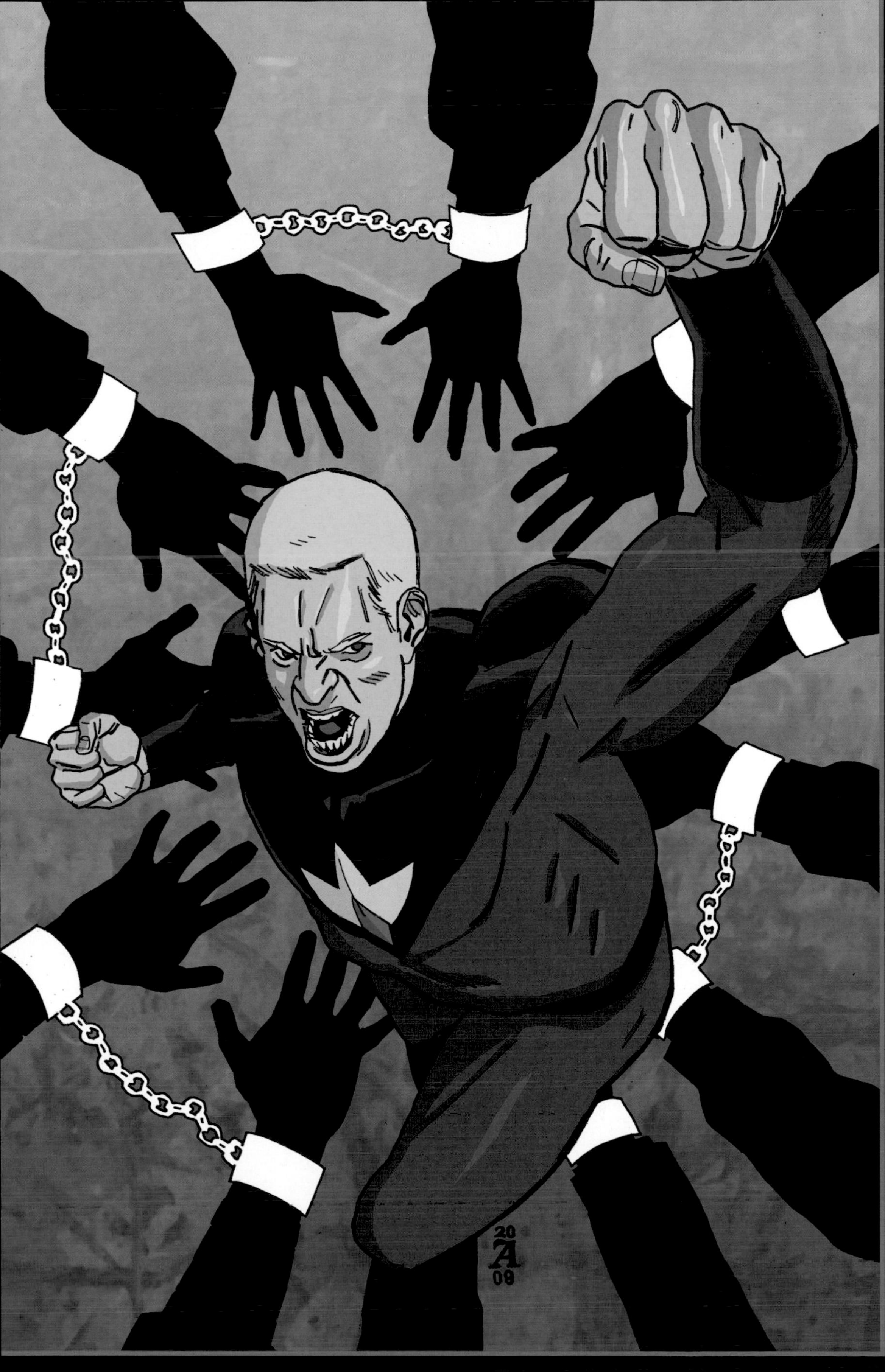
20
A
09

COVER 13A: PAUL AZACETA

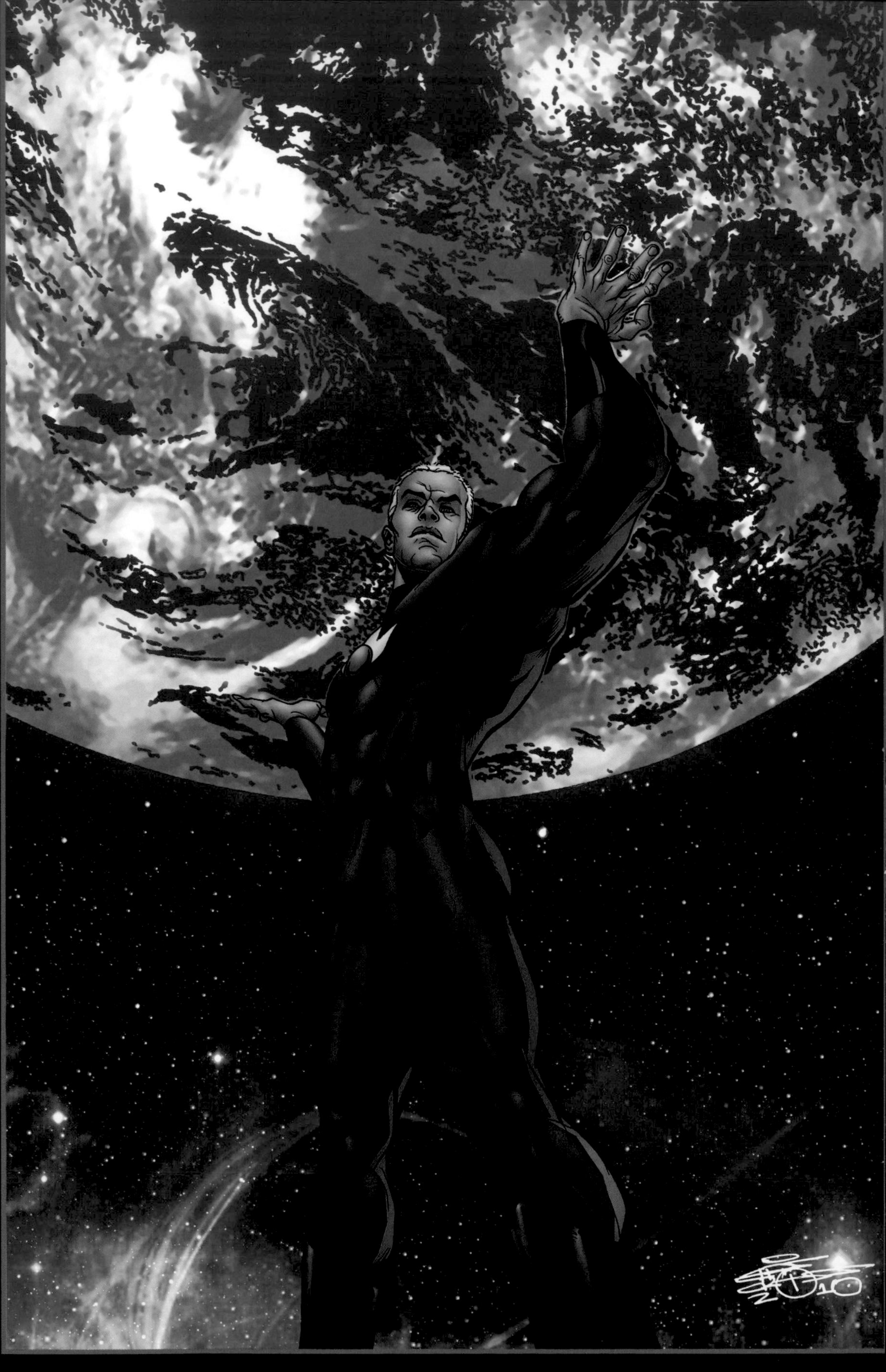

COVER 13B: CHRISCROSS

COLORS: ANDREW DALHOUSE

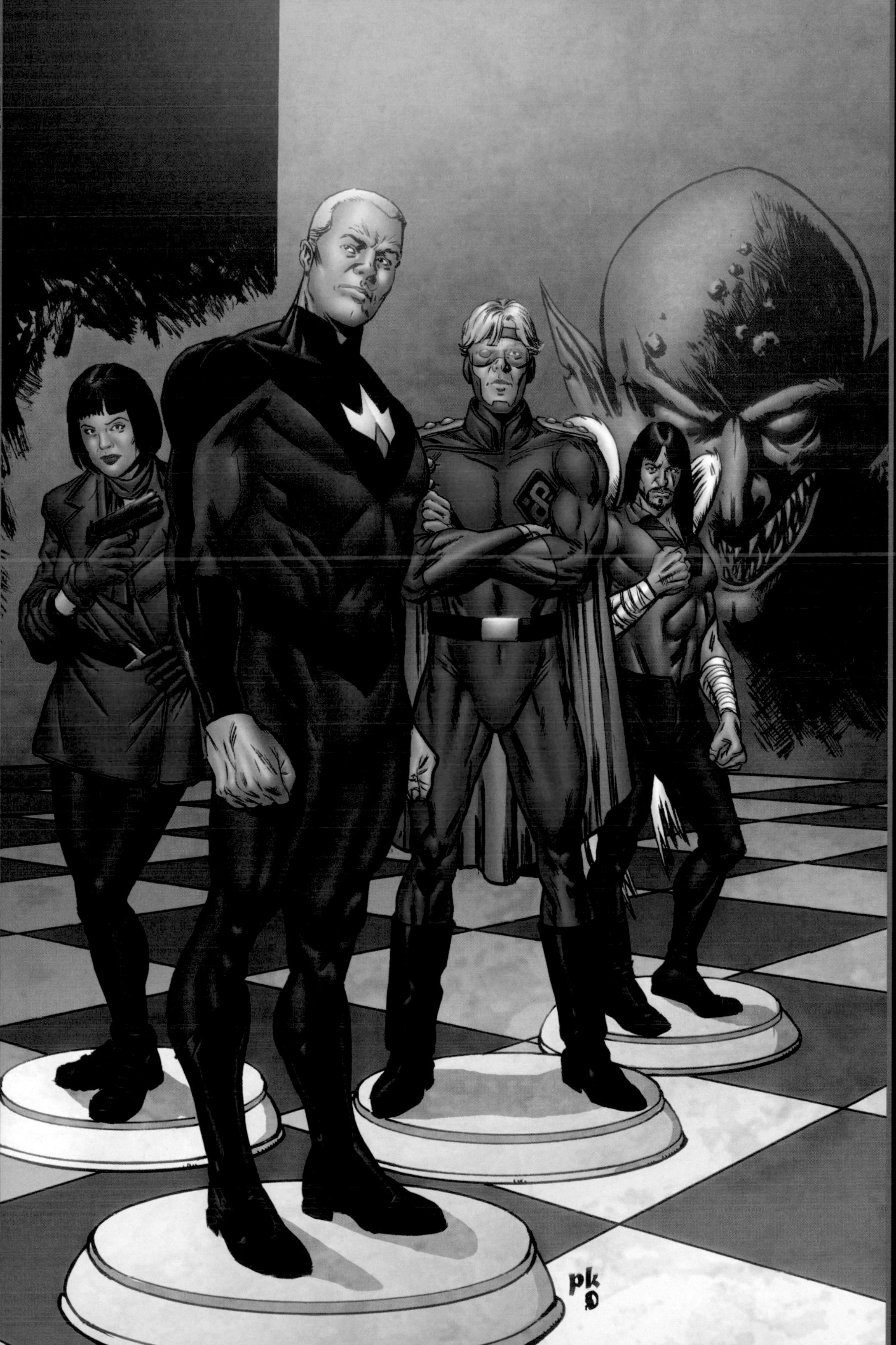
pk

COVER 14A: **PETER KRAUSE**

COLORS: **ANDREW DALHOUSE**

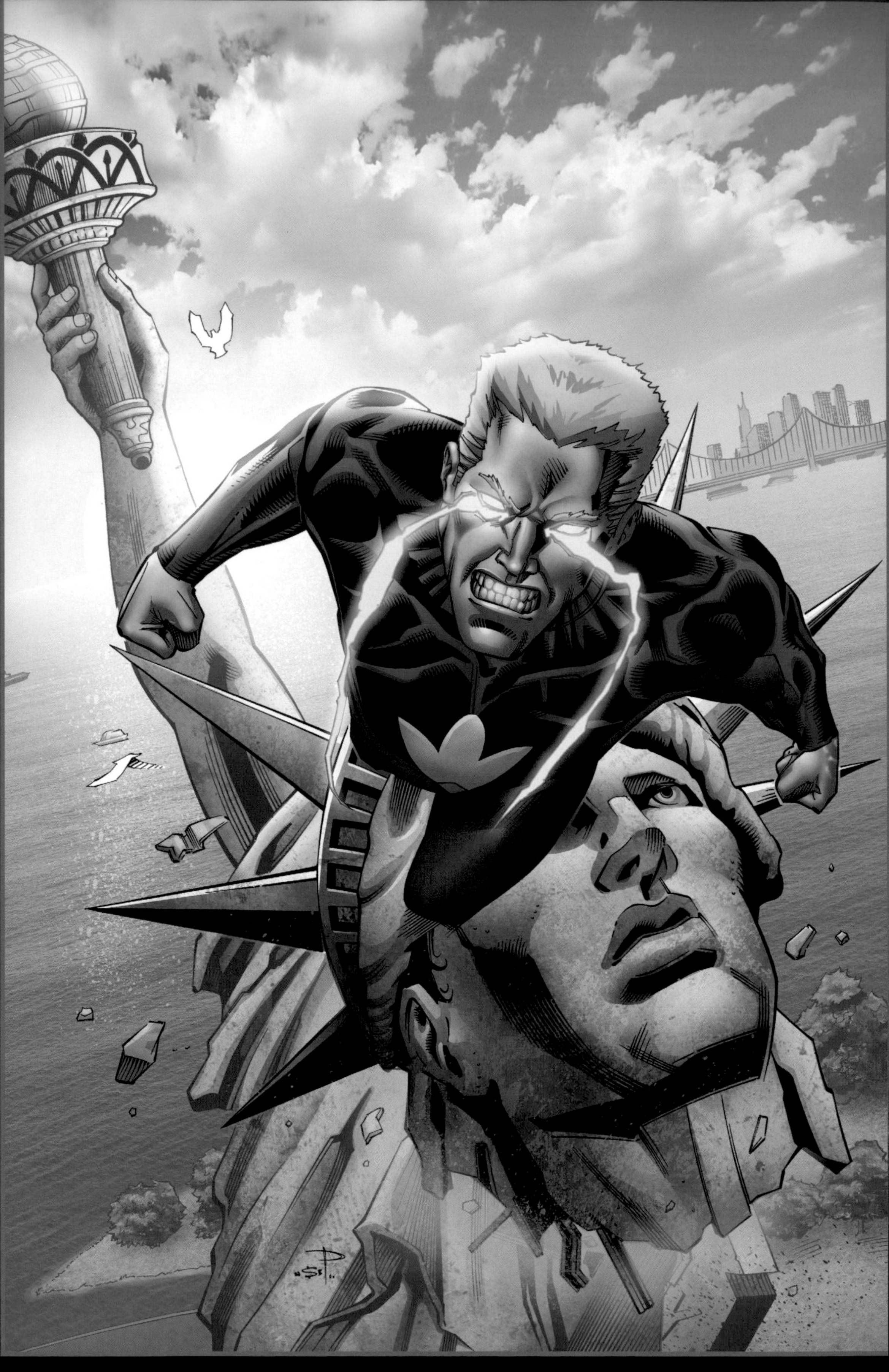

COVER 14B: TOMMY PATTERSON
COLORS: ALFRED ROCKEFELLER

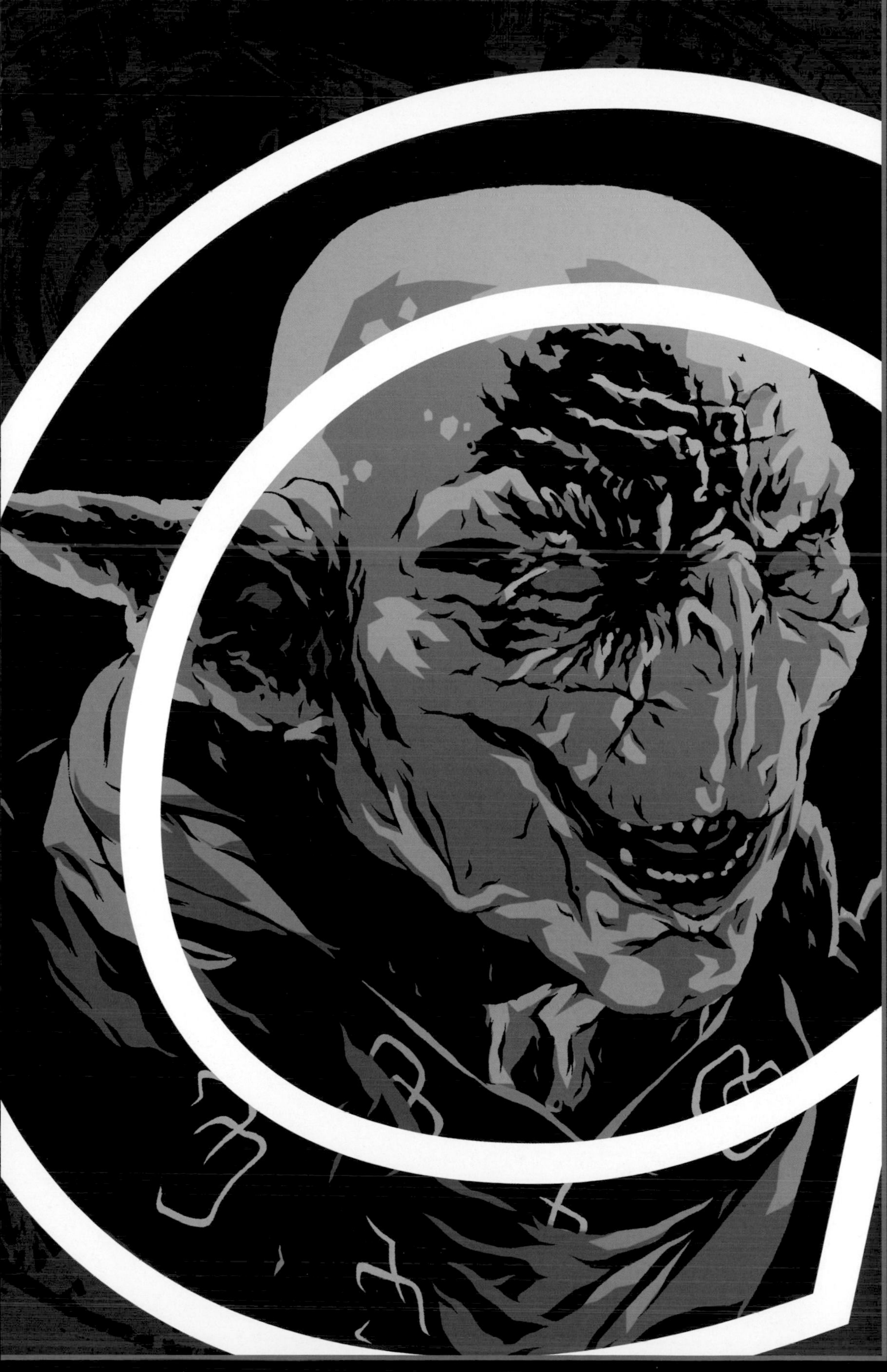

COVER 14C: JEFFREY SPOKES

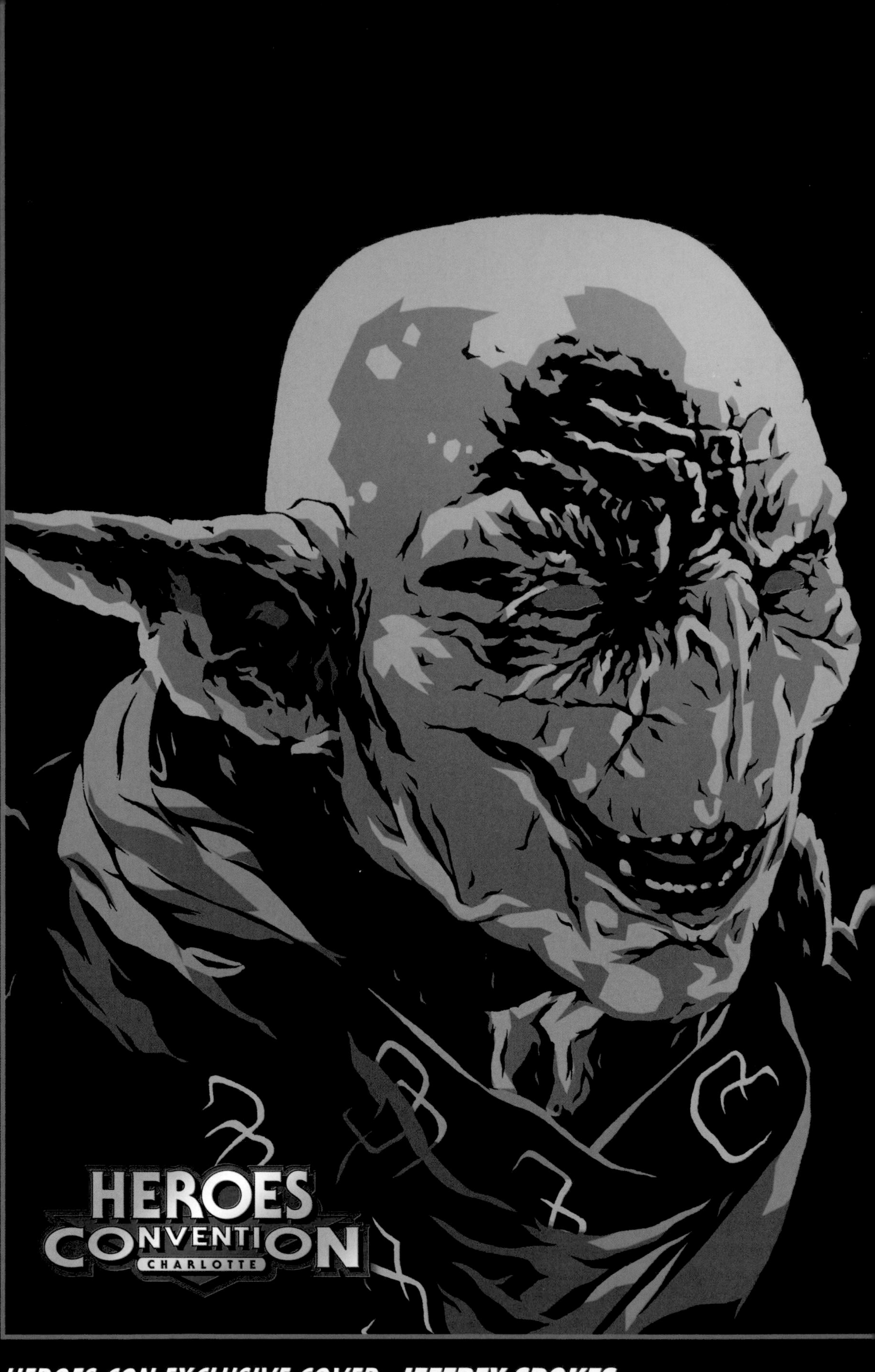
HEROES
CONVENTION
CHARLOTTE

HEROES CON EXCLUSIVE COVER: **JEFFREY SPOKES**

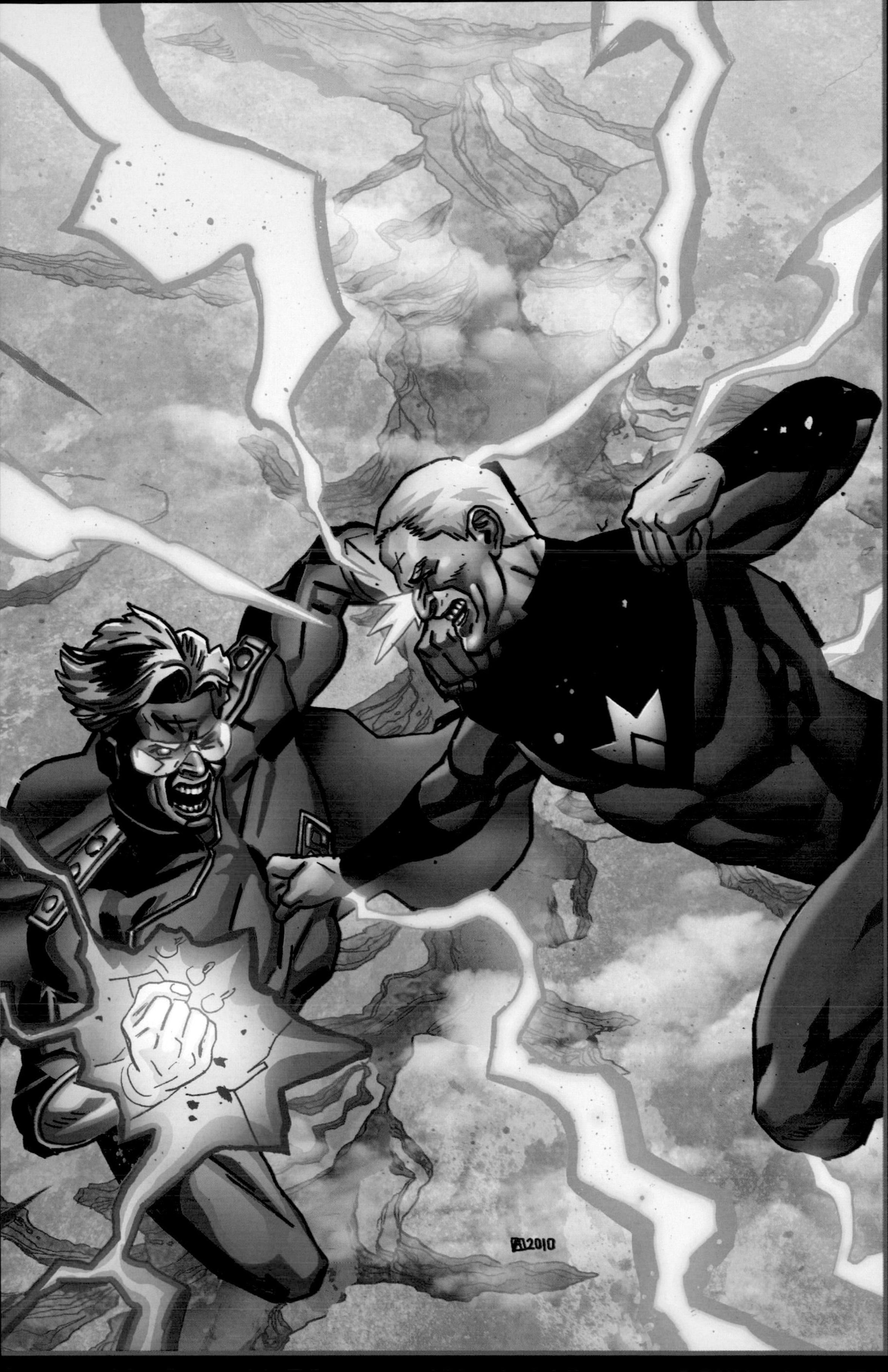
2010

COVER 15A: PAUL AZACETA

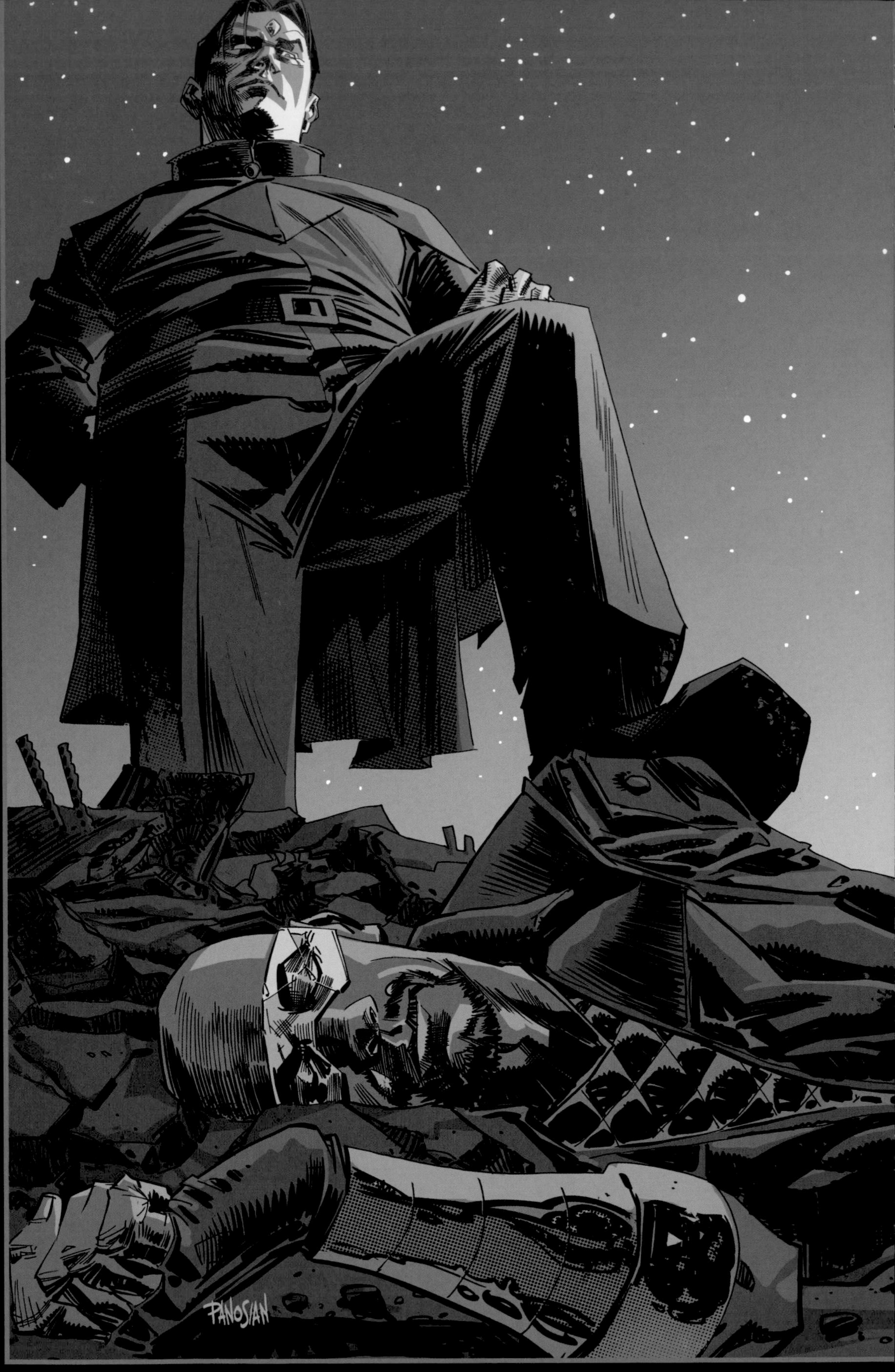
PANOSIAN

COVER 15B: DAN PANOSIAN

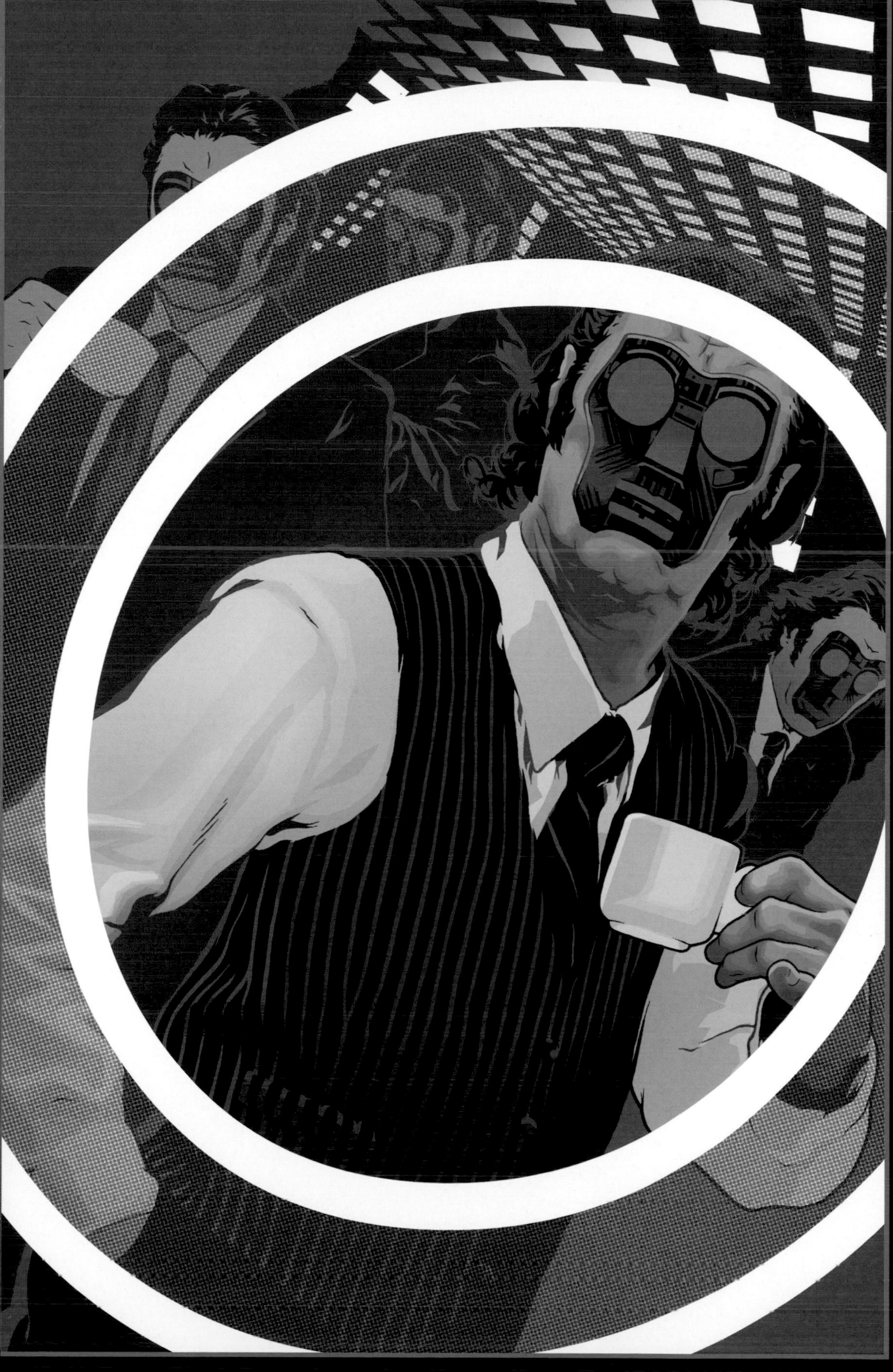

COVER 15C: JEFFREY SPOKES

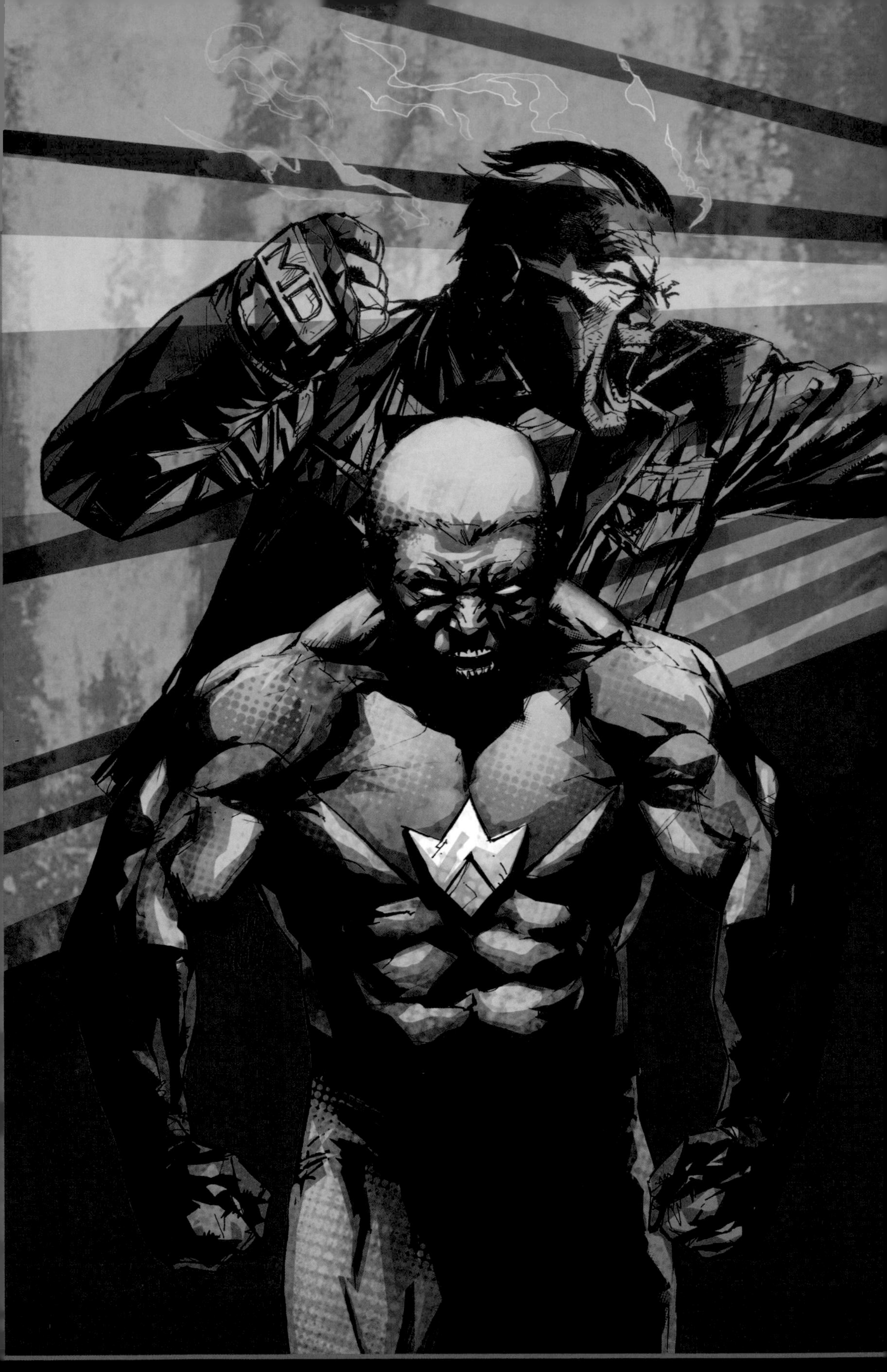
MD

SAN DIEGO COMIC-CON EXCLUSIVE COVER: **GARRY BROWN**

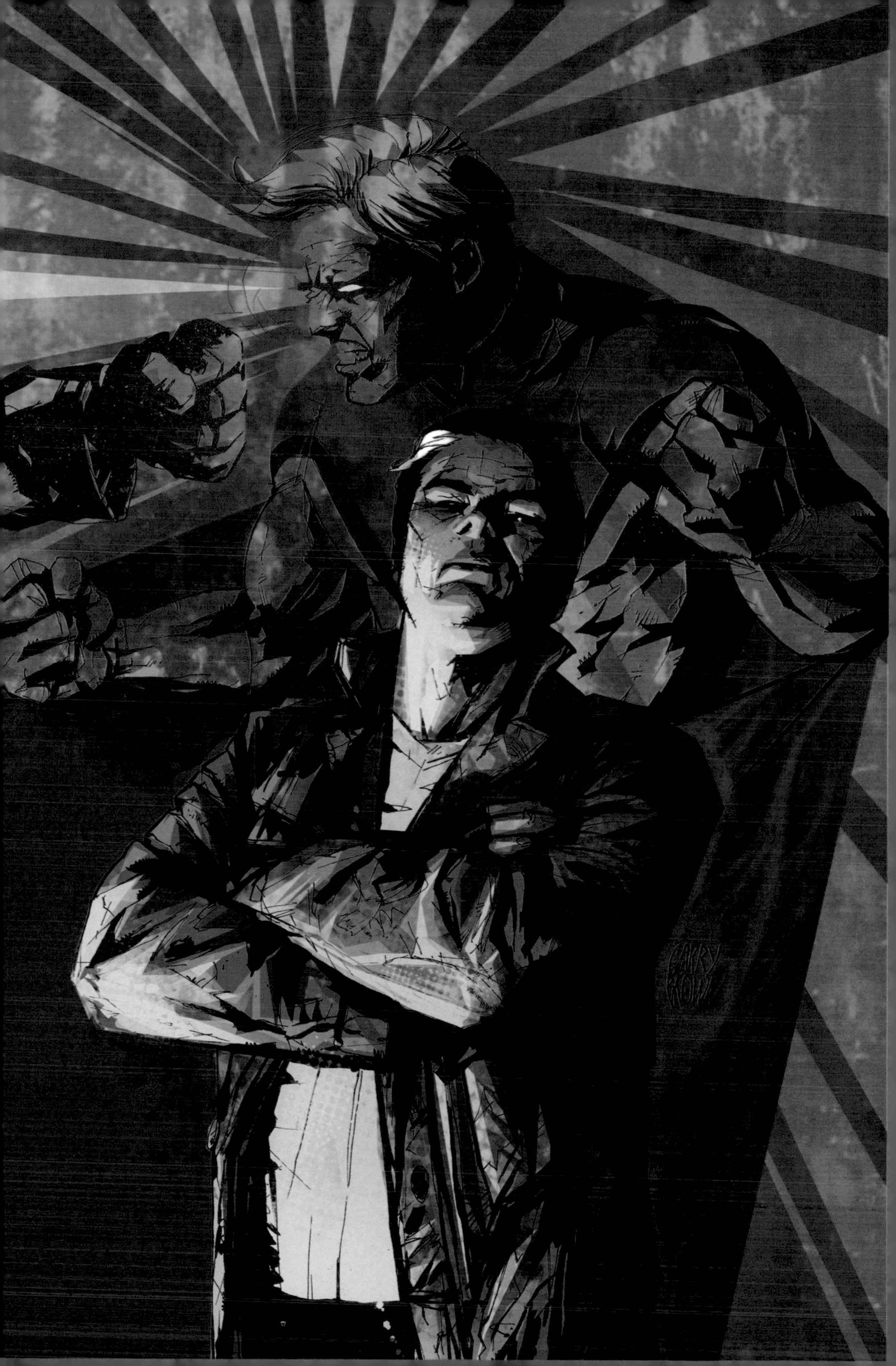

The UNKNOWN
WAID · OOSTERVEER
THE DEVIL MADE FLESH
SPECIAL 12-PAGE PREVIEW

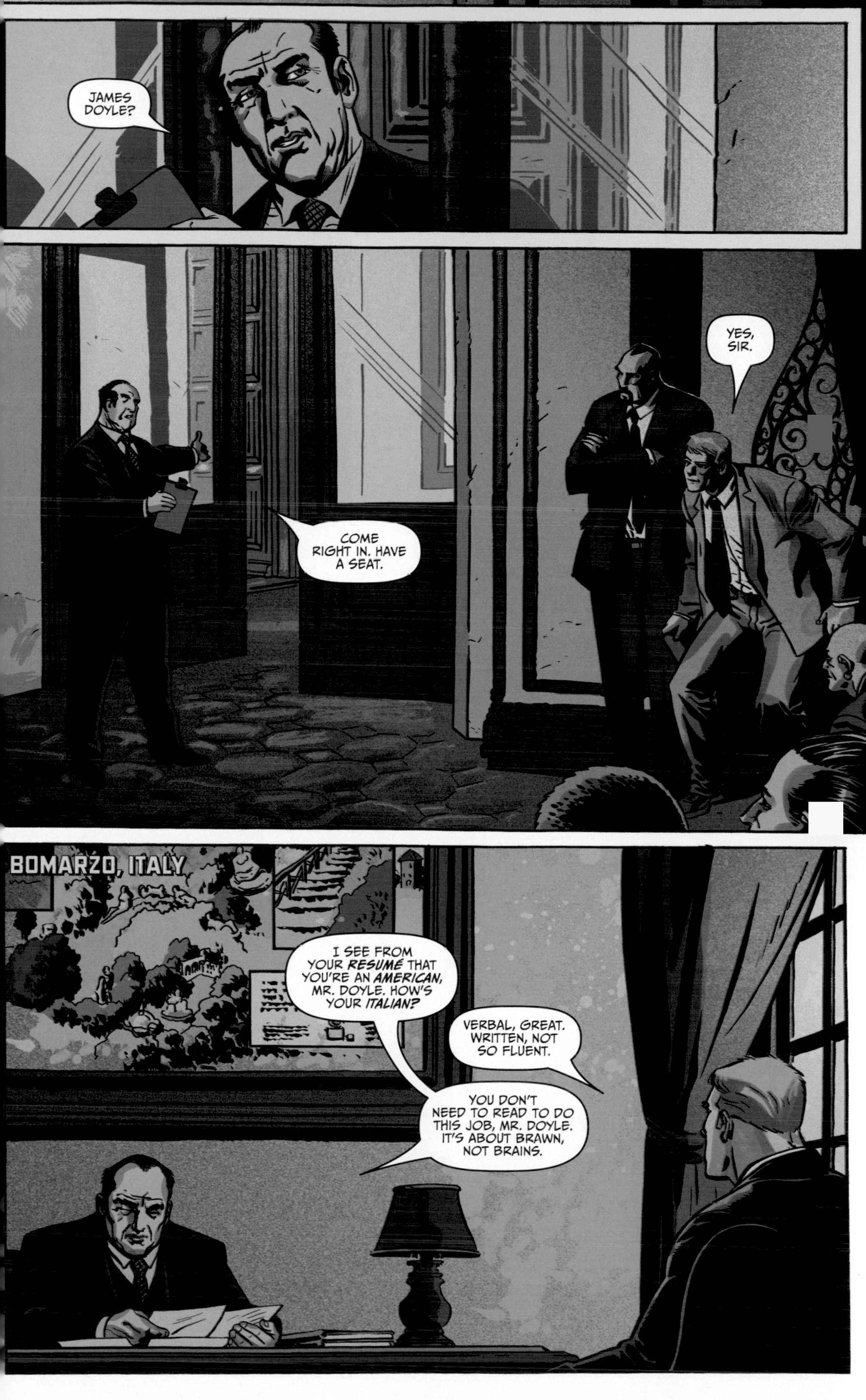
JAMES DOYLE?
COME RIGHT IN. HAVE A SEAT.
YES, SIR.
BOMARZO, ITALY
I SEE FROM YOUR *RESUMÉ* THAT YOU'RE AN *AMERICAN*, MR. DOYLE. HOW'S YOUR *ITALIAN?*
VERBAL, GREAT. WRITTEN, NOT SO FLUENT.
YOU DON'T NEED TO READ TO DO THIS JOB, MR. DOYLE. IT'S ABOUT BRAWN, NOT BRAINS.

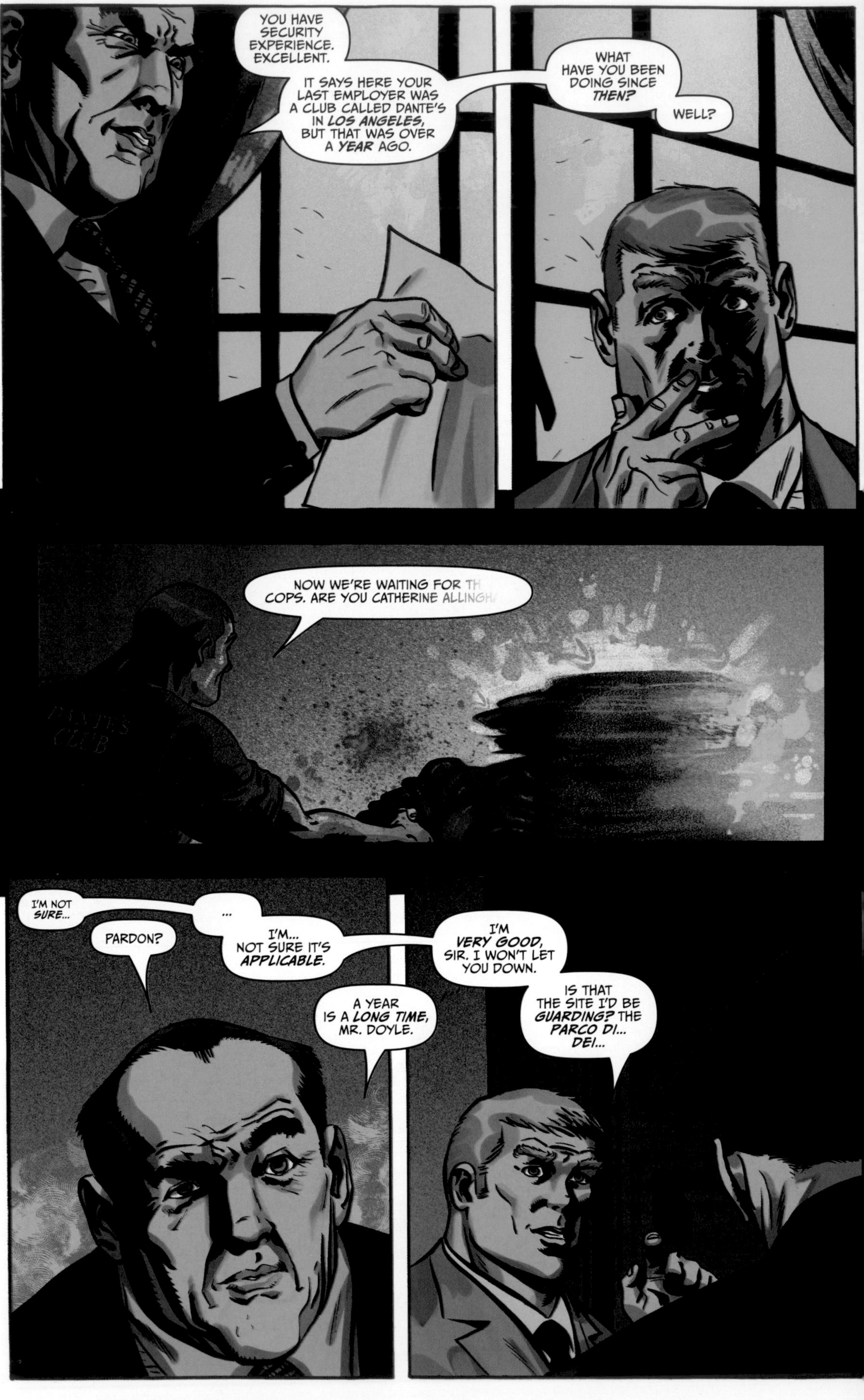

YOU HAVE SECURITY EXPERIENCE. EXCELLENT.
IT SAYS HERE YOUR LAST EMPLOYER WAS A CLUB CALLED DANTE'S IN *LOS ANGELES*, BUT THAT WAS OVER A *YEAR* AGO.
WHAT HAVE YOU BEEN DOING SINCE *THEN?*
WELL?
NOW WE'RE WAITING FOR TH
COPS. ARE YOU CATHERINE ALLINGHA
I'M NOT *SURE*...
PARDON?
...
I'M... NOT SURE IT'S *APPLICABLE*.
A YEAR IS A *LONG TIME*, MR. DOYLE.
I'M *VERY GOOD*, SIR. I WON'T LET YOU DOWN.
IS THAT THE SITE I'D BE *GUARDING?* THE *PARCO DI... DEI...*

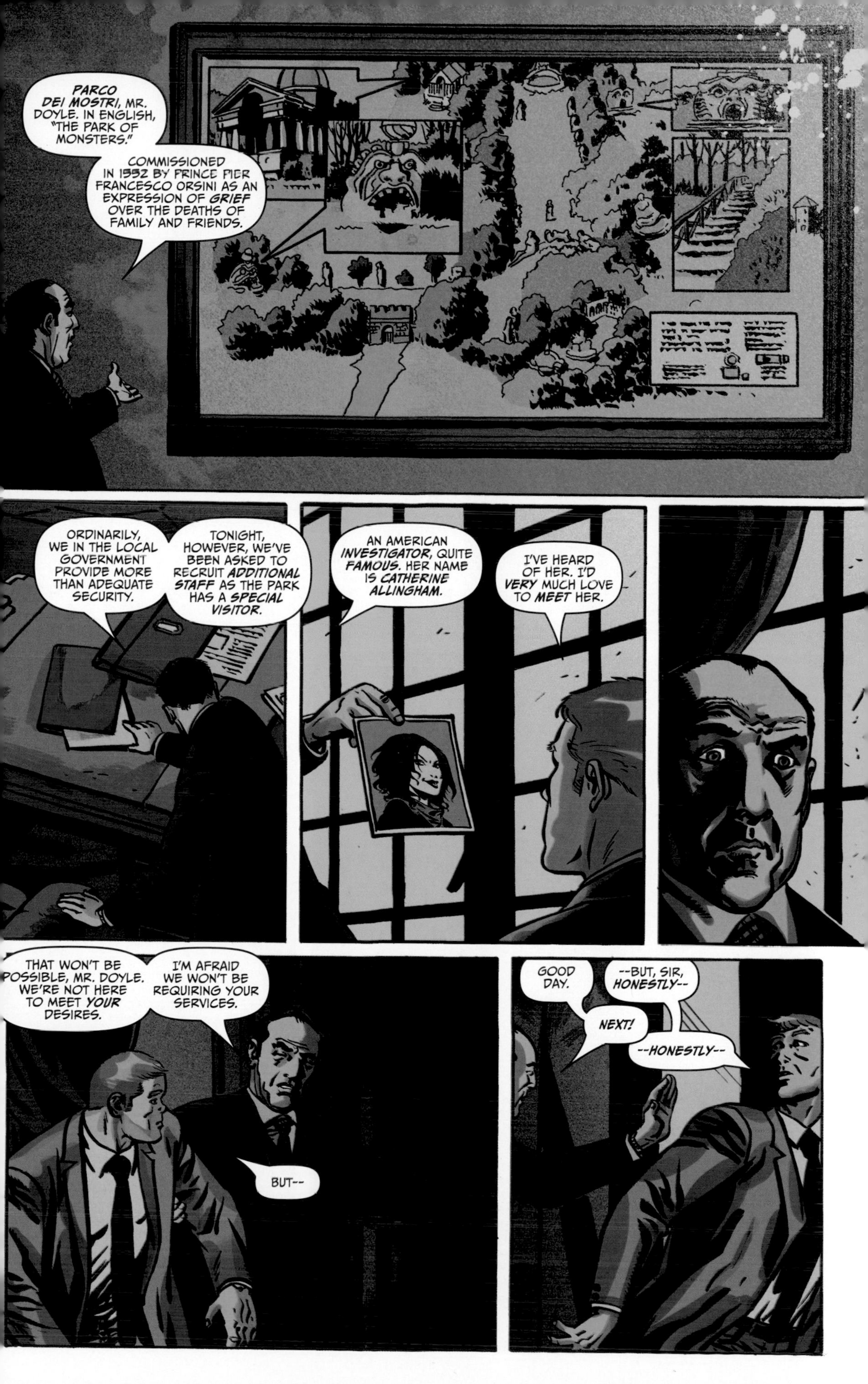
PARCO DEI MOSTRI, MR. DOYLE. IN ENGLISH, "THE PARK OF MONSTERS."
COMMISSIONED IN 1552 BY PRINCE PIER FRANCESCO ORSINI AS AN EXPRESSION OF GRIEF OVER THE DEATHS OF FAMILY AND FRIENDS.
ORDINARILY, WE IN THE LOCAL GOVERNMENT PROVIDE MORE THAN ADEQUATE SECURITY.
TONIGHT, HOWEVER, WE'VE BEEN ASKED TO RECRUIT ADDITIONAL STAFF AS THE PARK HAS A SPECIAL VISITOR.
AN AMERICAN INVESTIGATOR, QUITE FAMOUS. HER NAME IS CATHERINE ALLINGHAM.
I'VE HEARD OF HER. I'D VERY MUCH LOVE TO MEET HER.
THAT WON'T BE POSSIBLE, MR. DOYLE. WE'RE NOT HERE TO MEET YOUR DESIRES.
I'M AFRAID WE WON'T BE REQUIRING YOUR SERVICES.
BUT--
GOOD DAY.
--BUT, SIR, HONESTLY--
NEXT!
--HONESTLY--

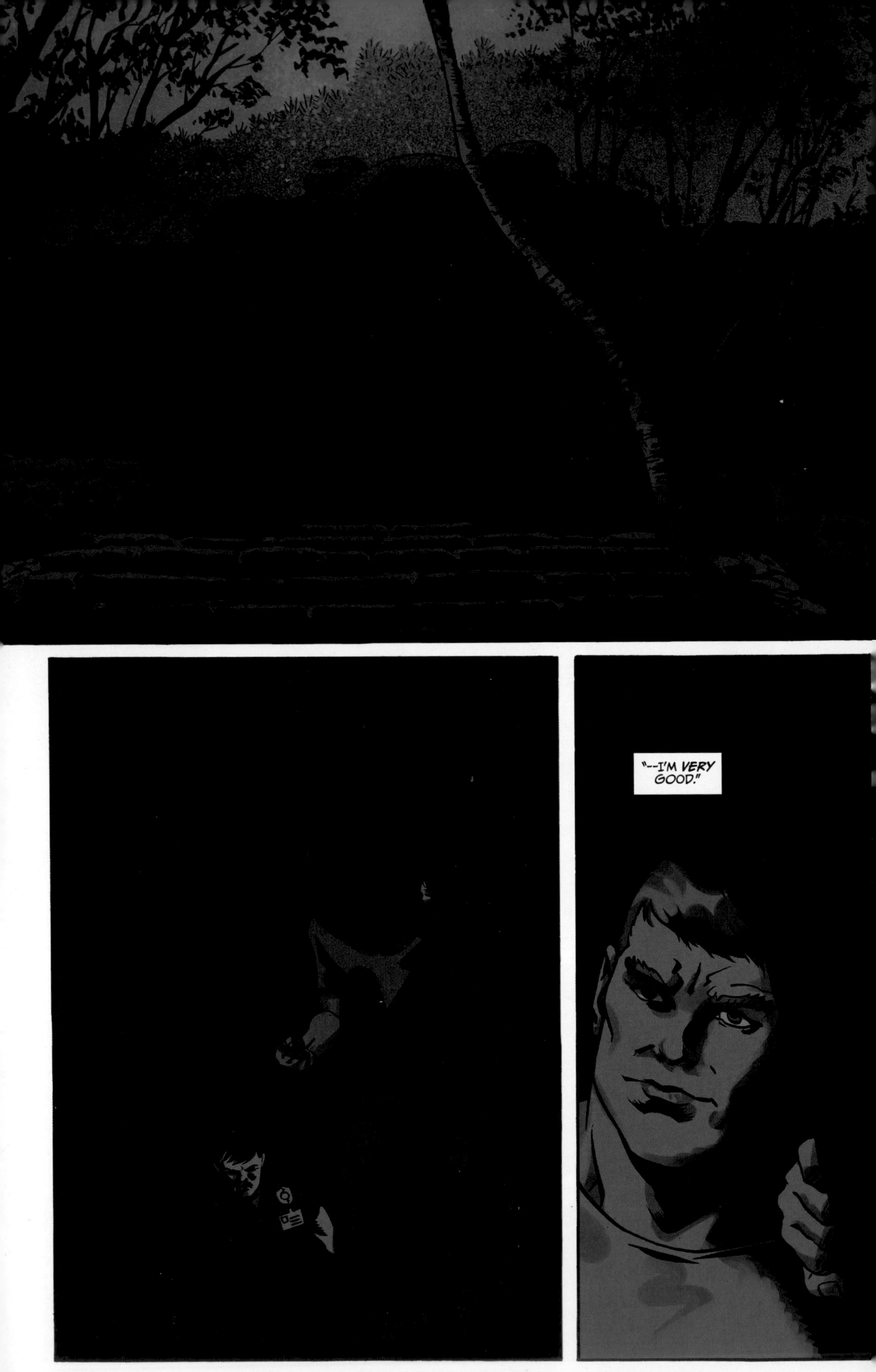
"--I'M VERY GOOD."

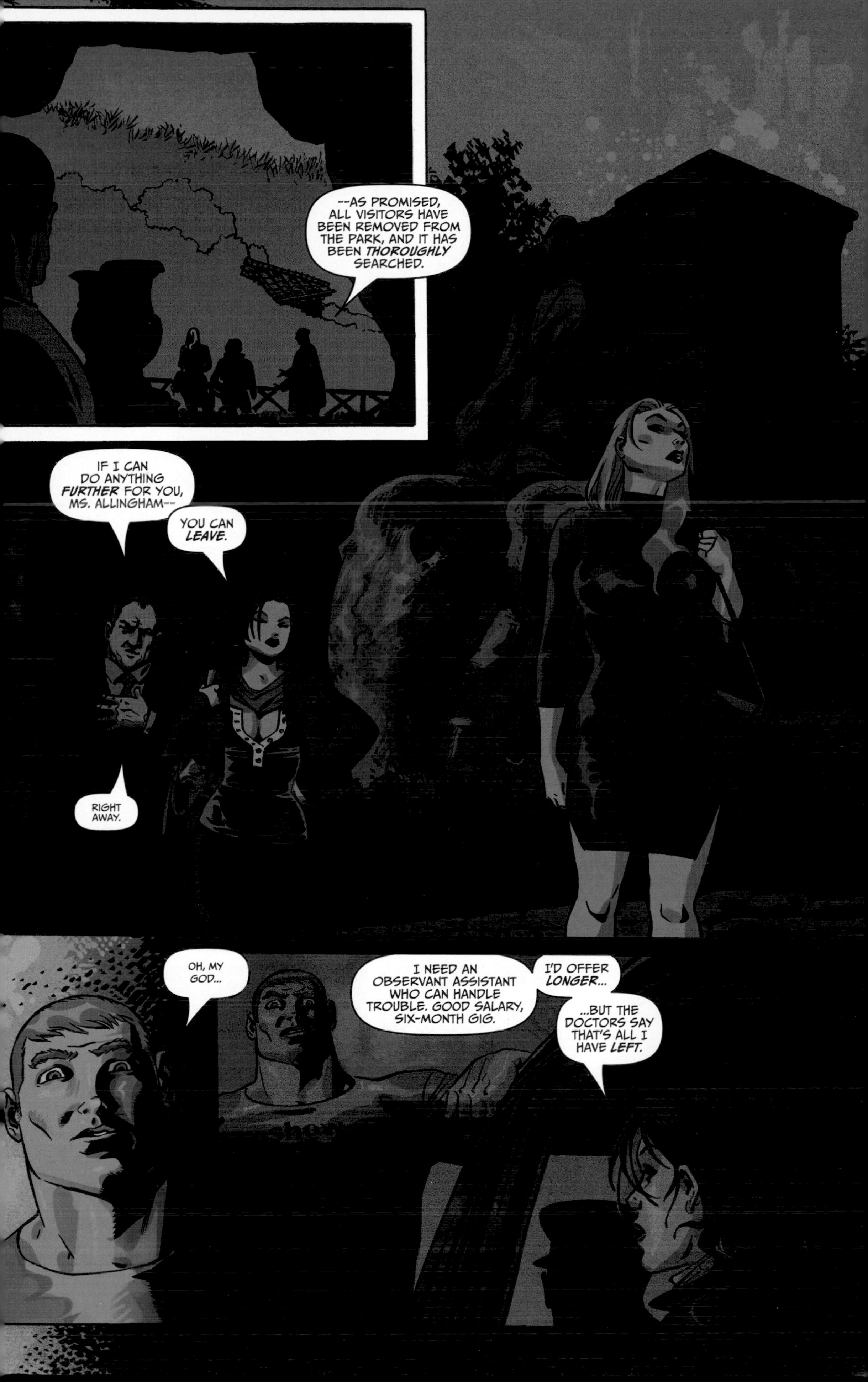
--AS PROMISED, ALL VISITORS HAVE BEEN REMOVED FROM THE PARK, AND IT HAS BEEN *THOROUGHLY* SEARCHED.
IF I CAN DO ANYTHING *FURTHER* FOR YOU, MS. ALLINGHAM--
YOU CAN *LEAVE.*
RIGHT AWAY.
OH, MY GOD...
I NEED AN OBSERVANT ASSISTANT WHO CAN HANDLE TROUBLE. GOOD SALARY, SIX-MONTH GIG.
I'D OFFER *LONGER...*
...BUT THE DOCTORS SAY THAT'S ALL I HAVE *LEFT.*

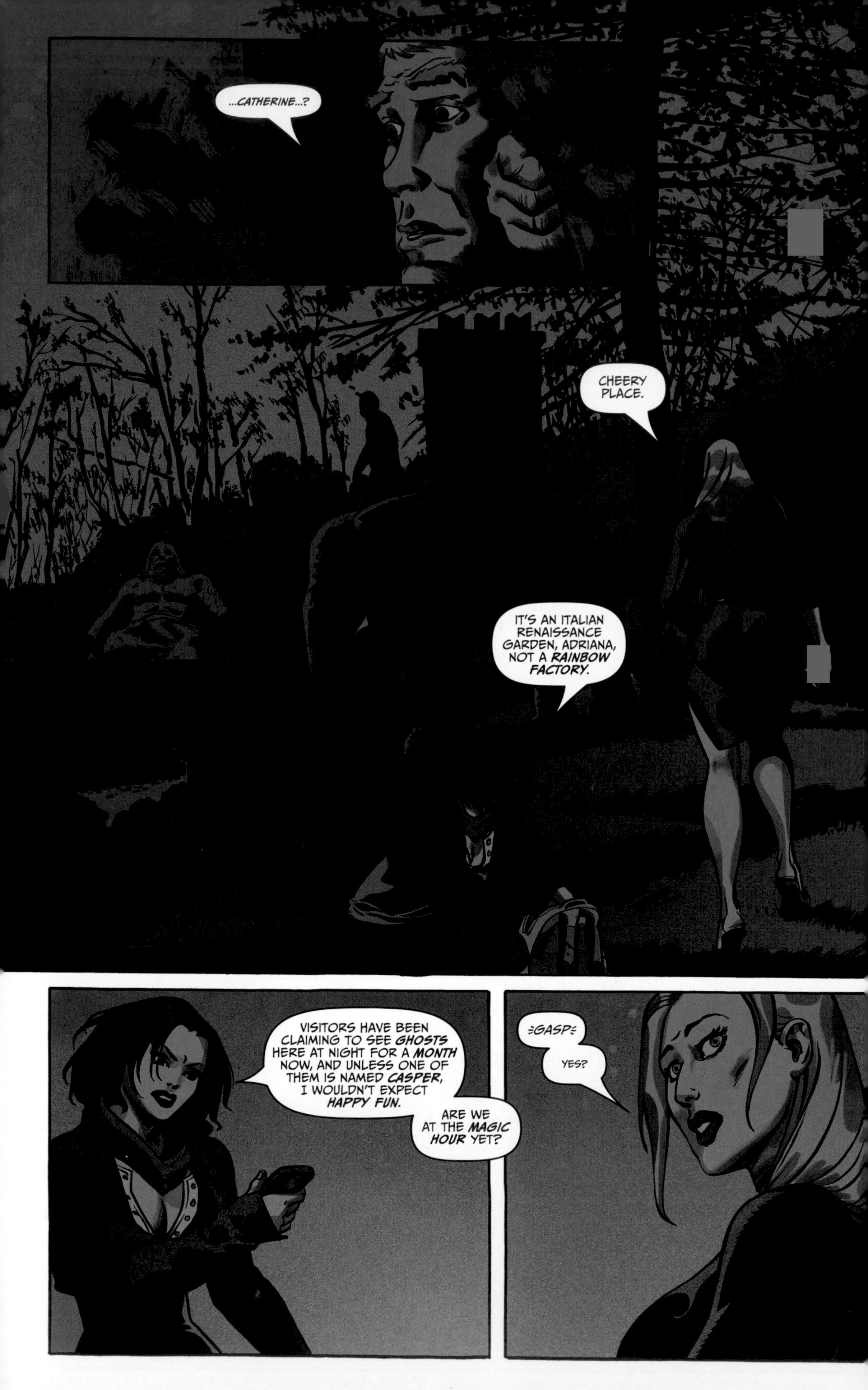
...CATHERINE...?
CHEERY PLACE.
IT'S AN ITALIAN RENAISSANCE GARDEN, ADRIANA, NOT A RAINBOW FACTORY.
VISITORS HAVE BEEN CLAIMING TO SEE GHOSTS HERE AT NIGHT FOR A MONTH NOW, AND UNLESS ONE OF THEM IS NAMED CASPER, I WOULDN'T EXPECT HAPPY FUN.
ARE WE AT THE MAGIC HOUR YET?
GASP
YES?

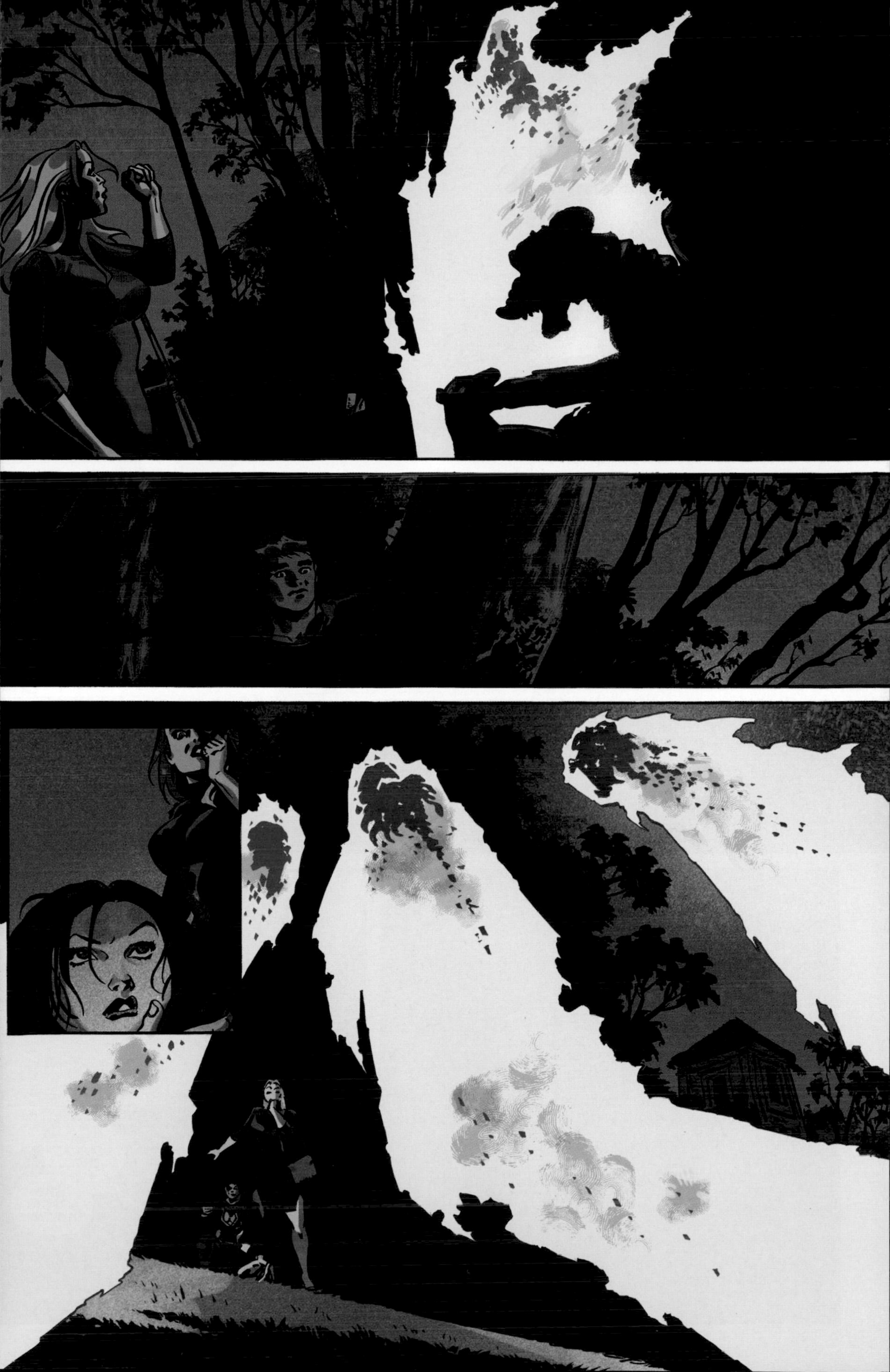

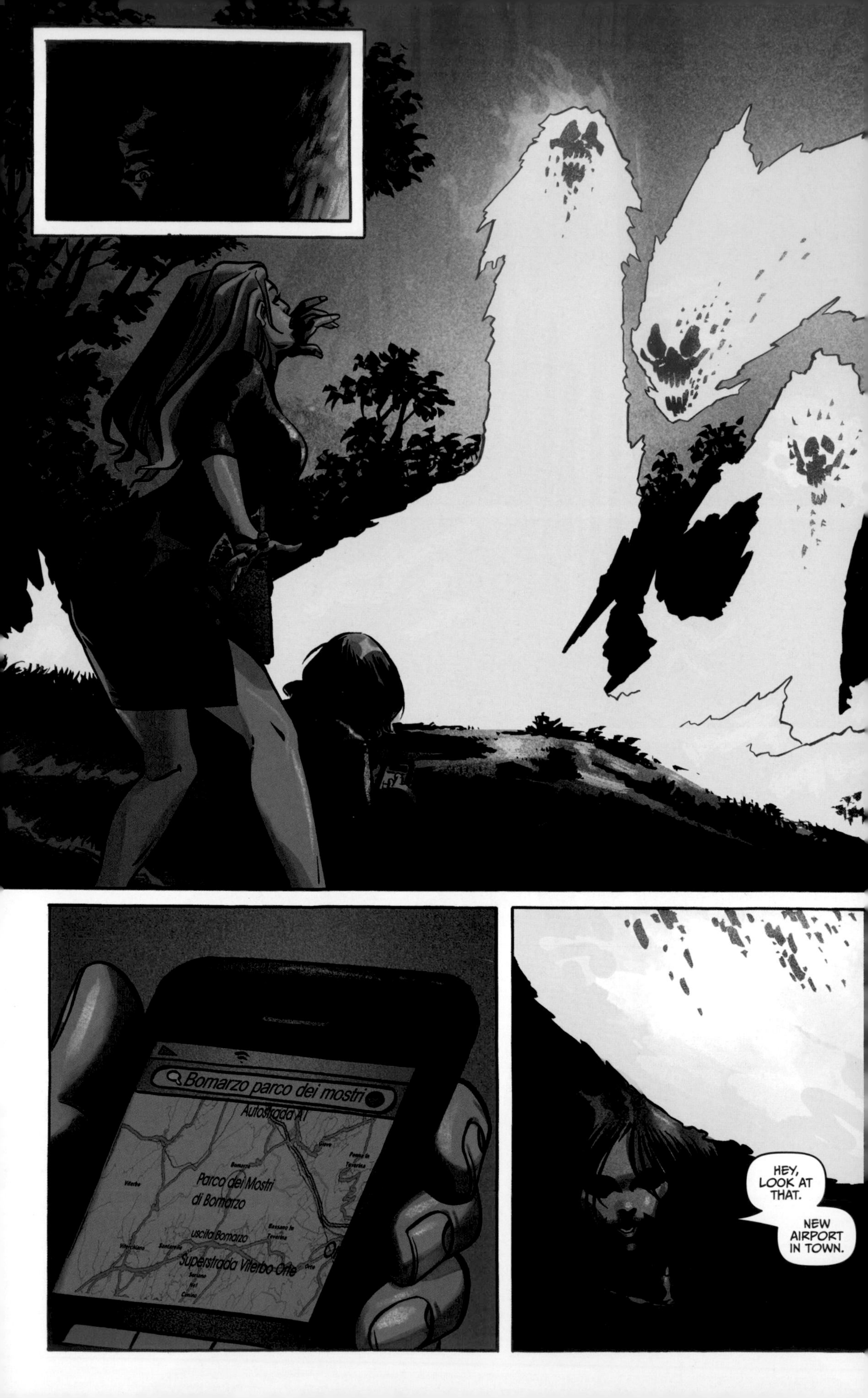
Bomarzo parco dei mostri
Autostrada A1
Parco dei Mostri di Bomarzo
uscita Bomarzo
Superstrada Viterbo Orte
HEY, LOOK AT THAT.
NEW AIRPORT IN TOWN.

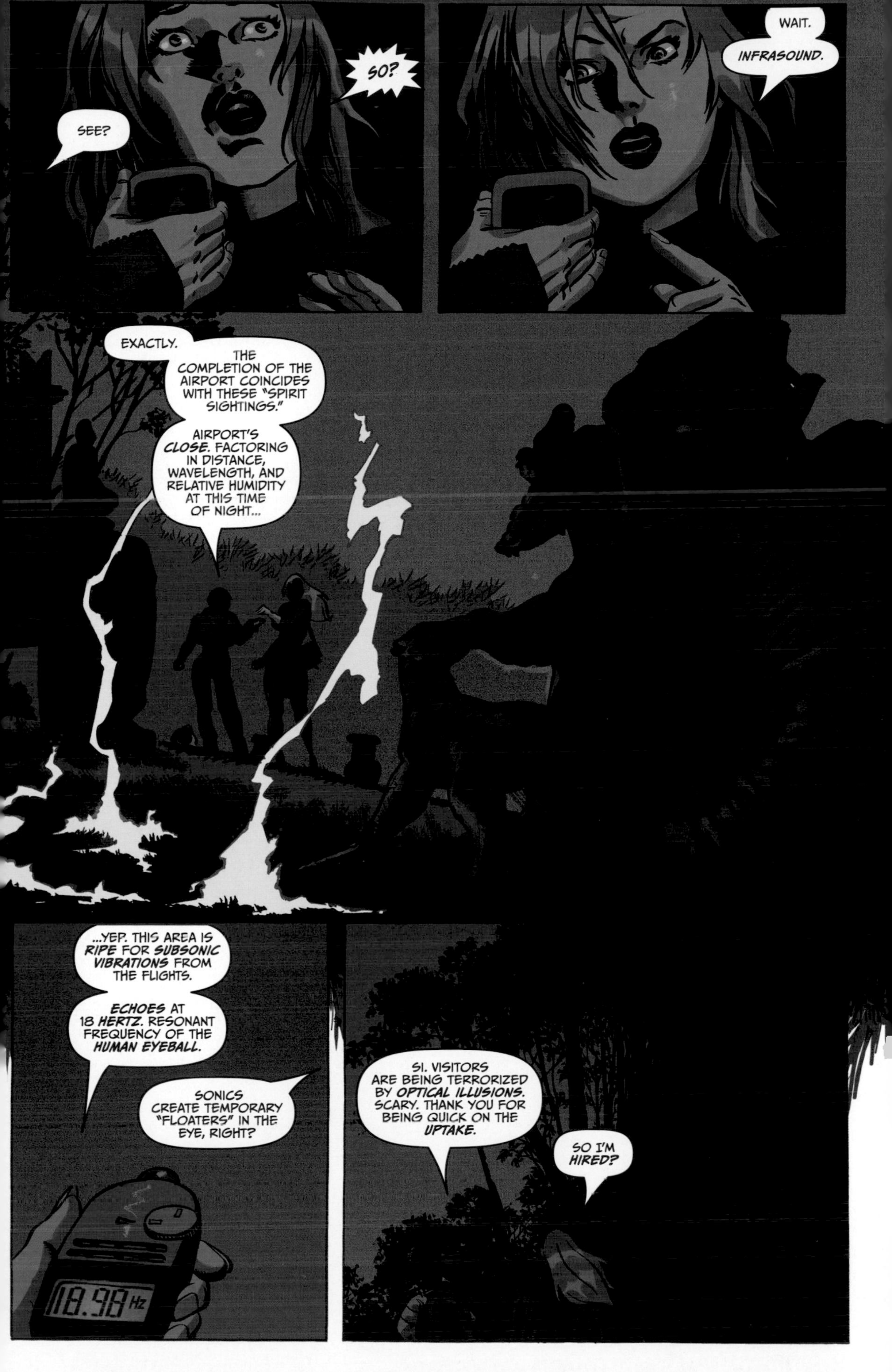
SEE?
SO?
WAIT.
INFRASOUND.
EXACTLY.
THE COMPLETION OF THE AIRPORT COINCIDES WITH THESE "SPIRIT SIGHTINGS."
AIRPORT'S CLOSE. FACTORING IN DISTANCE, WAVELENGTH, AND RELATIVE HUMIDITY AT THIS TIME OF NIGHT...
...YEP. THIS AREA IS RIPE FOR SUBSONIC VIBRATIONS FROM THE FLIGHTS.
ECHOES AT 18 HERTZ. RESONANT FREQUENCY OF THE HUMAN EYEBALL.
SONICS CREATE TEMPORARY "FLOATERS" IN THE EYE, RIGHT?
18.98 Hz
SI. VISITORS ARE BEING TERRORIZED BY OPTICAL ILLUSIONS. SCARY. THANK YOU FOR BEING QUICK ON THE UPTAKE.
SO I'M HIRED?

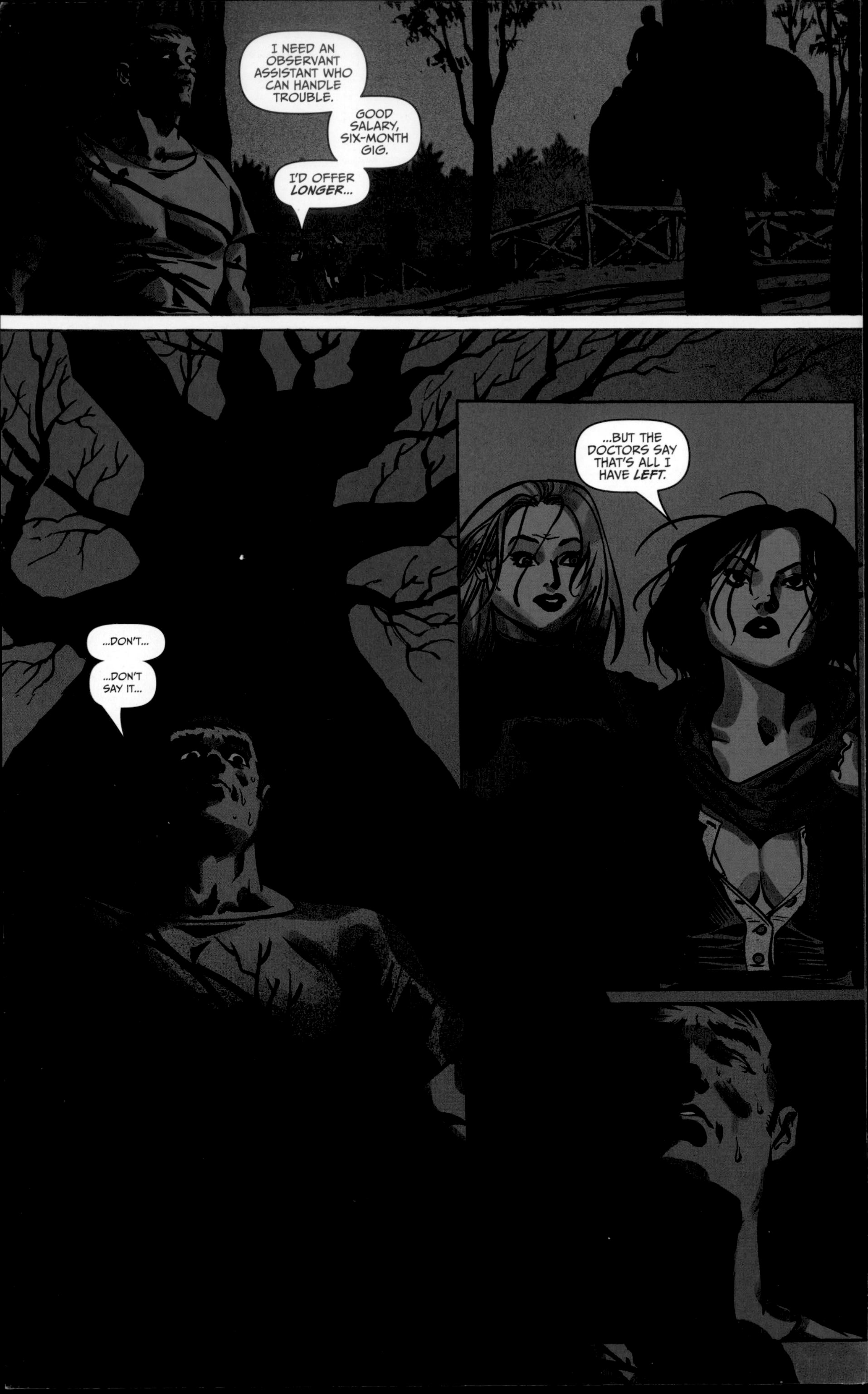
I NEED AN OBSERVANT ASSISTANT WHO CAN HANDLE TROUBLE.
GOOD SALARY, SIX-MONTH GIG.
I'D OFFER *LONGER*...
...BUT THE DOCTORS SAY THAT'S ALL I HAVE *LEFT*.
...DON'T...
...DON'T SAY IT...

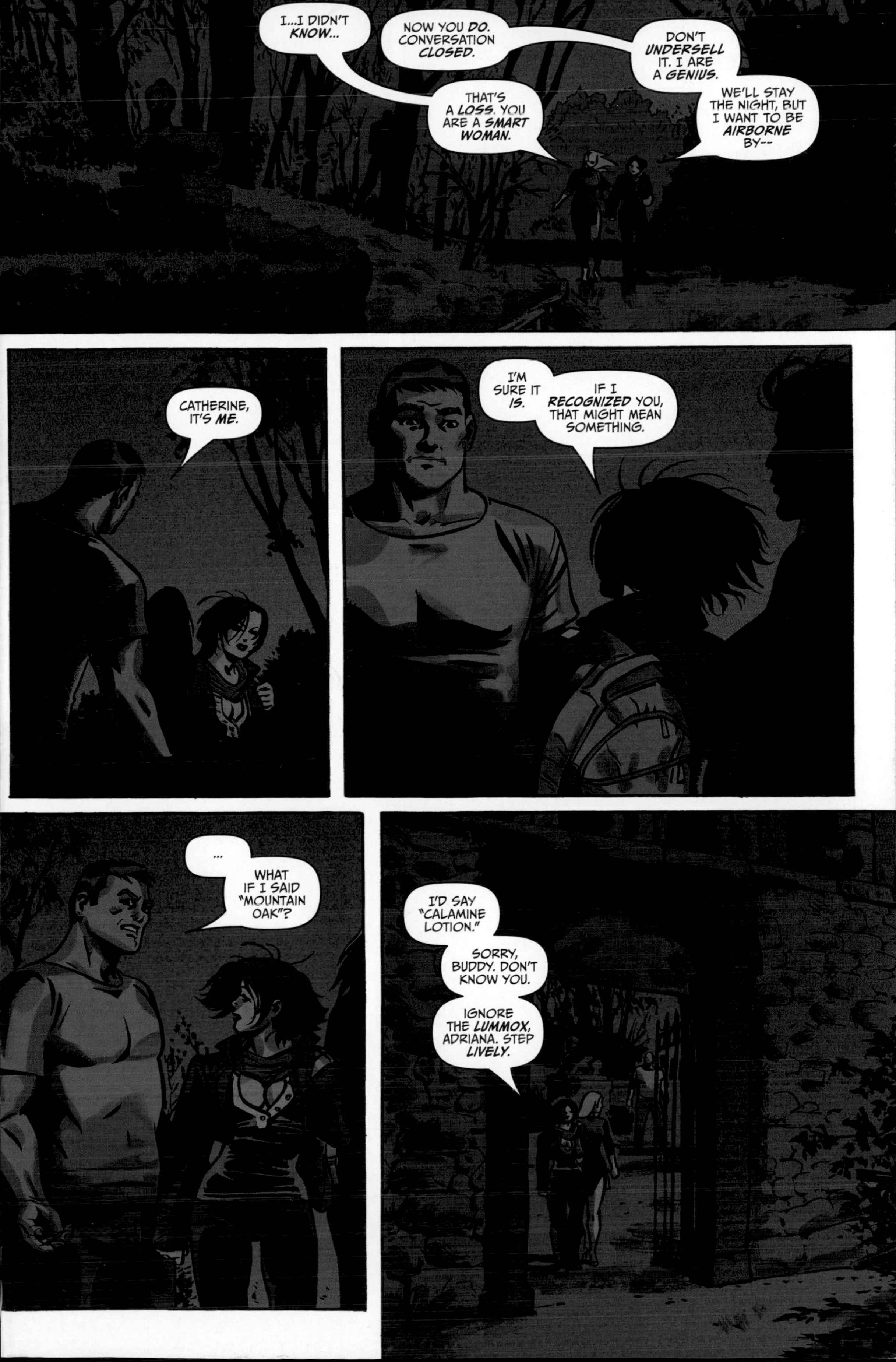
I...I DIDN'T KNOW...
NOW YOU DO. CONVERSATION CLOSED.
THAT'S A LOSS. YOU ARE A SMART WOMAN.
DON'T UNDERSELL IT. I ARE A GENIUS.
WE'LL STAY THE NIGHT, BUT I WANT TO BE AIRBORNE BY--
CATHERINE, IT'S ME.
I'M SURE IT IS.
IF I RECOGNIZED YOU, THAT MIGHT MEAN SOMETHING.
...
WHAT IF I SAID "MOUNTAIN OAK"?
I'D SAY "CALAMINE LOTION."
SORRY, BUDDY. DON'T KNOW YOU.
IGNORE THE LUMMOX, ADRIANA. STEP LIVELY.

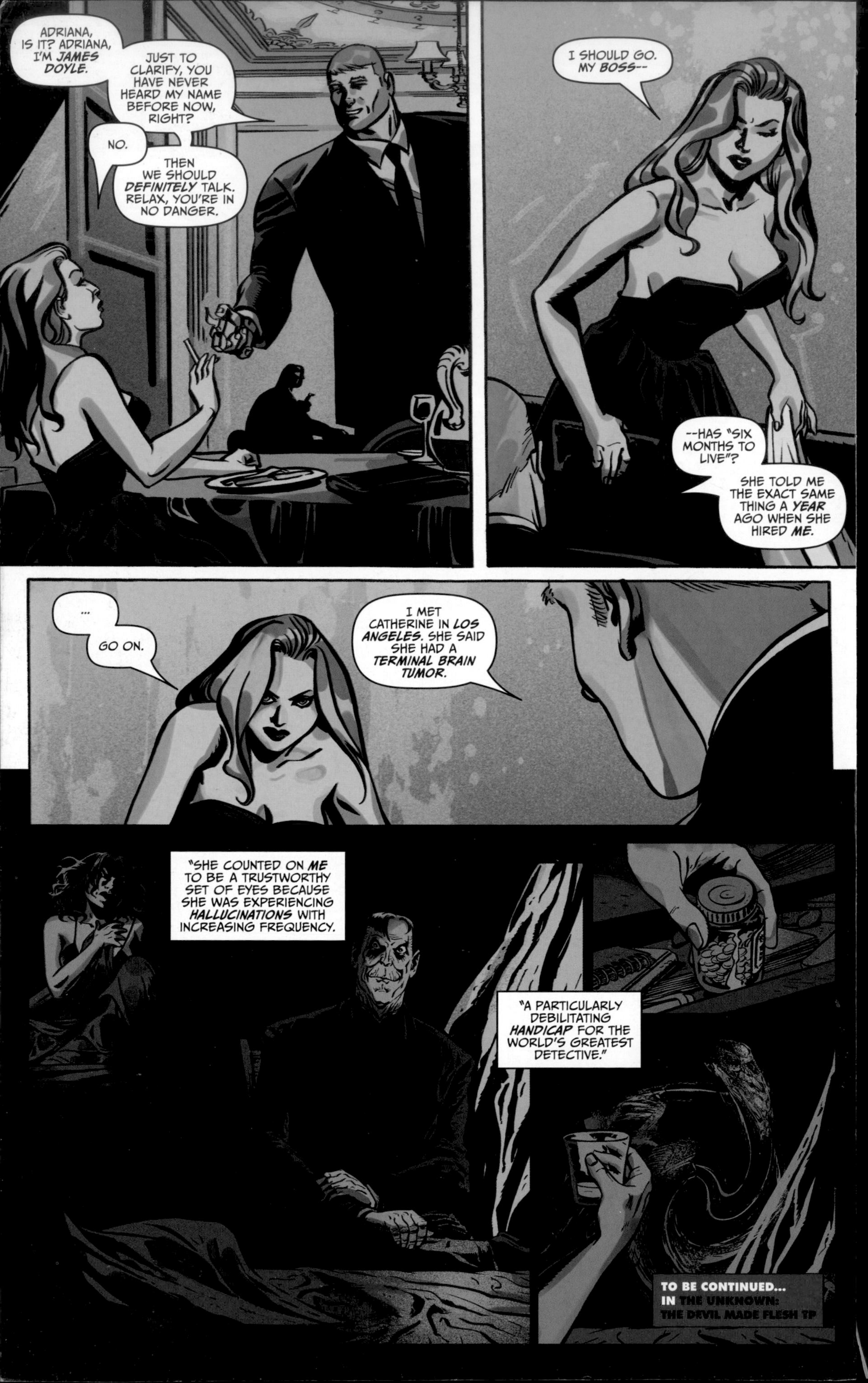
ADRIANA, IS IT? ADRIANA, I'M JAMES DOYLE.
JUST TO CLARIFY, YOU HAVE NEVER HEARD MY NAME BEFORE NOW, RIGHT?
NO.
THEN WE SHOULD DEFINITELY TALK. RELAX, YOU'RE IN NO DANGER.
I SHOULD GO. MY BOSS--
--HAS "SIX MONTHS TO LIVE"?
SHE TOLD ME THE EXACT SAME THING A YEAR AGO WHEN SHE HIRED ME.
...
GO ON.
I MET CATHERINE IN LOS ANGELES. SHE SAID SHE HAD A TERMINAL BRAIN TUMOR.
"SHE COUNTED ON ME TO BE A TRUSTWORTHY SET OF EYES BECAUSE SHE WAS EXPERIENCING HALLUCINATIONS WITH INCREASING FREQUENCY.
"A PARTICULARLY DEBILITATING HANDICAP FOR THE WORLD'S GREATEST DETECTIVE."
TO BE CONTINUED... IN THE UNKNOWN: THE DEVIL MADE FLESH TP